Memory-Theater and Postmodern Drama

THEATER: Theory/Text/Performance

Enoch Brater, Series Editor

Recent Titles:

Staging Place: The Geography of Modern Drama by Una Chaudhuri

The Aesthetics of Disturbance: Anti-Art in Avant-Garde Drama by David Graver

Toward a Theater of the Oppressed: The Dramaturgy of John Arden by Javed Malick

Theater in Israel edited by Linda Ben-Zvi

Crucibles of Crisis: Performing Social Change edited by Janelle Reinelt

Fornes: Theater in the Present Tense by Diane Lynn Moroff

Taking It to the Streets: The Social Protest Theater of Luis Valdez and Amiri Baraka by Harry J. Elam Jr.

Hearing Voices: Modern Drama and the Problem of Subjectivity by John H. Lutterbie

Mimesis, Masochism, & Mime: The Politics of Theatricality in Contemporary French Thought edited by Timothy Murray

Approaching the Millennium: Essays on Angels in America edited by Deborah R. Geis and Steven F. Kruger

Rooms with a View: The Stages of Community in the Modern Theater by Richard L. Barr

Staging Resistance: Essays on Political Theater edited by Jeanne Colleran and Jenny S. Spencer

Sightlines: Race, Gender, and Nation in Contemporary Australian Theatre by Helen Gilbert

Edges of Loss: From Modern Drama to Postmodern Theory by Mark Pizzato

Postmodern/Drama: Reading the Contemporary Stage by Stephen Watt

Trevor Griffiths: Politics, Drama, History by Stanton B. Garner Jr.

Memory-Theater and Postmodern Drama by Jeanette R. Malkin

Performing America: Cultural Nationalism in American Theater edited by Jeffrey D. Mason and J. Ellen Gainor

Space in Performance: Making Meaning in the Theatre by Gay McAuley

Mirrors of Our Playing: Paradigms and Presences in Modern Drama by Thomas R. Whitaker

Memory-Theater and Postmodern Drama

Jeanette R. Malkin

Ann Arbor

THE UNIVERSITY OF MICHIGAN PRESS

Copyright © by the University of Michigan 1999
All rights reserved
Published in the United States of America by
The University of Michigan Press
Manufactured in the United States of America
⊗ Printed on acid-free paper

2002 2001 2000 1999   4 3 2 1

A CIP catalog record for this book is available from the British Library.

Library of Congress Cataloging-in-Publication Data

Malkin, Jeanette R.
    Memory-theater and postmodern drama / Jeanette R. Malkin.
        p.   cm. — (Theater—theory/text/performance)
    Includes bibliographical references (p.   ) and index.
    ISBN 0-472-11037-3 (alk. paper)
        1. Drama—20th century—History and criticism.   2. Postmodernism
    (Literature)   I. Title.   II. Series.
    PN1861 .M278 1999
    792—dc21   99-6220
                                                                    CIP

To my most central and essential ones
Radi, Tali, Noga

Contents

Preface and Acknowledgments   ix

Introduction
Intersecting Scenes of Memory   1

Chapter 1
Memory, History, Postmodern Drama   17
Theoretical Accounts

Chapter 2
Samuel Beckett's Postures of Memory   37

Chapter 3
Heiner Müller's Landscapes of Memory   71

Chapter 4
Sam Shepard and the Anxiety of Erasure   115

Chapter 5
Suzan-Lori Parks and the Empty (W)hole   155
of Memory

Chapter 6
Thomas Bernhard's Resentment and the   183
Politics of Memory

Conclusion
Re-viewing the Performance of Recall   215

Notes   225

Index   253

Preface and Acknowledgments

Sprich—
Doch scheide das Nein nicht vom Ja.
Gib deinem Spruch auch den Sinn:
Gib ihm den Schatten.
  —Paul Celan, "Sprich auch du"

[Speak—
But don't split the No from the Yes.
Give to your speech too its sense:
Give it the shadow.]

The past has haunted me for as long as I can remember. I have always borne its shadow and have passed that shadow, knowingly and unwittingly, on to my children. My own past consists of the memories of Europe's Jews, of the absences and traumas rendered in broken images and narrative fragments by my parents and all the other adults I knew as a child. Later, when I began to read, I discovered a complex historical and cultural narrative to which my inherited images seemed to belong. But the history never fully adhered or "explained" the shadows I carried. And the images—the memories—to which my parents returned in the few breakings of the silence that surrounded their past, remained stronger than the historical accounts of which they were logically a part. The feeling of being an epigone, of coming "after," certainly directed my interest in the way memory and the anxiety of epigonism have found their way into contemporary culture—and especially into the theater, my area of professional interest. The "space" of memory, its circulations and echoings, fit naturally into the spatial art of theater. Studying the overlap of the two through plays and playwrights who have engaged me both intellectually and emotionally, exposed me to a broad range of artistic sensibilities "memoried" and activated by collective shadows; it also exposed me to a rich range of idioms through which this memoried state might be contemplated. For this I am grateful to the artists I address.

The pleasure of remembering, and acknowledging, the inspiration of friends and colleagues is particularly keen in a book dedicated to memory— even if that memory (in the case of my book though not of my gratitudes) is postmodern. The bulk of this book was written during an extraordinary sabbatical year granted to me by The Hebrew University, Jerusalem, and spent in Berkeley, California. Aside from the excellent library and restaurants of Berkeley, one of my great pleasures during that year was the friendship of Carol Cosman and Robert (Uri) Alter. Their generosity, no less than the grace of their conversation and writings, stimulated both my work and my leisure, for which I thank them. Deepest thanks to my friend and colleague Anat Feinberg for countless acts of assistance and comfort, and for carefully reading parts of the text. Linda Ben-Zvi enriched my work through her friendship, and by introducing me to the theater of Suzan-Lori Parks as well as to many of her Beckettian colleagues. Hjördís Hákonardóttir's moral fortitude, and mordant humor, invigorated my spirit when it waned. Two people who were willing to comment and inspire under any circumstances, and always succeeded in redirecting my energies, are my dear friends Felice Posner Malkin and Yaakov Malkin.

For his scrupulous readings of the typescript, his incisive comments and generous support, I am most grateful to John Rouse. Others who have read sections of the book at various stages, and whose valuable, often crucial, comments have made a difference, are David Bathrick, Hans-Peter Bayerdörfer, Michael André Bernstein, Stanton B. Garner Jr., Christopher D. Innes, Janelle Reinelt, Freddie Rokem, and Claude Schumacher.

With devotion, I thank my *Geschwister*—Ira, Jimmy, and Hanni Rosenzweig—who share so many of my memories; as well as my parents, Frieda and Samuel Rosenzweig.

This book is dedicated with unqualified love to the three people most effected by my disappearance into its writing, and who had the greatest stake in seeing it finally finished: Irad Malkin, and our daughters Noga and Tali.

Sections of a few of the chapters were previously published, in various modified forms. A section of chapter 2 appeared as "Matters of Memory in *Krapp's Last Tape* and *Not I*," *Journal of Dramatic Theory and Criticism* 11, no. 2 (1997): 25–39. A section of chapter 3 appeared as "Mourning and the Body: Heiner Müller's Fathers and *The Foundling* Son," *Modern Drama* 39, no. 3 (1996): 490–506. Part of chapter 6 appeared as "Pulling the Pants Off History: Politics and Postmodernism in Thomas Bernhard's *Eve of Retirement*," *Theatre Journal* 47, no. 1 (1995): 105–19. An additional section of that chapter was published as "In Praise of Resentment: Thomas Bernhard, Jews, *Heldenplatz*," a chapter of the book *Staging the Holocaust: The Shoah in Drama and Performance,* ed. Claude Schumacher (Cambridge: Cambridge University Press, 1998).

Introduction

Intersecting Scenes of Memory

Memory-Theater and Postmodern Drama targets the intersection of three central contemporary fields: the discourses on memory that have become so prominent in the last decades, the study of postmodern aesthetics, and the reading of late-twentieth-century theater texts. Memory is the subject, drama/theater is the object, and postmodernism is the form and worldview through which the former—memory—is processed and inscribed into the latter—drama/theater. Underlying this triangular relationship is the observation that an important group of theater texts written since the 1970s exhibit an exceptional preoccupation with questions of memory, both in terms of their *thematic* attention to remembered (or repressed) pasts, and in terms of the plays' "memoried" *structures:* structures of repetition, conflation, regression, echoing, overlap, and simultaneity. This book will argue that the way memory is conceptualized has changed in postmodernism and that, indeed, the terms used to discuss memory share a common ground—and often overlap—with the terms we have come to associate with a postmodern aesthetic. I will, moreover, propose the more far-reaching thesis that postmodernism is crucially bound up with agendas of remembrance and forgetting, serving, at least in part, to re-call the past from repression or from its canonized "shape" in order to renegotiate the traumas, oppressions, and exclusions of the past. The theatricalization of this new memory discourse has produced some of the most powerful and provocative works on the contemporary stage: works by Samuel Beckett, Heiner Müller, Sam Shepard, Suzan-Lori Parks, and Thomas Bernhard. These authors, in their various voices, give sophisticated and often moving expression to the ways we remember and forget, to the traumas we have repressed or obsessed, to the traces of a no longer cohesive past, and to the circulations of a (for the most part) collective memory spinning toward century's end.

But I begin my discussion with the story of another theater, a theater far removed from the postmodernism of my title, situated in late

Renaissance Italy, only large enough to hold one or two visitors, whose explicit function was the perfection of personal memory and the evocation of a transcendent memory, and whose creator, a stutterer, never got around to explaining the manner of its use. Giulio Camillo's "memory-theater"— both in what we know about it and, especially, in the incomplete body of knowledge that has come down to us—offers an evocative model as well as a loose, vitalizing metaphor, for the connection between theatricalization and recall. In fact, the story of the Italian rhetorician and occult philosopher Camillo (1480–1544) reads as though it might have been written by his future countryman Italo Calvino, as though the fragmentary tale of this stutterer might itself be a parable for a postmodern theater. Camillo spent his life perfecting a language of visual images, a theater of images meant to empower memorization and to inspire knowledge of the order of the world. In his book *L'Idea del Theatro,* published in 1550, he left us a detailed description of this memorial theater; but not, alas, the key to its use. His defense of its meaning and application—which Camillo planned to set out "when he can have quiet"—was never written.[1]

Camillo's fragmentary achievement, and the few texts that remain as witness to his grand design, were revived by the historian Francis Yates, whose study *The Art of Memory* did much to restore the memory of "the divine Camillo," considered to be one of the most famous men of the sixteenth century, yet lost to public memory for so long. Yates writes:

> His Theater was talked of in all Italy and in France; its mysterious fame seemed to grow with the years. Yet what was it exactly? A wooden theater, crowded with images, was shown by Camillo himself in Venice to a correspondent of Erasmus; something similar was later on view in Paris. The secret of how it really worked was to be revealed to only one person in the world, the King of France. Camillo never produced the great book . . . in which his lofty designs were to be preserved for posterity. It is thus not surprising that posterity forgot this man whom his contemporaries hailed as "the divine Camillo."[2]

In his theater, Camillo actualized the idea of "staging" memories by deploying a permanent set of images that were to provide a physical model for memorization. Based on the Roman theater described by Vitruvius, the auditorium of Camillo's small wooden amphitheater rose in seven levels divided by seven gangways, each of which was decorated with complex images drawn from Neoplatonic, Hermetic, Cabalistic, and Christian traditions. This created a mélange of occult and mythic icons that conserved traditions both hidden and past, while their placement was meant to act as a mental trajectory aiding its user toward remembrance and metaphysical understanding. In an important reversal of the usual workings of theater, Camillo's memory building was devised so that the spectator stood at its center, where the stage should have been, surrounded by the profusion of potent icons. These signs would become meaningful through their relationship with the specific viewer, and for each viewer the signs might read differently. As Camillo put it: "This high and incomparable placing not only performs the office of conserving for us the things, words, and arts which we confide to it, so that we may find them at once whenever we need them, but also gives us true wisdom"[3]—of what we cannot exactly know. But the plundering of diverse traditions, the theatricalization of images torn out of several contexts from varying periods, without determinate meaning, arranged not always transparently on one stage—all in the name of memory—and dependent for its meaning on the knowing viewer will be found again (this time without metaphysical claims) on the stages of our postmodern dramatists.

The story of the Renaissance stutterer who built a real theater of memory, placed the viewer at its center, flooded him (or, less likely, her) with a jumble of images—but forgot to supply the key for their exact use and interpretation—reads almost like a spoof on the outer workings of postmodern memory-theater. Yet neither theater—neither Camillo's nor the postmodern version—is as whimsical as this historical anecdote may make them seem. Camillo was a deeply serious Neoplatonic philosopher dedicated to unlocking hidden memories through an occult practice incomprehensible to the uninitiated. As to *postmodern* memory-theater, it is the aim of this book to convince the reader of its equally serious intent: the intent to evoke erased memories of national pasts, to recontextualize, reopen canonized memory-"narratives," rethink taboo discourses, intervene in the politics of memory and repression, and to engage (and occasionally enrage) the memoried consciousness of its audience—with whose memory, and repression, these plays are in constant dialogue.

Theater is the art of repetition, of memorized and reiterated texts and gestures. A temporal art, an art-through-time, theater also depends on the memoried attentiveness of its audience with whose memory (and memories) it is always in dialogue. For Aristotle, the pleasure of art, of mimesis, is lodged in our ability to recognize in symbolic representations something that we know in "real life." We remember and relearn the world through art. For Stanislavsky, there is no acting without the activation of memories from experience. His theory of "affective memory" turns the actor into coauthor who rewrites a character by channeling a fictive text through a remembered one. For Grotowski, theater is found foremost in the memory of the body, in the most primal psychophysical interiority of the actor. Vestiges of the past are always to be found in a nation's literature and theater; but the *ways* these memories are inscribed, and hence the ways we remember, are not constant and unchanging. Richard Terdiman begins *Modernity and the Memory Crisis* with the words: "Even memory has a history." Every culture depends on its memory of the past, he claims, "but how a culture *performs* and sustains this recollection is distinctive and diagnostic."[4] In the theater I address, memory is performed as unhinged, multiple, noncommensurate, traumatized. In many of these plays (such as Shepard's *Action,* with its fractured amnesiac characters; in most of Bernhard and Müller; in Parks's *America Play*), we find a no longer grounded past; a past that floats within the collective consciousness—as a place of (fragmented) collective identity. Within postmodernism, I contend, there has occurred a shift in *the way we remember,* and hence in the way culture, and for our purposes, the theater, represents and reenacts remembering. Where once memory called up coherent, progressing narratives of experienced life, or at least unlocked the significance of hidden memory *for* the progressions of the present, this kind of enlightenment organization has broken down in postmodernism and given way to the nonnarrative reproduction of conflated, disrupted, repetitive, and moreover collectively retained and articulated fragments. This shift in the workings of memory is reflected in plays shaped through fragment, recurrence, and imagistic tumult. The plays I discuss "remember" and represent memory in ways parallel to the theories of knowledge that inform them, and thus become, as has always been the case with mnemonic theories, paradigms for a vision of the world.

This was the case with the classical practice of mnemotechnics—the prized art of memory developed by Cicero and the unknown author of the first-century Latin work on rhetoric, *Ad Herennium.* A rational technology, this practice was meant to enhance rhetorical prowess. It also signified a view of man as self-reliant and capable of mastering a wealth of information that could be used to persuade or teach. Anecdotally attributed (via Cicero and Quintilian) to the Greek poet Simonides of Ceos (sixth century B.C.E.), the method developed and used by orators and scholars in the ancient world remained basically unchanged up through the Renaissance, and its main features can still be found in the "memory improvement" books sold today. The idea is simple and visually concrete: in order to memorize a text—a body of knowledge—and remember the order of its parts, mental images are attached to each section or idea, and then deployed in imaginary loci within a building or house that is set up in the imagination. The memorizer is encouraged to imagine an internalized architecture that remains constant and, if possible, is based on a real and known structure (such as a theater, for example). The orator then places the images along a mapped-out mental route, and by "following" them during recitation, recalls the order and ideas of a speech or argument. The images chosen for this purpose, Cicero insists, should be "sharply outlined and distinctive" and have "the capacity of encountering and speedily penetrating the mind."[5] The author of *Ad Herennium* went into greater detail: "Ordinary things easily slip from the memory while the striking and novel stay longer in mind," he wrote. We should thus aim to set up images "as striking as possible . . . images that are not many or vague, but doing something" exceptional.[6] Classical mnemonics was, thus, a *visual* endeavor, a vivid inward seeing into the theater of the mind that performed the mental act of "staging" unforgettable images as an aid to pragmatic recall. Cicero writes pressingly of the primacy of sight—"the keenest of all our senses"[7]—and its importance in stimulating recall. Despite the temporal aspect we might tend to associate with memory, *place* (siting), rather than time (or returning), is the central factor. With very different effect, and for very different reasons, sight and site remain the central elements found in postmodern dramatizations of memory as well.

Plato's doctrine of anamnesis—his theory of memory that posited correspondences between recall and eternal Forms—diverged from the rhetorical aim of mnemotechnics and expressed a different vision of the world. Plato postulated that memory is directly expressive of a transcendental reality, and that through the objects of the world we can "remember" the ideal Forms or Ideas of which we had direct knowledge in a prior disembodied existence. Things in the world, properly understood, function to remind us of the ideal world and can be employed to restore lost knowledge of it—and thus *interpret* reality. This spiritual view of memory as a route to recovering hidden truths (in addition to memorizing rhetorical ones) led in the Renaissance to memory systems that employed occult signs and magical abodes—wheels, palaces, theaters—believed to provide its initiates with a *clavis universalis,* a master key to the workings of the universe.[8] Camillo's memory-theater was one of several occult developments of the classical art of mnemonics aimed at creating a physical paradigm that would reflect, and help to realize, the promise of Plato's anamnesis.

Freud, in a modernist inversion of this Neoplatonic attraction to external magical abodes, sought life's secrets within the caverns of the unconscious individual mind. With Freud, the theater of memory moved inward, beyond the imagination, into the psyche; and its drama was played out between repression, symbolic encodings, and therapeutic retrieval (these

theories are discussed in chapter 1). The revolutions of modernity brought
about a profound preoccupation with matters of memory and inspired a
new set of questions as to its place and function. According to Terdiman,
the upheavals provoked by political change, technological progress, urban-
ization, and shifts in economic production—changes that dislodged long-
established customs of rural life and communal ways of marking time—generated the powerful perception of "a massive disruption of traditional forms
of memory." The relation of the changed present to the heritage and representation of the past became problematic questions, resulting in a widespread sense of conflicted recollection and a crisis of representation—which
themselves shaped the evolving ideas about "the modern."[9] Modernist
searches for ways to present a no longer "natural" or common sense of continuous memory found paradigmatic expression in the vitalist philosophy of
Bergson, in Proust's idealizing of involuntary memory, in Joyce's stream of
consciousness, and, not least, in the psychology of Freud. These transformations of memory, writes the historian Pierre Nora, imply a decisive shift
in the way memory was imaged and conceived, a shift "from the historical
to the psychological, from the social to the individual, from the objective
message to its subjective reaction." Exemplary articulations of this transformed view of memory are of course found in the works of Freud and
Proust, to whom we owe, writes Nora, "those two intimate and yet universal sites of memory, the primal scene and the celebrated *petite
madeleine.*"[10] These "universal sites" exist within the common structures of
the individual psyche, home to (in subjectivist terms) the whole of the
remembered past.

     For Proust—whose renowned faith in memory may be usefully con-
trasted with postmodernist perceptions—memory was both the tool of his
craft and its object, reflected and discussed throughout *Á la recherche du temps
perdu*. Like Freud's repressed memory, which is hidden but never lost,
Proust too believed that the best part of our memory is "concealed from our
own vision in a more of less prolonged forgetting."[11] True remembrance—
Proust's *mémoire involontaire*—can, however, reveal those hidden memories
and redeem the past from its obscurity. This is accomplished through two
moments: the "salvationist" moment of involuntary memory—an irrational
sensation that occurs outside of time, unwilled, never mechanical, and that
miraculously "restores" a lost or forgotten past; and the temporal process of
remembrance in which we give that unwilled epiphany concrete form.
Potentially triggered by a smell or a taste or by tripping over the roughness
of a stone, Proust's involuntary memory rejects the tyranny of forward-
moving and segmented temporality. It has the power to restore fully what

willed memory cannot—the nuance and significance of the past. Restoration is, however, not given to cognizance through the miracle of sensual recall alone. For this we require a subsequent unfolding and retelling that allows the past to take its place in the present—as narrative. "The important thing for the remembering author," wrote Walter Benjamin of Proust, "is not what he experienced, but the *weaving of his memory,* the Penelope work of recollection."[12] That is, the irrationally experienced past only becomes significant once it is recollected through time, in all its detail, and organized into a cognitively convincing shape. This shape is the narrative structure of the *Recherche* through which a previously forgotten history is restored to conscious memory—and simultaneously returned to the progressions of time.

This description of memory's potential recoverability is no longer relevant for postmodernism—which allows for neither a real remembering "self," nor for narrative "weavings," nor for unambiguous epiphanies. Postmodernism's changed view of memory is expressed in the theater by a set of new characteristics. In postmodern theater, voice and image is privileged over narrative and character, the collective over the individual, the interactive over the self-sufficient, intact text. In this reformed reality, the question of *who* is doing the remembering is problematic. Unlike memory in modernist plays (in Chekhov or Strindberg or Arthur Miller, discussed in chapter 1), where a protagonist, or group, is the explicit source of remembrance, postmodern drama has no psychologically endowed characters who can act as the locus of recall. For postmodernism, individual recall is no longer the relevant paradigm, since the rooted, autonomous self, the subject-as-consciousness, is no longer available. When, as in Beckett's late plays, recall appears to arise from a specific subject, that subject is him/herself fractured, "falling to bits,"[13] and placed at a remove from the "remembering" voice(s). The link between an experiencing subject and articulated recall is severed, as is the faith in memory to capture truth, find origins, or heal. "Ya' know, you'd be O.K., Becky, if you had a self," Hoss says to his manager in Shepard's *The Tooth of Crime;* "So would I. Something to fall back on in a moment of doubt."[14] Hollowed out, lacking an ego or a core of human essence, these are not characters who develop in time and inspire audience identification. In the plays I discuss we'll see the subject in fragments (Beckett), in a relay of moments (Shepard, Müller), as an ideological construct (Bernhard, Parks); mostly, as a collective collage. Such a "subject" cannot be the source of memory; memory works *through* these figures, but never originates in them. The fragmentation of experience and the dissolution of a unified self—basic topoi of postmodern thought—banish memory from the security of individual control, rendering it sourceless, without a psychological home, as though emanating from a culturally determined collective subconscious.

Collective remembrance implies collective memories. Aside from Beckett, whose late plays will be discussed in terms of their theatrical representations of memoried "states of being," all of the plays I consider evoke a historical or cultural terrain common to the audience for whom they were intended. Memory-theater, like postmodern thought, contains the marks and traces of cultural discourses and historical remains—but torn out of context, ungrounded, returned in the shape of dreams. Memory in these plays is rarely polemical, and its uses are never dogmatic, but a variety of agendas do radiate through the memoried images advanced. These "agendas" are sparked by a collective store of images, by specific social situations, and by the audience toward whom they are directed. The pasts we find in the texts I discuss are drawn (largely) from the failures of Western history—ranging from the French and socialist revolutions (Müller) to the American destruction of its native populations (Shepard), from slavery and deracination (Parks) to Communism and Nazism (Müller, Bernhard). Memory-theater might be doubly defined as a theater that *imitates* conflicted and sometimes repressed or erased memories of a shared past; and as a theater that *initiates* processes of remembrance through practices of repetition, conflation, regression, through recurrent scenes, involuntary voice, echoing, overlap, and simultaneity. Some of the texts I discuss are written with the hallucinatory openness of voices in memory—without designated speakers, without punctuation, without stage instructions. Some consist of long repetitive monologues, or of static stage images surrounded by piped-in voices. The immobility of many of these plays—the suspended head of *That Time,* the isolated mouth of *Not I,* Bernhard's static speakers on the abstracted stages of Europe's past, Parks's black Lincoln, forever fixed within the moment of his death—and the often derealized "voicings" of the past through echoing speeches dispersed and shared among speakers, turn these stages into composite *mindscapes* flooded by the collective voice of memory.

Postmodern memory-theater involves an explicit (and usually "loaded") evocation of a collective past (Beckett, here as elsewhere, is the exception), confounded by pastiche procedures, by a destabilized perspective, or by other deconstructive tactics. The past erupts on these stages with contradictory images and irrational transformations. In Müller's *The Task* (*Der Auftrag,* 1979), for example, scenes shift from the French Revolution (or rather, memories of the Revolution), to an elevator leading into the future (in which the unnamed passenger has forgotten his task). The Revolution, and its betrayals, is remembered through shifting voices of the dead, the unattributed, the parodied, even through the voice of the Angel of Despair. This collage of voices and sitings disallows narrative organization and denies closure. One of the themes that I isolate in these plays is the affinity between the structurally chaotic influx of memories, and pathologies of trauma. Postmodern memory-theater is often overburdened by disconnected stimuli: conflicting discourses, unexplained objects, intruding images, overlapping voices, styles that veer and shift in baffling and sudden ways. The same play (Müller's *Task,* for example), may include ghosts and angels, Grand Guignol and epic masks, past and future, as well as long, static, unattributed monologues. There is no unity of enunciation, no closure, no easy way to "read" or organize the sensual and discursive overload. Moreover, the past is rarely actually "recalled" in these plays: it encroaches, intrudes, forces its way in and possesses the figures. Often, the memories burst upon the stage without order, causality, direction, or coherence, as though in reaction to what Heiner Müller (following Stephen Daedalus) has called the "nightmare of history."[15]

This overabundant influx of stimuli echoes Freud's description of trauma as a climactic occurrence that rips the *Reizschutz,* the protective filter of consciousness, resulting in an uncensored "flooding" of images— and memories (discussed in chapter 1). By releasing and "bringing up" the past, the plays I discuss remember (and perhaps mourn) the past; by conflating and displacing the chronologies of the past, they distance, and perhaps try to forget, the past. This dialectic of remembrance and forgetting works on many levels. Shepard returns to the defunct myths of the American past, to the repressed voices and the forgotten oppressions as though, writes John Lahr, he were "yearning for a new history."[16] Bernhard's characters constantly quote from the past, releasing taboo discourses that target, and aggravate, the repressions of his audience. Müller's shaping of memory is often a conscious effort to stem forgetting, as well as to complicate the remembrance of Germany's recent past, Nazi and Communist. Suzan-Lori Parks combats forgetting by "inventing" memory, theatrically. Speaking for an African-American community bereaved of its memory and history, she aims to "recover" an erased past by "re-membering and staging historical events which, through their happening on stage, are ripe for inclusion in the canon of history."[17] Clearly, the plays I address have varying memory agendas and are not all doing the same kind of "memory work"; but the sense of a *conflicted and traumatized relation to the past* is common to them all. These plays are knowing, self-reflective, consciously positioned within a specific discourse. They forge a dialogue with the memory of the audience, forcing on us the tasks of remembrance; while their chaotic form and thematic conflations deny the possibility of reconstruction, recuperation, or of a Proustian "salvationist" restoration of the past.

The memoried obsession of postmodern drama is not an isolated phenomenon. It is part of a broader cultural longing for—and inability to—return to and have done with, the past. The present preoccupation with memory and memoried art probably has as much to do with loss and endings—the loss of faith in what Jürgen Habermas calls the "unfinished project" of modernity, and the ending of this violent century—as with a desire to retrieve or restore. Andreas Huyssen has suggested that the "turn" to memory in postmodernism is a reaction to the modernist structure of temporality that celebrated the new as utopian.[18] The optimism of "make it new" (which failed, in the eyes of many, to make it better) is mocked in postmodern techniques of pastiche and repetition, in its stress on the circulations and conflations of recall. Ideologically, postmodernism differs from the modern in terms of the foundational concept of "progress." Progress implies linear and causal increase through time, development, improvement, teleological faith. The virtues of progress and goal-oriented history—compromised beyond repair by this century's ideological excesses—are rejected in postmodernism and replaced by concepts stressing synchronicity: the simultaneous, repetitive, plural, and interactive (discussed in chapter 1). It has become a commonplace to speak of modernism as privileging time, while postmodernism privileges space. Space, in modernism, writes Michel Foucault, "was treated as the dead, the fixed, the undialectical, the immobile. Time, on the contrary, was richness, fecundity, life."[19] Temporality underlies historical thinking and allowed in modernism for the development of utopian models and emancipatory explanations such as, for example, Marxism. Spatial paradigms—such as Camillo's theater—which embrace the synchronous and simultaneous in place of the temporal and stratified, are, on the contrary, implicitly ahistorical. Concern for origins and hierarchy is replaced in postmodernism by discussions of remains and traces, of the displaced and dispersed incursions of a once causal, rooted world. That is, a conceptual vocabulary based on process, development, causality, and thus suited for historical thought, is replaced in postmodernism by concepts more compatible to the field of memory.

Memory has, indeed, been a constantly recurring theme during these last decades of the millennium. "We speak so much of memory because there is so little of it left," claims Pierre Nora, who undertook to chart

French national identity through the *lieux de mémoire*—the collective "sites," or remains, of memory—within present-day France (discussed in chapter 1).[20] Numerous books on memory and memorialization have been written over the past two decades. History, ethnicity, psychology, architecture, literature, film—have all been viewed through questions of memory formations and as carriers of memory traces. Simon Schama's *Landscape and Memory* (1995) is only the latest attempt to read even woodlands and fjords as the projections of a memoried consciousness, and as the bearers of national identities. The desire for memorialization has also been carried over onto the public spaces and official sites of Europe and the United States. Museums and monuments commemorating the Holocaust of Europe's Jews, the devastation of Hiroshima and Nagasaki, the fallen American soldiers in Vietnam, grew incomparably—and not without controversy—in the eighties, decades after the events being remembered had ended. This monumentalizing mania is not without its irony. "The less memory is experienced from the inside," writes Pierre Nora, "the more it exists only through its exterior scaffolding and outward signs."[21] Or, as James Young rightly notes, "once we assign monumental form to memory, we have to some degree divested ourselves of the obligation to remember."[22] Thus the obsession with marking memory may in fact portend an awareness of its erosion, perhaps even the desire to forget.

This observation—that monuments often replace memory and sanction forgetting—was overtly incorporated into some of the memorials designed during the eighties. One fascinating example of such self-reflexivity is the *Monument against Fascism, War, and Violence—and for Peace and Human Rights,* designed by the conceptual/performance artists Jochen and Esther Gerz, and erected in Hamburg, Germany, in 1986. Termed by its creators as a *Gegen-Denkmal* (a counter-monument), this astonishing project is as much a meditation on—and theorizing of—the implications of memorialization as it is a historical edifice. Moreover, it demonstrates the convergence between markers of recall, performance, and postmodern aesthetics, and thus shares a common ground with our subject here. The Gerzes wanted to give sculptural and kinetic shape to a history of fascism without producing an object that would absorb (and replace) the act of memory it was meant to mark, and without aesthetically imitating the ideology their monument was meant to mourn. The memory of Nazism's monumental architecture, and the aspiration of the "thousand-year Reich" to permanence, were concepts against which they wished to react. Another consideration that directed their design was the tendency of monuments to immobilize their spectators, turning the object of commemoration—the remembering community—into passive receivers of meaning. The result of these reflections was an interactive, mobile, mutable, and self-effacing monument that acted as a provocation rather than a sanctified representation of the past.

Set in the midst of a commercial center in Harburg, a community of working-class Germans and Turkish guest-workers on the outskirts of Hamburg, the Gerz monument was a plain, one-meter square, twelve-meters high pillar made of hollow aluminum covered by soft lead. The performative goal of this self-negating shaft was explained on a plaque at the column's base, in German, French, English, Russian, Hebrew, Arabic, and Turkish:

> We invite the citizens of Harburg and visitors to the town, to add their names here to ours. In doing so, we commit ourselves to remain vigilant. As more and more names cover this 12 meter tall lead column, it will gradually be lowered into the ground. One day, it will have disappeared completely and the site of the Harburg monument against fascism will be empty. In the end, it is only we ourselves who can rise up against injustice.

In order to facilitate and encourage spectatorial participation, the artists attached steel-pointed pens on long cables to the corners of the column. And in fact, as reachable sections of the shaft were covered with names, mottoes, graffiti of every sort—and not always reverent in content—the monument was lowered into the ground, allowing for further participatory inscriptions. The speed of its immersion into a hole prepared for this purpose depended entirely on the active engagement of the "spectators."[23] The viewer thus became both witness and coproducer, determining the behavior as well as the appearance of this marker of memory. An additional performative element of this extraordinary monument was the public ceremonies held at each lowering of the pillar. As was the case at the original 1986 unveiling, these subsequent lowerings were attended by dignitaries, media, and members of the community. (It was lowered six times, and totally immersed in 1991; only a stone remained as commemoration to the *act* of its erasure.) These repeated performances, each time with an altered memorial object, underlined the mutability of memory, its unfixed and yet repetitive nature; while the immersion itself signified the disappearance of memory's "exterior scaffolding and outward signs"—similar to the "disappearance" of theatrical performance, which leaves its trace only in the memory of the participating viewer.

The Gerzes' monument, like the plays I discuss, is dedicated to memory. Yet, again like these plays, it neither represents the subject *of* that mem-

ory through mimetic (figurative) imitation, thus prescribing a fixed object
of memory, nor does it predetermine the viewer's reaction *to* the memorialization. The Gerzes' ungainly shaft, scorned by some for its lack of aesthetic charm, likened by others to a chimney, compared by the Gerzes
themselves to a great black knife in the back of Germany[24]—thus recalling
the Nazi rhetoric against Jews and Communists—is not a self-sufficient
monument at all. It can only become meaningful, or become more than an
unsightly graffiti-trap, when perceived by a knowing and "remembering"
viewer. It only exists *as* a monument when it engages the memory and
engenders, activates, a dialogue. In fact, the discussions and "memory
work" stimulated by this postmodern artifact are similar to those that followed Thomas Bernhard's *Heldenplatz* in Vienna (discussed in chapter 6),
which created a serious political scandal in Austria. Like the Gerz monument, it drew its effectiveness from its positioning within a public memory
wound, to which it appealed, and out of which dialogue—and sometimes
cacophony—emerged.

The problem with evaluating postmodern shapings of memory in the
arts has much to do with the dependence of this art *on* its positioning, on the
specific memory discourse in which it intervenes. In addition, evaluation is
problematized by the lack of didacticism, of fixed perspective and determinate meaning available through such shapings. In its open, unfinalized, multiply inscribed form, postmodern art often mingles kitsch and irony, humor
and mourning, ventriloquistic "quotings" and the simultaneous deconstruction of the quoted object. These contradictory perspectives disable unambiguous response and evoke sometimes radically different readings of the
same art object. Bernhard's *Eve of Retirement,* for example, has been hailed
for exposing the hidden memories that continue to thrive in present-day
Germany, and thus for posing a moral challenge "to the historical compulsions which continue to preoccupy it."[25] It has also been accused of a postmodern "disruption of time and memory" in which remembrance is
weightless and any political stance is reduced "to secret caprice, repression
and perversion."[26] Both radically opposed readings refer to the same object,
viewed by two differently situated critics. In a different genre, but in similar terms, the paintings of the German artist Anselm Kiefer, paintings that
recall Germany's Nazi history in both mythic and ironic terms, simultaneously quoting that past and framing it in a manner that might connote
mourning, have aroused drastically variant responses. During the late eighties, Kiefer was hailed in America as having lifted postmodern art to singular
heights through his profound evocations of history and his expressive use of
ideas and materials. During that same period in Germany, Kiefer was

accused of fascist aesthetics, of inspiring and conjuring up Germanic myths imbued with neo-Nazi tendencies. In 1984, that same Kiefer was accorded a retrospective exhibition at the Israel Museum in Jerusalem, a then unusual event for a German artist. His evocation of mourning is considered the source of his success among his Jewish audience.[27] In each case, responses to Kiefer's extraordinarily complex and multicoded art hinged on the type of memory read into it from within varying communal contexts. His work's appeal to "memory" is undisputed; but the interpretation of that memory— as in the case of Bernhard—had everything to do with the type of memory it aroused and inspired in differing circumstances. The dialogue carried on with the paintings, the meeting between viewer and art, finally determined (though this determination may not be final), the way it was valued.

The indeterminacy of the art object within postmodernism brings me to a word concerning my own choice of objects, of dramatic texts. The five playwrights in this book—representative of a memoried theater—were chosen, first and foremost, because, to my mind, they are among the most original and exciting dramatists writing within a postmodern aesthetic. They share a certain set of postmodern characteristics, although variously shaped in each, and directed toward varying types of "memory work." Aside from the still young but already acclaimed African-American Parks, none of my choices are, I think, surprising. The broader reception of these playwrights has confirmed them, in their own countries and internationally, to be among the most powerful and influential voices of the contemporary stage. The importance of their work might, in fact, be considered "canonic" (a paradoxical concept, admittedly, when dealing with the postmodern) to any discussion of the connections between a postmodern form of drama and the fertile field of memory studies. In addition, all of these playwrights— with the exception of Beckett—belong to the two dramatic literatures I know best: German and American. It is striking that so much excellent memory-drama has emerged from these two very different cultures, with such divergent histories. American postmodernism is the effect of an advanced capitalistic society whose ubiquitous technology and mediated forms of communication have given new meaning to notions of simultaneity and the interactive. With Germany or German-language drama, postmodern expressions are more closely connected to the historical chasm following World War II, and to the consequent break with earlier modes of thinking and representation. Not surprisingly, as I show in my reading of the plays, these two cultures have produced opposed approaches to memory in their theater: Shepard and Parks explore the erasures of American memory, its disappearance into amnesia and capitalist commodification. These losses lead to anxiety, nostalgia, and—particularly in the case of Suzan-Lori Parks—mourning. Müller and Bernhard, on the contrary, theatricalize a surfeit and saturation of historical memory and a chaos of ideological traces. Born of historical rupture and ideological ruin, their plays work with repression, taboos, and trauma.

Despite the apparent divisions between American and German-language authors, the overlaps among them crosses national lines. Shepard's collage monologues and character transformations are closer to Müller than to Parks. Bernhard's static theater and "talking heads" have more in common with Beckett's dramaturgy than with Müller's. Memory has a far more political tenor for Müller, Bernhard, and Parks, for example, than it does for Beckett and Shepard. Müller, Bernhard, and Parks also share a demanding relation to their audiences, insisting upon the spectator's coproductive work in their theaters, and carrying on overt dialogues with the knowledge and memory of their viewers. There is much diversity among these writers, and I would agree with Geoffrey Hartman that "memory [has] many shapes, which should not be prematurely unified."[28] Despite this diversity, I will claim that all of these playwrights stand (in at least a portion of their work) at the onerous intersection between a theatrical postmodern aesthetic and the commands of a memoried consciousness: and that is precisely the intersection that this book undertakes to study.

Chapter 1

Memory, History, Postmodern Drama
Theoretical Accounts

Coming to Terms: On the Postmodern

My use of the term *postmodern* is pragmatic as well as formal. It refers to the way plays function and are received in the world, as well as to how they are shaped aesthetically. Certain characteristics distinguish postmodern litera-ture: fragmentation, indeterminacy, reflexivity, intertextuality, montage techniques, temporal conflation, randomness. Postmodern theater is addi-tionally characterized through its emphasis on voice and image, rather than on narrative and character, emphasizing the collective and interactive over the individual and self-sufficient text. The distinctiveness of postmodern theater, especially in terms of its difference from the modernist or avant-garde drama and theater it sometimes resembles, has been convincingly argued by the theater semiotician Erika Fischer-Lichte. Her discussion is especially useful for connecting the aesthetic shaping of a postmodern dra-matic vision with the social mind-set—the zeitgeist—within which it was created and to which it appeals.[1]

As Hal Foster had already shown, postmodern art cannot be discussed merely in terms of an aesthetic, as though it existed "apart, without 'pur-pose,' all but beyond history" and formally self-sufficient.[2] Indeed, he sug-gests that postmodernism must be viewed ideologically as an *antiaesthetic* that problematizes the very notion of a separation of realms, and insists on a rela-tion between a world and artistic form. In a similar vein, Fischer-Lichte problematizes the idea of postmodernism's difference from modernism. Asking how the most prominent characteristics of postmodern drama differ from those we might find, for example, in the expressionism of Kokoschka, the surrealism of Apollinaire, the dada texts by Tzara or Goll, or the reflexive plays of Pirandello, she concludes that they cannot be differenti-ated either on the semantic, the pragmatic, or the metasemiotic levels. In

one form or another, she claims, the early avant-garde plays display the same
dissolution of the self, redefinition of the relationship between time and
space, focus on the interaction between text and audience (dada, especially),
parallelisms, pluralisms, and emphasis on performance over representation
that we associate with postmodern drama. She then shifts her inquiry to ask
of the relations—or structures—formed by and among the distinctive characteristics; and to ask about "the historical, social *Zeitgeist* of the age to
which the structure of relations corresponds." In the avant-garde theater,
Fischer-Lichte writes, these factors form clear links with one another so
"that a structure is formed"—a structure that, in turn, related to a culture
crisis of the period.[3] The various semiotic factors, disparate and disjunctive
though they be, cohere in avant-garde theater to form an enunciation that
has to do with audience provocation and a consciousness of imminent social
and cultural transformation—goals no longer relevant in the age of postmodernism. In the case of dada, for example, the audience was to be
shocked, provoked into aggression through the nonlinearity, incoherence,
and conflated devices used. Postmodern drama, on the contrary, assumes an
audience with changed attitudes of reception, within whom cultural change
"has long since been effected," and thus shock is neither intended nor relevant. Fragmentation and collage, for example, are not meant to shock the
spectator into a reformed view of reality; rather, "the device should encourage spectators *already oriented toward the principle of randomness* to apply their
own meanings" to the given form.[4]

David Harvey put it this way: a central difference between modernist
and postmodern art is not the question of wholeness or fragmentation, but
how the fragment is understood. The tendency to splinter in order to form
a better whole characterizes modernism. On the other hand, the idea of the
splinter as a reflection of the available reality is found in postmodernism.
The multiple perspectivism and relativism of modernism—in surrealism, for
example—is an epistemology through which "the true nature of a unified,
though complex, underlying reality" was to be revealed.[5] In postmodernism, equally complex and split, no such underlying assumption exists.
Along similar lines, Fischer-Lichte argues that avant-garde and postmodern
performances differ in the philosophical and ideological assumptions that
precede and produce the theater event, and through which the event is subsequently received and interpreted: the existing zeitgeist. The role of the
spectator cannot be overestimated in establishing this distinction. Postmodernism shifts the locus of attention from the object—so central to modernism—to the transaction between spectator and object. It does not
assume, and in fact deconstructs the idea of, a representative objective

viewer.[6] Thus, a theater in which the represented object, and representation itself, is unfixed, is aimed at an audience already oriented toward such a view: an audience able to productively read multiple meanings through a mind-set that has internalized multiplicity and contradictions.[7] In this way, Fischer-Lichte writes, "Beckett's later dramas (*Play, Not I, That Time, Ends and Odds*), Heiner Müller's plays since *Germania Tod in Berlin* (*Germania—Death in Berlin*), and the dramas of Peter Handke and Thomas Bernhard can actually be identified through the very distinctive characteristic . . . that they are open to the reader/spectator"—without pregiven hermeneutic designation—precisely because their various levels do not cohere.[8]

The discussion of postmodernism can now be expanded to include the social and political expressions of a postmodern zeitgeist that helped shape, and within which must be read, the splintered forms of postmodern memory-theater. On the social level, postmodernity has been broadly interpreted as a shift from the ordering impulse of modernist rationality to a release of control, a collapse of boundaries, a rejection of center and hierarchy. From the dominance of a "culture of control" that imposes structuring, regulating, and legislative reason, emphasizing foundations and universalizing concepts, we move with postmodernism toward the contingent, provisional, fragmentary, plural, and interactive. This opening up of boundaries and hierarchies is reflected in the remapping of political and social power since World War II, and in the general trend toward rereading the past. A destabilization of the West, loss of European hegemony, decolonization of the third world, the dispersal of economic power, migrations, and a new class of intellectuals drawn from previously oppressed populations, all contribute to renewed thinking about history—which has itself become contested territory. Gender, ethnic, racial, sexual and social perspectives have been reconfigured and expanded, leading to new and multiple power bases, as well as multiple, and unstable, redefinitions of the self, the body, society, and the past. New technologies of communication, of computer memory and information retrieval, give the individual greater options, but put in question the old organizational categories, the old criteria and hierarchies through which the multitude of new information might be read. Thus, greater freedom and greater chaos seem to occur simultaneously.

Postmodernism is considered by some to have a serious emancipatory agenda, opening hierarchies and margins, freeing thought from outworn ideologies and totalizing metanarratives.[9] Others see it as a playground of pastiche and *jouissance* "where pluralism and difference contrast with the older 'terrorism' of totalizing discourses."[10] Steven Connor's analysis of the double nature of postmodernism, especially in terms of its theories of cultural politics, directly addresses the polar views of postmodernism as a world-changing paradigm (an emancipatory agenda) and, alternatively, a structureless fluff of playfulness (a playground of pastiche). Postmodern theories, Connor suggests, offer the "dual prospect, on the one hand of a transformation of history by a sheer act of imaginative will, and on the other, of an absolute weightlessness in which anything is imaginatively possible, because nothing really matters."[11] Both "prospects"—seriousness and weightlessness—coexist in the theater I will discuss, defeating any attempt at easy position-taking, while forcing the viewer to bear and sift more than he or she can (cognitively, and emotionally) carry, as Heiner Müller put it.[12] Another version of such double inscription has been theorized by Linda Hutcheon, who argues (too forcefully, perhaps) that the ruptures of postmodern fiction are never neutral or detached, but rather contain within them the paradox "of complicity and critique, of reflexivity and historicity, that at once inscribes and subverts" the ideologies and conventions of a given culture.[13] The plays I discuss are all deeply serious and often seriously ironic. They build on the audiences' knowledge of the past (or, rather, of how the past is usually represented), in order to question and disrupt that knowledge through multiple, conflated perspectives. As Umberto Eco put it, the past must be "revisited"—"since it may not be destroyed, for its destruction results in silence";[14] but the revisiting must be ironic, knowing, in collusion with the reader/viewer. These knowing "revisits" are often—certainly in plays by Thomas Bernhard, Heiner Müller, or Suzan-Lori Parks—provocations that challenge the usual representations of that past, or of the present in its light.[15]

The bulk of this book deals with postmodern configurations of memory in the theater. The uniqueness of these configurations may be easier to grasp by way of a preliminary contrast with memory formations and devices found in some of the plays central to the modernist canon. Willy Loman (*Death of a Salesman,* 1949) and Tom Wingfield (*The Glass Menagerie,* 1945), for example, come to us in the forms of remembered pasts, in flashbacks and conjured-up moments; both are the protagonists of "memory plays." Arthur Miller originally planned to call his subjective remembrance of a life "Inside His Head." Willy relives past encounters with his brother, his sons, his lover—encounters that are signified as hallucinatory, and thus as psychological aberrations. The play merges a realistic present with a past experienced by Willy in his *mémoire involontaire.* These subjective remembrances "return" Willy to a past that may perhaps "explain"—to us, if not to him—the reasons for a failed life. In Tennessee Williams's play, rationalizing life's effects is even more explicit. The entire play is a narrated flashback "framed" by the "rememberer" (Tom) who tries to exculpate his guilt at leaving his mother and sister by reinvestigating his actions. The play is an act of confession, of psychoanalytic recall publically performed. In the "Production Notes," Williams terms *The Glass Menagerie* "a memory play" through which Tom learns that "to escape from a trap he has to act without pity."[16] In both of these plays, memory has a restorative and explanatory function; it is seen as psychological and individual, constructed through narrative recall, introspection, flashback. "I turn back time," Tom says in his opening "frame" monologue: "The play is memory. Being a memory play, it is dimly lighted, it is sentimental, it is not realistic."[17] These memory plays use subjective conventions in order to "see" into the mind, to reconstruct a life, and thus to find interpretive frameworks for personal or social failure. In the plays I discuss, subjectivity is no longer unified or given to reconstruction; and memory is neither psychologically formatted nor rooted in an originary impetus toward some future goal. Narrative devices (flashbacks, realistic frames) are abandoned, as are appeals to a teleological understanding of the past.

Other, less individualized examples of modernist uses of memory can be found, for example, in Chekhov's *Three Sisters* (1901)—where a group of characters, all deaf to the desires and memories of the others, speak parallel monologues of longing and recall that almost disrupt communication or plot. However, as Peter Szondi notes, despite the characters' intoxication by memory and dreams and their "psychic absence from social life," the play retains formal devices that uphold those categories necessary for it to be dramatic and forward moving.[18] Memory, as nostalgia and illusion, functions in Chekhov as a sign of the impotence and ultimate irrelevance of an entire social class; it doesn't so much recall the past as identify stagnation in the present. Again, and despite the poetic voice of longing, its use is rational and explanatory. Another example might be Strindberg's *Dream Play* (1907), in which a world is recalled in all its illogical transformations. Although there appears to be no unified self or world in this play, everything emanates from one consciousness "transcending all," as Strindberg writes—"the consciousness of the dreamer," and thus returns to the psychological unity discussed above. In all of these plays, and here is the difference from our postmodern memory-theater, we find paradigms of a basically unified (personal or group) consciousness, employing coherent dramatic enunciations in order that a past be illuminated and a present explained—rather than diffused, decentered, problematized—through memory.

A final, more recent example, precisely pinpoints the structural differ-

ences. Harold Pinter's 1978 play *Betrayal* does not work through personal
flashback or through an internalized reliving of a failed past. It is, rather, a
formal study of the relationship between three people over time, functioning through a series of realistic tableaux that move backward into the past.
The play begins with the meeting of the two estranged lovers and with the
question—do you remember, do you? It then goes backward—*structurally,*
not psychologically—placing the emphasis not on what the characters
remember or thought, but on how the audience experiences knowledge
that is constantly being revised backward. The unfolding of the play acts to
constantly displaces what we (the viewers) know through additional archae-
ological layers of the hidden. And yet, although inverted, the structure of
Betrayal is still fully "realistic" and centered, assuming and moving toward a
source—a moment of inception (of desire, of the first betrayal) that becomes
a moment of longing and loss, or perhaps of regret, in the light of its consequences. We understand the play's story—and are motivated *to* understand
the story—by constantly putting it back together again in our own memories, from end to start. Thus, although Pinter's play moves backward and
forward at once, and although memory is never simplistic or stable or even
necessarily reliable, Pinter's relentless retrospective structure retains its faith
in linearity, causality, in the unified subject and world, and in a source
(however trivial) that can be recovered through memory: all terms that are
questioned and exploded in postmodern drama.

In the following sections, I present some aspects of a memory discourse that
will inform my subsequent discussions of postmodern memory-plays and
performances. The four contexts I isolate could be categorized as a historical, a philosophical, a psychological, and an apocalyptic view of memory.
But although all of these aspects exist, they do not neatly separate: they
overlap and intertwine. By confronting memory from a variety of angles
and disciplines, "prismatically" rather than through a single system, I hope
to afford a rich and nuanced vocabulary—rather than a coherent and "totalizing" model—for viewing the never stable or systematic, yet the recurrent
and persistent intersections between the opulence of memory, and the varieties of postmodern drama.

Horizontal Memory: "Lieux de Mémoire"

In the 1980s, the French historian Pierre Nora proposed a new method for
studying the past: a "cartographic" method that charts the sites and symbols

that, at a given moment, codify and anchor national memory. In a seven-volume collaborative work containing one hundred and fifty articles by historians and intellectuals, arranged thematically rather than chronologically, Nora amassed discussions of objects, places, texts, concepts, even verbal coins (such as "Liberté, Egalité, Fraternité") that contain or rupture collective identity. His project, titled *Les Lieux de Mémoire*,[19] involved a rereading of the French past through its symbolic, functional, and material traces, creating a horizontal "mapping" of the "'places' where memories converge, condense, conflict, and define relationships between past, present, and future" in a world no longer suffused with memory.[20] Nora noted that the impetus for his study of memory—as inscribed in concrete *loci memoriae*—was Francis Yates's study of classical mnemonic practices that taught orators to remember speeches by associating ideas with images mentally deployed in real or imagined architectures. By developing the concept of spatial mnemonics, Nora continued a tradition of memorization-through-localization by circulating the individualized "theater of the mind" advocated by Cicero and Quintilian, through the public sites and shared icons that constitute *collective* memory formations and dissipations.

What, however, is "collective memory"? The pioneer analytical study of this subject was undertaken in the 1920s by the French sociologist Maurice Halbwachs. Originally a student of Henri Bergson, Halbwachs opposed his teacher's idealist approach to memory. Bergson, influenced by Freud, placed all memory—collective and private—within the recesses of the individual mind; past experiences, he thought, are abstracted and vaulted within the ephemeral site of the psyche.[21] Halbwachs, on the contrary, believed that individual memory is only possible, and is itself formed, within the concrete spaces of a public social world. There is no private memory that is not linked to the verbal conventions, traditions of thought, and sited stimuli of the collective, he argued. Mikhail Bakhtin's poignant image of language as "overpopulated" with the intentions of others, as never private but always collective, always already filled with meaning, approximates this view.[22] For Halbwachs, as also for Bakhtin, time itself is a social construction rather than a subjective experience, forged and sustained through the conscious efforts—and changing agendas—of institutions and the group. As such, memory for Halbwachs is not about the retrieval of a possibly repressed but essentially unchanging past, but rather about the shifting "social frames" that allow the past's *reconfiguration* to emerge in the present.[23]

Nora's work emerges from Halbwachs's. Like Halbwachs, he begins his discussion with the way collective memory—affective and magical—was replaced in modernity by the intellectual and secular pursuit of history. Until the collapse of a rural peasant culture during the nineteenth century, and the ensuing "acceleration of history," memory and history had been experienced as coeval. In the "organic" memory of old, Nora writes, the assumption was "that the past could be retrieved" by a present that was, in fact, no more than its continuation. This synthesis came apart under the pressure of secularization and with new forms of historical thinking (historiography) that rendered the past abstract and philosophical. With the rupture between memory and history, a world that had appeared continuous and thus predictable collapsed, leaving us with nothing more "than sifted and sorted historical traces."[24] So have we gone "from the idea of a visible past to an invisible one," Nora writes; "from a solid and steady past to our fractured past; from a history sought in the continuity of memory to a memory cast in the discontinuity of history."[25] The current obsession with collecting and commemoration, Nora suggests, testifies to the anxiety caused by such discontinuity, and to a nostalgia for shared memorial traditions. It testifies as well, to their loss. "There are *lieux de mémoire,* sites of memory," Nora writes, "because there are no longer *milieux de mémoire,* real environments of memory."[26]

Nora's monumental study aimed to collect the discontinuous remains of a fractured communal memory and dispersed history, and to chart them in two respects: spatially, by identifying concrete "markers" as sites of memory; and by showing the capricious and shifting significations of those sites over time, that is, the instability of their meanings. Through a methodology that is synchronic and thematic and places theatrical emphasis on the uses of space, Nora eludes the narrative demands of historical progression, emphasizing instead an ever-changing, often conflicted collective identity that emerges in the synchronic concrete remains of the present. Through this, Nora also creates a historical memory model that coincides with the tenets of postmodern thought. Nora's new index of national identity is not anchored within a predeterminate historical pattern or presumed telos (no longer available), but is rather, like postmodern memory-theater, multiple and horizontal, shifting, pluralistic, unfinalized. Memory cast "in the discontinuity of history" gives us, for example, the meetings of Napoleon and the Nibelungs at Stalingrad (Müller's *Germania Death in Berlin*), or of a black Lincoln look-alike lost in the Great Hole of history (Parks's *The America Play*). It gives us parallel and simultaneous memorial images without hierarchy or connections, without a clear tradition of interpretation, devoid of grounding, and liberated from the "historicism" and "official" historical narratives so despised by, for example, Walter Benjamin.

Walter Benjamin and the Ruins of Memory

In a different vein, and in a period further in the past, the memory traces of a discontinuous history is also the subject—or rather the object—of Walter Benjamin's "Theses on the Philosophy of History" (completed 1940). Benjamin's "Theses" is best known for its creation of the "Angelus Novus," one of the most ubiquitous icons of postmodern historical consciousness and of its cultural forms. Wim Wenders and Peter Handke quote the "Theses" and emulate its "angel" in their memory-film *Wings of Desire* (*Der Himmel über Berlin,* 1988). Müller, in constant dialogue with Benjamin, creates counter-angels, angels of despair (discussed in chap. 3), while Tony Kushner, in his *Angels in America,* offers us a redemptive angel of hope. Even Laurie Anderson, in her performance-piece *The Nerve Bible,* includes passages from the "Theses." Through quote and image, through textual reference and thematic development, these postmodern artists expand our "angel's-eyed" view of history and become, like those angels, witnesses to history's wreckage in the present. Witnessing the ruins is indeed the major function of Benjamin's airborne angel. Ever in motion, he is depicted as being helplessly blown into the future by a storm from Paradise, tumbling into time while looking to the past—"His eyes are staring, his mouth is open, his wings are spread." Like a helpless spectator forced to witness the spectacle of the past, the angel views the fragments and havoc of history, the "wreckage upon wreckage" growing skyward before him. A strange angel this, most unlike the romantic Hollywood messengers who can restore or teach or bring hope to the suicidal on Christmas Eve. Benjamin's angel of history is more like Damiel and Cassiel from Wenders and Handke's film-poem about the ruins of Berlin: a passive angel caught between past and future, that is: lost in the eternal present. He is unable to act, and despite his pity he cannot "stay, awaken the dead, and make whole what has been smashed," to quote Benjamin. With eyes staring and mouth agape, he can only bear witness to the wreckage.[27]

The view of modern Western history as a "catastrophe," as a succession of ruins—from the failed French Revolution to the successful mass-murders at Auschwitz—is central to the postmodern historical sense, to its offshoot in *posthistoire,* and to its depiction of the past. The unique twentieth-century intersections of rationality and genocide, of advanced technology and nuclear destruction, of an ideology of progress and a praxis of barbarism, have become constitutive paradigms for the postmodern mind. Benjamin contributes to this store of images not only through his view of history as "wreckage upon wreckage," but through his view of the past as a formless

potential that responds to, and emerges from, the needs of the present—
which is the only incontestable reality. Like St. Augustine, Benjamin could
say, "There are three times: the present of the past, the present of the present, the present of the future."[28] For Benjamin, the present dictates the past
we use and remember; the past is called forth and "saved" by the needs of
"now," of Benjamin's *Jetztzeit*. Unlike the Hegelian idealist perspective in
which historical Reason shapes historical evolution in an ever-perfecting
progression, for Benjamin, memory, especially Proust's involuntary memory, is the central category of an historical consciousness. But for Benjamin,
unlike Proust, this memory is not individual and ephemeral: it is collective,
material, historically potent.

Rejecting the pretensions of historicism to attain objective knowledge
of the past, Benjamin's historian is guided by the concrete demands of the
present, its political constellations that preserve traces of a forgotten or
repressed past. The present animates, "redeems," and also thinks about itself
through the past to which it is drawn. In his "Theses," Benjamin wrote,
"To articulate the past historically does not mean to recognize it 'the way it
really was' (Ranke). It means to seize hold of a memory as it flashes up at a
moment of danger" in the present.[29] The "needs" of the present—especially
in times of crisis and change—determine the past that the present remembers. By recalling the past to memory, the (repressed, often marginalized)
past is saved from oblivion and becomes an extension of the present it illu-
minates. As Stéphane Mosès put it, the "Proustian experience of resurrect-
ing the past in the illumination of recollection is elevated to the status of a
historical category" by Benjamin.[30]

Since the past is created through the needs of the present, history cannot be seen as a linear continuity, as a narrative with fixed and causal
episodes. It is, after all, the victors who compose the "narrative" of the past,
and they compose a "continuum" that always excludes the story of the van-
quished. In Benjamin's famous formulation (thesis 16): "The historical
materialist leaves it to others to be drained by the whore called 'Once upon
a time' in historicism's bordello. He remains in control of his powers, man
enough to *blast open the continuum* of history."[31] The continuum, that closed
and causal narrative of the past, silences the memory of the defeated and
powerless for whom the past is an uneven succession of fragmented and
interrupted moments. "The history of the oppressed is a discontinuous history," Benjamin wrote; "continuity is that of the oppressors."[32] Thus, in
order to overcome this historicist hold on the past, and to open the past to
those excluded, Benjamin proposes a view of history that would *imitate*

memory, stressing the breaks and interruptions of the past and created in the form of discontinuous fragments.

Benjamin's imagistic descriptions of a historical/redemptive methodology based on memory-moments inspired by the needs of the present is highly evocative for the plays I will be studying. The past as a vast unformed heap of ruins and wreckage reaching skyward, spread out, available yet incomprehensible, is a distinctly theatrical image, reminiscent of Hamlet's opening lines in Heiner Müller's *Hamletmachine:* "I stood at the shore and talked with the surf BLABLA, the ruins of Europe behind me." These ruins are recaptured in the stage Jannis Kounellis designed for Müller's *Mauser* project (discussed in chapter 3)—a stage clogged with disconnected furnishings from various periods, and at their center a huge smokestack and train-tracks recalling Auschwitz. For Benjamin, as well as for the postmodern imagination, "a preoccupation with fragments and ruins became, as it were, a literary signature."[33] The past as multiformed, as intersecting and *coexistent* with the present, and the rejection of deterministic historicism and causal progressions as principles of historical retrievals, all feed directly into the memoried visions of the past in these plays. In Suzan-Lori Parks's *Imperceptible Mutabilities in the Third Kingdom,* for example, the present of her black-American figures is inspired and viewed through the choral voices of a people lost in "middle passage," on slave ships forever moored between Africa and America. The past in her play, as in Benjamin's thinking, is never prior or linear. It coexists with the present—but hidden and oppressed, needing to be sought out, blasted out, reformed, re-created, re-membered.

The centrality of the fragment and the explosion, of the "blasting open" of history and the collapse of linear and controlling "grand narratives," has been subsequently addressed by Jean-François Lyotard, especially in *The Differend*. Lyotard locates the breaking point of scientific reason, the "blasting open" and destruction of the Enlightenment narrative of progress and rationality, at Auschwitz. His famous image of the seismic end of an era parallels the topos of trauma that I will discuss below:

> Suppose that an earthquake destroys not only lives, buildings, and objects but also the instruments used to measure earthquakes directly and indirectly. The impossibility of quantitatively measuring it does not prohibit, but rather inspires in the minds of the survivors the idea of a very great seismic force. The scholar claims to know nothing about it, but the common person has a complex feeling, the one aroused by the negative presentation of the indeterminate.[34]

The long-term result of this explosion, which, as Heiner Müller has said, left a mark on the entire European subconscious,[35] was the shattering not only of the continuum of history, but also the *shape of its representation.* Lyotard writes that thought itself "cannot be phrased in the accepted idioms" after the destruction of its groundings (the rational instruments of measurement) at Auschwitz. Thus, Lyotard requires of the historian of Auschwitz, or the historian of the trauma of history, to lend an ear "to what is not presentable under the rules of knowledge"[36]—a task implicitly undertaken by many of these playwrights. Anton Kaes, writing on "the return of history" to German films, explains how Lyotard's requirement might apply (in a more concretely historical vein) to the postmodern filmmaker who, as visual artist,

> can shed light on the social imagination, perverse as it may be, that underlies the unspeakable deeds. It is the filmmaker who can translate the fears and feeling, the hopes and delusions . . . into pre-verbal images and thereby *trigger memories, associations, and emotions* that precede the kind of rational reasoning and logical-linear discourse needed in historiographical writing. If it is agreed that the cataclysmic mass destruction that occurred a half-century ago defies not only historical description and quantitative determination but also rational explanation and linguistic articulation, then a new self-reflexive way of encoding history is called for.[37]

Kaes's call for a self-reflexive postmodern art that encodes history through "pre-verbal images" that trigger memories in a Benjaminian materialist mode, and that employs strategies other than a "logical-linear discourse" of reasoned historical explanations in order to achieve political effect, is answered in the plays of Müller, Parks, Shepard, and Bernhard—each of whom deals explicitly, and politically, with memory within a problematic historical context. Self-reflexivity takes various forms, but it almost always entails an extravagant and overabundant theatricality that prevents clear, reasoned reactions. Heiner Müller calls this type of theatricality "flooding" (discussed below) and recommends it as a political strategy for reforming easy habits of reception and uncritical historical memory. Saul Friedlander has also written about "overabundance," referring to the profusion of accounts of twentieth-century history that, he claims, have produced a paralysis in attempts at global interpretation of the past, and particularly of the Holocaust. This paralysis is translated into writings that, in their various designs, tend to convey either "surplus meaning or blankness."[38] These two extremes precisely define the mystifying images found in many of the plays I will discuss: images at once overdetermined by the fragmentary, noncausal

nature of postmodern dramaturgy, and underexplained within their context. "Surplus meaning or blankness," like Connor's description of the double nature of postmodern theories (quoted above) which lead to either
transformation or playfulness, offers us a way to view, for example, Shepard's characters, who suddenly crawl like tortoises, can't find their place in
the book whose story they've forgotten, grow older and younger and transform at will; Bernhard's characters, who are killed by voices from the past,
and who lay claim to great drama through endless (epic) monologues;
Parks's theme-park of history, her carnival of animated historical stereo-
types; Müller's historical icons—Danton, Robespierre, Lessing, Hitler,
Stalin, the Nibelungs—who walk through the horizontal stages of memory
competing for our attention, recalling pasts and futures and, especially, their
coexistence in the eternal postmodern present. Are we to view these
excesses as examples of "surplus meaning," of chaotic renderings of a too
enormously burdened past? Or do these rather represent a "blankness," a
stylized and empty playfulness that can no longer offer "global interpretation" for the trauma of history?

The "Trauma" of History: Flooding and Repression

One of the distinguishing features of postmodern memory-theater is its
overabundance of disconnected stimuli: conflicting discourses, intruding
images, overlapping voices, hallucinatory fragments. There is no easy way
to "read" or organize—or *bind*—this sensual and discursive overload. The
images often reach back into the pasts of a society, but their arrangement
does not suggest historical reconstruction; rather, chaotic memory—perhaps
even *traumatized* memory—seems to be at work.

Trauma is a broad term lacking precise definition, but it is generally
agreed to be the result of an overwhelming event or events, not fully
experienced by the victim during its occurrence, which leads to repeated
hallucinations, intrusive dreams, uncontrollable actions, along with a
numbing that distances the emotional effect of the event. Psychologists
working with war-shocked soldiers tell us that traumatic memory is experienced as a profusion of "disconnected fragments" or "disconnected body
states and sensations" *shorn of the event* that caused those sensations; that is,
torn out of narrative and deprived of origin.[39] Trauma does not remember its source; rather it replays, in gestures or body experiences, the
moment of cognitive disruption. This state leads to a wide set of psychological problems, from memory loss and depression to psychotic urges to
return to, and eternally repeat, the traumatic moment. According to

Cathy Caruth, the pathology of trauma cannot be defined by the event that caused it; rather, it consists

> solely in the *structure of its experience* or reception: the event is not assimilated or experienced fully at the time, but only belatedly, in its repeated *possession* of the one who experiences it. To be traumatized is precisely to be possessed by an image or event.[40]

The result of such traumatization is a syndrome termed "post-traumatic stress disorder" (PTSD) that has three basic components, all of which are relevant to the memory-dramas I study. First, it is provoked by an *external* event of such force as to elude integration into the personality of the victim(s) or into the customs of a culture. Second, trauma expresses itself only belatedly; thus it is always displaced, or "placeless." As psychiatry, psychoanalysis, and neurobiology suggest, the history expressed through trauma is "a history that literally *has no place,* neither in the past, in which it was not fully experienced, nor in the present, in which its precise images and enactments are not fully understood."[41] Finally, PTSD resulting from a historical event—Vietnam, enslavement, the Holocaust—must be seen as a pathology not of the unconscious, "but *of history itself.* . . . The traumatized, we might say, carry an impossible history within them, or they become themselves the symptom of a history that they cannot entirely possess."[42] Generalized into a collective event, historical trauma—displaced, shorn of an object or a cognitive origin, fragmented, repetitive, not "owned" by a subject—has a remarkable resemblance to postmodern dramatic components.

In *Beyond the Pleasure Principle,* Freud describes the physiology of trauma thus:

> We describe as "traumatic" any excitations from outside which are powerful enough to *break through the protective shield* [*Reizschutz*]. It seems to me that the concept of trauma necessarily implies a connection of this kind with a breach in an otherwise efficacious barrier against stimuli. Such an event as an external trauma is bound to provoke a disturbance on a large scale in the functioning of the organism's energy and to set in motion every possible defense measure. At the same time, the pleasure principle is for the moment put out of action. There is no longer any possibility of preventing the mental apparatus *from being flooded with large amounts of stimulus,* and another problem arises instead—the problem of mastering the amounts of stimulus which have broken in and of binding them, in the psychical sense, so that they can then be disposed of.[43]

Freud defines trauma as a rip in the protective shield of consciousness that normally filters out excessive stimuli. Shock tears that filter, influx is no

longer regulated—and flooding results. The reliving of chaotic memories is
the mark of trauma; the inability to "place" or make sense of these memories is one of its effects. Cathy Caruth goes so far as to claim that what dis-
tinguishes traumatic memory is "the force of its *affront to understanding*" and
that this rational "affront" guarantees "both *the truth of an event,* and *the truth
of its incomprehensibility.*"[44]

Freud further theorized trauma as the outcome of a lack of prepared-
ness, a deficiency of anxiety that could have alerted the mind and prevented
the upheaval of shock. The absence of appropriate anticipation, rather than
the event itself, is what leads to traumatization—that is, the incapacity to
fully experience and thus "own" the meaning of that shock. Until such anxiety has been recuperated and *worked through,* Freud claims, the trauma will
continue to live in us as a past that refuses to go away. Postmodern procedure—repetitive and obsessive, fragmentary and dislocated, imagistic,
scrambled, sometimes incomprehensible—might be seen as a way of inducing anxiety, of evoking memory fragments and conflations that provoke
audience engagement. Heiner Müller has spoken of sensual onslaught, or
"flooding," as one of the aesthetic principles to be aimed at in contemporary theater. "I think we can only proceed now through *Überschwemmung*"
(flooding), runs Müller's postmodern argument. "You have to pack more
into a play than the viewer can carry." Unlike Brecht's theater in which,
according to Müller, one thing follows another with dialectic prescience,
today "multiple views must be presented—simultaneously," thus forcing
the spectator to reexperience the (traumatic) explosion of an irreparable
past.[45] Müller's aesthetic of simultaneity, overload, flooding, can be seen as
imitating the psychoanalytical effects of the "trauma" of history, a subject
that underlies much of his writings. This excess—found also in the plays of
Parks or Bernhard—allows the spectator access to consensual memories as
well as taboos, to the iconic and repressed, to the familiar and the forgotten,
thus prevailing upon the audience to actively *coproduce* the spectacle being
seen, and, perhaps, "work through" a collective historical wound.

This is not to say that postmodern drama has a therapeutic agenda, or a
therapeutic affect. While it engages the shards of memory in a way that
impedes emotional indifference, its form does not allow for closure or integration—that is, for overcoming the effects of trauma—as might, for example, a *narrative* construction of the past. Narrative forms of memory are inte-
grative by nature; they tend to "restore or establish coherence, closure, and
possibly a redemptive stance," writes Saul Friedlander, thereby side-step-
ping the more profound mires of memory. The real memory of trauma,
so-called deep memory, is, however, resistant to such rational order and

unaffected by it. Unmediated and inexpressible, trauma remains unrepresented by narrative constructions.[46] "When I speak to you of Auschwitz," said French author and playwright Charlotte Delbo, "my words don't come from deep memory; they come, so to speak, from external memory, intellectual memory, reflective memory"—the memory Friedlander associates with coherence and closure. This, Delbo explains, is the socially constructed way she has learned to translate the past for others. When, however, "deep memory" comes, "I feel it again, through my whole body, which becomes a block of pain, and I feel death seizing me, I feel myself die."[47] The rational "emplotment" of the past, the turning of memory into controlled narrative, operates in such cases as a "cultural silencer," displacing real anxiety and inhibiting the expression—bodily, performative, irrational—of trauma.[48] Friedlander asks whether at the collective level too, historical trauma may not "leave traces of a deep memory beyond individual recall"[49] inscribed in a society, traces that continue to exist despite rational formulations, that cannot be tamed as a social construction. Such traumatic traces might be seen as the result of the rending of a collective *Reizschutz*. Eric Santner has reminded us of the *textual* quality of the *Reizschutz*. Rather than view this protective covering through the positivist metaphor of a shield or screen, he suggests it is composed of symbolic material that forms "a culturally constructed and maintained organization of individual and group identities."[50] Thus, collective trauma would tear into collective identity, leaving widespread scars and deep traces of recognizable, perhaps repressed, certainly no longer constructed or controlled, cultural memories.

The abundant anxieties in the memory-plays I study, the unattributed voices, the massive influx, the structures of mourning, the recurrent images of loss, are, I suggest, often an expression of such deep collective memory traces. Both the Freudian view of trauma and the workings of postmodern form in the drama display a chaotic fracturing of the whole and the failure to filter out the marginal. The need to return and "rehearse" past moments or images, to repeat, quote, recycle, is also common to both. And as with deep memory, the "traumatized" design of postmodern memory-drama offers no integration and no aesthetically constructed release from the past.

Memory and Forgetting: Agendas for the End-of-Millennium

It has often been noted that our current fin de siècle is marked by the double, and paradoxical, aspect of ever-accelerating amnesia—inspired by the overabundance of new media and technologies; and by a fierce return to, even an obsession with, matters of memory. Critics point to the waning of historical consciousness combined with the "recovery" of alternate pasts; to the disappearance and simultaneous "invention" of traditions; to a renewed appetite for museums and monuments that exists side by side with talk of *posthistoire*.[51] This Janus-faced logic is typical of the apocalyptic imagination, and is hardly new. Double fantasies of doom and redemption, of Armageddons and second comings have been common coin for two thousand years—as shown by Hillel Schwartz in his study of *Century's End*.[52] But the current expression of this logic seems to involve less of an outside "coming" than a willed attempt at "overcoming" the past. The terms repeatedly used by critics point to a reformation of our sense of temporality itself: consisting of simultaneous acts of remembrance and of forgetting.

This is the area Jean Baudrillard has long plumbed. Time, Baudrillard postulates, has come to an end in our hyperproductive technological age and can only repeat or go back upon itself. In his 1988 article "The Year 2000 Has Already Happened,"[53] he joined theorists such as Alexandre Kojève, Arnold Gehlen, and Gianni Vattimo in equating the loss of an organic past, and thus a predictable future, with the postmodern sense of an "end of history"—that is: an antiapocalypse of stasis and entropy, of repetition and simulation. For the Italian philosopher Vattimo, the postmodern is itself "an experience of the end of metaphysics and the end of history which accompanies the most advanced phases of modernity" and contains within it the melancholic experience of epigonism, of "coming-after," of "belatedness." History is no longer seen to have a telos; it has simply become a routine part of consumer society, a necessity without a goal.[54] As Lutz Niethammer put it in his critical study *Posthistoire: Has History Come to an End?* "The problematic of posthistory is not the end of the world but the end of meaning."[55] History and progress, in this view, have reached their limit. They merely "recycle" traces and remains without offering any extension into the future; they have come to a standstill—like Heiner Müller's "hapless angel" buried under the weight of the past (discussed in chapter 3). This obsession with the obliteration of history and the erasure of progress is given a concrete social reading in Baudrillard's recent *Illusion of the End* (1992), which explains that the apocalyptic marker "the year 2000" offers only the *illusion* of an end, but is in fact being approached as the index of a new beginning. Baudrillard details the immense process of historical revisionism that he sees as characterizing our present fin de siècle, attempting, as he puts it, to efface the entire twentieth century and modernity itself, to write out the catastrophes but also the "glory," reversing time in a fantasy of new beginnings, of redemptive rebirth that still belongs to a linear vision of history. In an example of such revisionism, Anton Kaes, speculating on the meaning of Germany's obsessive preoccupation with the apocalypse in its cinema of the 1970s and 1980s, wondered whether it "does not express Germany's subconscious wish to eradicate its traumatic past once and for all," and "to begin once more, to create a pure moment of origin that is not contaminated by history."[56] This melancholic rejection of the past (Baudrillard speaks of a process of mourning) that "consists in reviewing everything, rewriting everything, restoring everything, face-lifting everything, to produce, as it seems, in a burst of paranoia a perfect set of accounts at the end of the century, a universally positive balance sheet," is an attempt to level and reverse time, to go backward to a time before memory, even while seemingly moving forward. We are, Baudrillard claims, rushing through revision toward amnesia.[57] The paradox of willed oblivion in an age of archival amassing is not lost on Baudrillard, who sees the present attempts to record and save, to restore and remember as merely the inverse of this denial. We "arm ourselves with the whole battery of artificial memory," he writes, "all the signs of the past, to face up to the absence of a future" that, in our millennial fantasy, will in any case consist only of the—rewritten and improved—replaying of that past.[58] Despite his apocalyptic (and embarrassingly "totalizing") pessimism, Baudrillard does convincingly tie memory and amnesia together. We recall in order to rewrite, we collect in order to reform. The past is evoked in order to be overcome and forgotten.

Freud claimed that forgetting *is a memory*. We remember to forget what we would do better not to have in consciousness—that is: repression has its advantages, although its cost may be psychic wounding.[59] Similarly, historical "forgetting" also has its uses.[60] Ernest Renan, writing on nationalism in 1882, argued that forgetting is an absolute necessity for nation building. Nations, he claimed, are bound and created not only through shared memories, but also through "a shared amnesia, a collective forgetfulness."[61] This historical process of valorizing some pasts and covering up others, of disguising origins (such as the variety of forgotten French ethnicities discussed by Renan), of confounding victors and victims, has today both accelerated and been made apparent, even self-reflectively apparent. The process of recalling and repressing is being openly played out today in a struggle for (and against) the past, a struggle that, according to Baudrillard, obsesses our entire culture. Our fin de siècle is fascinated "to the point of distraction by the horror of its own origins"—and thus incapable of letting them go, or of letting them remain unrevised.[62] Pierre Nora's description of contemporary collective memory as lodged in horizontal traces of the past (discussed above), contains this same doubleness—of memory and amnesia.

"[T]he most fundamental purpose of the *lieu de mémoire*," he writes, "is to stop time, to block the work of forgetting"—thus proving the affirmative function of these sites; "it is also clear," he continues, "that *lieux de mémoire* only exist because of their capacity for metamorphosis, an endless recycling of their meaning and an unpredictable proliferation of their ramifications."[63] That is: sites of memory, those cultural and historical remnants within which we define our collective identity, can only fulfill their function through constant adaptation and transformation that *is*, in a sense, a forgetting. The American flag no longer holds thirteen stars and stripes "representing a new constellation,"[64] and the Eiffel Tower no longer commemorates either Alexandre Eiffel's design or the optimism of modernist technology. The origins of these sites of national identity have been obscured through time and change. Are the sites then, asks Nora, expressions of their original intentions? Or are they what they have become through "return in the cycles of memory? Clearly both: all *lieux de mémoire* are objects *mises en abîme*"[65]—which thus both preserve and erase the past.

The same can be said of much postmodern memory-drama. Memory sites in these plays coexist and conflate as origin and "return," as recall and revision. Indeed, the entire enterprise of voicing and imaging the past theatrically—but not linearly—creates an interplay between memory and forgetting. The abundance of pasts deployed in these plays inform us of the centrality of remembrance; but the shapes these images take—Shepard's futuristic Indians, Parks's black Lincoln theme park, Müller's French revolutionary entering an elevator into the future—alert us to the transformations that postmodern form attends upon memory and time. The past is not reinscribed in these plays through narrative and linearity, and the absence of narrative coherence questions the very temporality *of* those pasts. Thus, a new collective memory is not formed through the plays—as was the case, for example, in eighteenth-century German historical tragedy, which both commemorated the past and *created* national identity.[66] Since no new narrative or unifying memory structure is offered here, a process of relinquishing hold on the shaping of the past, and thus relinquishing the past, may be inferred.

The paradox is clear: this form of theater—which obsessively recalls the past, and especially the wounds of the past, in a form that frustrates remembrance (or re-membrance) of the past—consequently defeats unambiguous memorialization. Brought up as "images" but obscured by being torn out of context, it is left to the audience to construct—or not—a future for the pasts that appear, but do not cohere, in this theater. Self-reflective and always consciously positioned within a specific contemporary discourse, these plays create a theater that insists we remember—while it prepares us to forget.

Imitating the trauma and chaos of history torn out of narrative and context, these postmodern theater convulsions may almost be seen as a *rite de passage* from the affliction of our shared past, toward the emptiness and openness of a future marked by the approaching millennium. Looking both backward and forward, these janiform plays seem a fitting form of theater for the century's end, a theater that both "sums up" the past of Western modern history—and seeks to clear it out, to go beyond.

Chapter 2

Samuel Beckett's Postures of Memory

Estragon: All the dead voices . . .
Vladimir: They all speak together . . .
Vladimir: To have lived is not enough for them.
Estragon: They have to talk about it.
                    —*Waiting for Godot*

In 1965, seven years after writing *Krapp's Last Tape,* Beckett wrote a filmic version of "man and his memory-machine" titled *Eh Joe.* Less amusingly than in *Krapp's Last Tape,* more blatantly than in *Not I* or *That Time,* this short film sets up a context and frame for the study of obsessive introspection, of unwilled memory. Before the words start "coming," Joe, "seen from behind," moves from window to door to cupboard to bed, checking for intruders, locking out potential infiltrators, drawing "hangings"—like curtains—over all ominous gaps and openings. Finally feeling secure, "beginning to relax," he finds that he has after all been invaded: by self-perception, by a voice within.[1] Beckett tells us that the camera moves in nine measured zoom-ins from three feet back, to nine inches from Joe's face, moving ever closer into the mind-machine of memory. This movement suggests a connection between the static head we see and the steady woman's voice we hear, an accusing and taunting voice, rather mechanical, almost like a tape recording. The mimetic frame, the mechanical voice, the focus on the memories of one character, still connect *Eh Joe* to *Krapp's Last Tape;* the sourceless voice, the close-up on an isolated body fragment (head), the need for viewer intervention to make a connection between the two disparate elements (image and voice), already look forward to *Not I, That Time, Footfalls, Rockaby.* In *Eh Joe* we still find the mimetic link missing in Beckett's later memory-plays: the link between the voice and posture of remembrance, and a narrative frame. Beckett "frames" his film script with Joe's attempt, and failure, to keep memory at bay; we follow his dread of intrusion, and witness its onset. Beckett's later rememberers, from *Not I* to *Ohio Impromptu,* are all already in media res of remembering; it is their

basic *modus vivendi*. No "frame" or moment of inception directs our understanding of these later remembering voices, severed, as they often are, from
the remembered and (just as often) *dis*membered body. What we experience in the later plays is a memory eruption given through a simultaneity of
voices, overlapping time-frames, disconnected images, sawed-off bits of
narrative, the disparate fragments and floating signifiers so typical of postmodern art.

    In his set of short plays scattered between 1972 (*Not I*) and 1980 (*Ohio
Impromptu*), Beckett advances a range of dramatic strategies—of theatrical
"postures"—for imaging memory. He grapples in these plays with formal-
izing devices, with ways to give theatrical shape to remembrance. The two
primary, and often disconnected, elements he emphasizes in these plays,
image and voice, constitute the two dimensions within which memory
lives: space and time. Beckett's (usually) static, (always) stunning images are
markedly spatial—floating eight feet above stage, pacing, rocking, frozen in
a duplicated stance of eternal repetition. His voices, remembering or
remembered voices, develop in, cut through, and often conflate time. Time
and space, voice and image, interact in a multitude of ways. Through them,
Beckett sets up a theatrical vocabulary of remembrance in a series of physical postures and derealized voices: a dismembered mouth, moved by
unwilled words, tells of an absent body and a past that we can only restruc-
ture, if at all, in our own memory; a floating, disembodied head listens, as
we listen, to three entangled, yet separate, voices from various and simultaneous pasts; a rocking body calls forth, and tries to stem, the inner voice of
ceaseless consciousness, of ceaseless recall; the rhythms of pacing, of footfalls, structure the voice of memory through which the present pacing
action is viewed; or two duplicate bodies function as Reader and Listener,
as rememberer and perceiver of a past, and still repeating, memory of
bereavement.

    In all these cases, Beckett's voices do not reconstruct or explain a past,
and his images have, on their own, little narrative value. Rather, they show
a variety of modes of being, or just barely being, *as* and *in* memory. The
memories recalled are often incomprehensible, and just as often negligible,
almost objectless. What we know about Mouth, Listener, Woman, May,
Reader, and Listener is less than fragmentary. Unlike Heiner Müller, whose
fragments of memory are always also about the fragments themselves—Hamlet, Hitler, the French Revolution, displaced and unendingly present on the
"desolate shore" of memory—for Beckett it is not the memories revealed or
the words that suddenly "come" that are of the essence. Rather, it is the
manifold memoried states of being that are theatricalized. Beckett represents

existence as a constant replay of memoried moments through ghostly figments—ever "slightly off centre"—who can never evoke present selves. And it is within their lack of presence that the act of recall is positioned.

Beckett's careful shaping of the fragments of memory is in many ways paradigmatic for a postmodern memory-theater. Speaking of Beckett as a postmodernist requires, however, taking a position in what H. Porter Abbott has called the modernist/postmodernist "turf war" surrounding Beckett. Abbott admits that Beckett remains a "categorical rift, giving the lie to categories,"[2] but appeals to a modernist cohesion found in the auto-graphical persistence of Beckett's "signature" throughout his texts, which give a certain modernist unity to the diversity of his writings. This stylistic "cohesion" does not, however, negate the profound indeterminacy and "ungroundedness" at work within each of these late plays, as I will discuss. Beckett's late texts enact a typically postmodern reshaping of our notions of theatrical space and time; they perform multiple dissolutions of the bound-aries of the (mostly absent) self and stress the process of viewer reception over the self-sufficiency of the text. These texts are self-reflexive, open-ended, multiply fragmented—from the fragmentariness of the image on stage (Mouth, Listener), to the fragmenting of speech and text and percep-tion.[3] I would go so far as to argue that each of Beckett's late plays be seen as a memory nugget, an individually shaped shard of remembrance, while, taken as a group, the plays render ambiguous, shifting perspectives of the notion of recall. The fact that Beckett's "signature" is evident in each of the interrelated shards does not determine the manner of relation among them, a relation that I see as open and indeterminate. The suggestion that Beck-ett's late plays gravitate around each other, and toward a common intuition, has already been put forward by Enoch Brater in the following terms: "Though the works since Not I may not have been conceived together, and though the style and subject matter of each one carries its own mood and its own inner determination, their various metaphors . . . reveal the almost epic adventure that lies behind a much larger work." Brater sees Beckett's metaphors as centering on "rest, night, and approaching death."[4] I would propose that the liminal and fragmented states they portray open up inward into the shifting, "unepic" variations of memoried states of being that, while interrelated, relate in a fluid and noncohesive manner, creating a theatrical lexicon of objectless remembrance, a postmodern discourse on the dramatic ontology of memory.

In addition to being paradigmatic of a postmodern memory-theater, Beckett's memory-plays differ in important ways from those of the other playwrights I will consider. Beckett does not lend himself to discussion through terms such as "collective memory" or "historical trauma"—terms I will be using in subsequent chapters. Memory in Beckett's plays is not motivated by historical wounds, nor is it the memory *of* those historical inscriptions. Yet, it would also be wrong to view these plays as expressing *individual* memory. The individual collapses in Beckett's late plays, comes apart in ways that are crucially different and more basic than the splintered modernist figure. Beckett himself remarked upon this when he said, in interview: "The Kafka hero has a coherence of purpose. He's lost, but he's not spiritually precarious, he's not falling to bits. My people seem to be falling to bits."[5] Beckett goes to great lengths to signify this disintegration as beyond repair, and to frustrate our ability to hear his texts as the narrative of any cohesive personal past. But while Beckett "undoes" psychology or narrative, and refrains from invoking a common context or history, his texts still speak to, and of, the common ontological state of memoried being. The duplicate rememberers of *Ohio Impromptu* are the best example of what Beckett is doing: through the play's repetitive and reflexive structure, they reenact the *act* of obsessive recall, of melancholy remembrance. It is not the specific memory of loss (which the play never clearly renders) that is of interest here, but rather the embodied form and theatrical reflection that that remembrance takes. Beckett's late plays provide us with a complex net of memoried being—the interplay of inner voices, the pluralism of self-perception, the complexity of agency, of volition or its lack, the simultaneity of pasts and present, of traces and patterns. Thus, they have the double importance of evoking ontological senses for our memoried selves, and of providing theatrical models for their performance.

From pulsating Mouth to the duplicate old men shading their faces in *Ohio Impromptu,* all of these plays center on a vivid visual image that, to quote Enoch Brater, "is simultaneously character, stage prop, and stage set,"[6] and is always both surprising and moving. Striking images, writes Cicero, are at the heart of successful mnemotechnica, allowing and *inspiring* recall. The story of how the legendary founder of mnemonics, the poet Simonides of Ceos, stumbled onto his memory method, focuses on the imprint of a compelling visual image under dire emotional circumstances. As Cicero tells it: at a banquet given by a nobleman, Simonides recited a poem in honor of his host and (much to the host's irritation) honored as well the twin gods Castor and Pollux. Soon after, he was told that two gentlemen requested his presence outside. Once he was out, the roof of the house suddenly collapsed, crushing all the guests to death. Simonides could not find the two men (Castor and Pollux?) who had called him away from the celebration, and was stunned by his miraculous salvation. The emotional impact of the event impressed the image of the large banquet table from which he was saved indelibly into his imagination; and through this stirring image Simonides was able to recall where each of the guests had sat, and thus identify each of their unrecognizable, mangled bodies for the families.[7]

Beckett's late "memory plays" do something similar: each impresses a strong, evocative single image onto our memories, images—a displaced mouth, a floating toothless head, a pacing ghostly figure, an ashen rocking woman—that are disturbing and difficult to forget, that, as Cicero suggests in his discourse on memory, have "the capacity of encountering and speedily penetrating the mind."[8] In production, writes Brater of Mouth, for example, "one is all but overwhelmed by the sheer persuasiveness of the image: a mouth staring out at us from otherwise 'empty' theater space. Disembodied, suspended in space, and throbbing with a constant pulsation of lips, teeth, tongue, and saliva."[9] "You may find nothing in it," said Jessica Tandy, who played Mouth in the 1972 New York production, "but I suspect you will never forget it."[10] The texts spoken by or "above" these images provide the emotional and intellectual pinning, but are less easy to penetrate or recall. "I am not unduly concerned with intelligibility," Beckett told Tandy when she complained that his suggested speed for the monologue of Mouth made the words unintelligible; "I hope the piece may work on the nerves of the audience, not its intellect."[11] And indeed, when we think of these plays—even of *A Piece of Monologue,* named for its verbal dimension—it is not the words, the monologue, the "story" we recall: but rather the static, stirring images floating, pulsating, pacing, rocking, sitting in duplicate huddled postures, or standing, white-socked and ghostly in a spot of light surrounded by the dark. The images function as memory triggers, evoking the sense and sensations of the plays, the "nerves," rather than the words or stories. It is through the image—rather than through any plot line or character development—that we intuit the complexity of these dramas of absence and fragmentedness.

This focus on image, "nerves," and fractured text places distinct pressure on the dimension of reception. Some of Beckett's short texts are unusually difficult to follow in production—*Not I* and *That Time* present definite cognitive dilemmas. Mouth is small and distant, isolated and mispositioned eight feet above the stage; and the prone head of *That Time* offers even less visual stimulation. The question "what are we seeing" is likely to precede "what does it mean." In *That Time* three separate stories intercut each other, provoking and frustrating spectator understanding. Mouth, speaking too quickly and with various inner voices intervening, is no less difficult to follow. The spectator, deprived of cognitive "sense," is forced to find a perspective—or perspectives—through which to view the plays, to imagine some form that might "accommodate the mess." Typically, writes Michael Vanden Heuvel, "Beckett creates a kind of 'environmental space' that seeks an open-ended transaction with the spectator, who is invited to make connections, fill in the narrative gaps of the *troué* script, and otherwise actively engage Beckett's 'undone' texts."[12] Beckett, as S. E. Gontarski has so definitively shown, purposely instills difficulty and distortion into his plays, with the "intent of undoing" narrative cohesion[13]—thus too undoing the easy habits of narrative reception. Beckett was always aware of the "impure" mimetic drive that induces most audiences to seek causal constructs in even the most abstract art. In his *Proust* book (1957) he writes of the ideal and formless abstraction of music that is "distorted by the listener who, being an impure subject, insists on giving a figure to that which is ideal and invisible."[14] But even if a "figurative" reading of these late plays is a distortion, the plays still reach out for some form of interaction with a viewing public. "The engagement of the audience in the speculative process of establishing a narrative context and an image of character," writes Charles Lyons, "and, at the same time, recognising the hypothetical nature of these constructs, transforms the static scene . . . into dynamic theatrical experiences."[15] Reception is posited by Lyons as an *activating* context that transforms a theater with little action into a theater of essential *inter*action. In addition, most of these plays are highly self-aware and reflective of their status as theater. When Mouth speaks of the "stream of words . . . in her ear," of "straining to hear . . . [to] piece it together" she describes not only "her" dilemma, but the audiences' strain of reception as well. Thus is the spectator invoked and assumed within the abstractions of the play. Reception is implicit.

Spectating, like writing, occurs within the parameters of a zeitgeist. The relativism and lack of closure of postmodern art has often been related to—and found to perhaps emerge from—new forms of knowledge. This is exemplified, for example, by quantum physics that teaches that multiple realities occur simultaneously, and that what we chose to view, or observe, of those simultaneous realities, changes the reality itself. "[T]here is no exact correspondence between the world outside and that in our minds," writes Natalie Crohn Schmitt: "Thus we must turn from the idea of knowing reality in itself to an account of the observation of it." As with the theory of relativity, facts and perceivers "are joined in an observation," and "no occurrence or object can be defined apart from an observer."[16] That is, the reality is *shaped* by how we observe and describe it. Applied to audience observation of plays such as these—plays in which perception is challenged, interpretive centers are lacking, and multiple perspectives defeat any single receptive strategy—observation would seem to assume a multiplicity and *diversity* in the spectatorial role as well. These late Beckett plays accommodate fluidity and uncertainty, showing always unfixed and protean fragments of being; not surprisingly, the audience too is treated as equally unfixed and multiple. The audience of contemporary theater, writes Herbert Blau, is brought together in theater "as *alienated*,"[17] as ruptured and split, not as a unified community. Similarly, the acts of memory in these plays do not target a communal experience; rather, multiple ways of being encourage each spectator to complete the images, or not, to take them on as her own, or not. In this view, there is no one way to "read" a stage performance since, as Crohn Schmitt writes, if the object depends for its completion on the gaze of the observer, the very idea "of a single true account of reality is challenged."[18]

Beckett's stage rememberers can themselves almost be viewed as a succession of "accounts" of reality; a succession of voices, perspectives, angles, positions, dialogically interrelated. Within these "accounts," being is recalled and reformulated. Beckett's entire late corpus, as I have already suggested, might be viewed as a series of memory perspectives and postures that hold "open-ended" dialogues with each other—and with an audience composed of remembering observers. The varied "accounts" thus offered encourage varied states of recall within the audience and render the varieties of remembrance as templates for modes of being. In the following discussion I will focus on the ways these plays "remember," on their theatrical strategies of recall, and on the various forms of audience reception implicit within them.

From Krapp's Tape to Mouth's "Mind"

Krapp's Last Tape (1958) embodies memory and the dislocations of time; in *Not I* (1972) even the "body" disappears—"whole body like gone"—and only a dislocated memory, visualized as a "subjectless" mouth, is left us. Theatrically, we can locate here the break between a mimetic theater (however reduced), and postmodern dissolutions. Krapp may be drawn as a metaphor for man as clown or bum—white face, purple nose, short pants, large shoes—but for all the pregnant minimalism he still retains a distinct character, a discernable story, a room, a name. Mouth obviously has none of these; she also has no body or head attached to the red orifice we see, no logical placement on stage—floating as she (it) does eight feet above stage level—no context or frame, beginning or end to the unstoppable monologue we hear her speak. Separated by fourteen years, both of these related plays investigate memory within highly visual—and very different— organs of remembrance. Beckett's ever-moving fragment of body, Mouth, recalling a being that slips away and disperses even as it is being evoked, reflects an ontologically different notion of memory and self than does the static memory-machine (the tape recorder) we find in dialogue with Krapp. Inversely, we might say that this changed perspective governed Beckett's reformed strategy in *Not I* for imaging and theatricalizing memory.

There has never been a lack of "rememberers" in Beckett's theater: Hamm's ongoing story of a remembered life, probably his own (*Endgame*); Winny's struggle to remember bits of her cultural past (*Happy Days*); the divergent testimonies given by the three complicit figures of *Play*. But in *Krapp's Last Tape,* the past remembered is problematized through Beckett's experiment in physically *imaging* memory and memory processes on stage. Thus we must negotiate between two versions of self—Krapp, the banana-eating body, and Krapp the memory-box, dependent on the whim of the man. With *Not I* and Beckett's ensuing short plays, this dualism is itself problematized, and a completely different view of memory, and selfhood, is advanced. The differences between *Krapp's Last Tape* and *Not I,* especially in terms of memory and selfhood, can be used to gauge a break between a mimetic, dualistic theater, and a postmodern theater of dispersal and irreducible fragmentation.

In *Krapp,* memory is imaged as a large two-spooled (double-lobed) tape recorder. This choice of metaphor—a mechanical, material box—presupposes and shapes the way we view memory function, and thus the "self," in *Krapp.* It also entails a set of concepts and dramatic moves—mechanistic, dualistic, basically still mimetic—that, I will claim, are no longer relevant in *Not I.* Memory in a box means memory localized within a concrete, material form. No longer elusive or diffuse, memory seems self-contained, redeemable, very present, depending for its "use" on finding the right reel, twisting the right levers, locating the desired section of tape. The comic ironies wrested by Beckett from Krapp's difficulty in locating the exact memory he seeks (his need to fast-forward and rewind) only underscore the dualism of rememberer and memory, where memory is imaged as an objectified "other" that cannot be completely controlled. The play shows Krapp, "a wearish old man," sitting in his den trying to record his memories of the past year—as he does every year on his birthday; but instead, he is drawn to listen, again, to a recording from his past, the memory of "farewell to love." The past that Krapp seeks is elicited from his box at will; it is also ironized and contextualized through Krapp's present behavior: his visual doubling of the traits described in memory (eating bananas, drinking, writing notes on an envelope), his difference from the self in memory (more lonely still, more depleted, and there is also forgetting). This objectification of memory is a brilliant way to theatricalize dual consciousness; it is also a way to give a one-man play "company." *Krapp* presents us not only with the act of remembering a life, but with a dialogue between living and remembrance, present and past: Man and his Memory.

Remembering is, in a sense, an inherently dualistic activity. The one part of the mind *re*calls, brings up the past; while the other watches, listens, is reminded, reacts, sometimes refuses the memory brought up and rejects it (Mouth: "try something else . . . think of something else").[19] Memory, writes St. Augustine,

> is like a great field or a spacious palace, a storehouse for countless images of all kinds which are conveyed to it by the senses. . . . When I use my memory, I ask it to produce whatever it is that I wish to remember. Some things it produces immediately; some are forthcoming only after a delay, as though they were being brought out from some inner hiding place; others come spilling from the memory, thrusting themselves upon us when what we want is something quite different [Mouth: "not that either? . . . nothing to do with that either?"]. . . . These I brush aside from the picture which memory presents to me, allowing my mind to pick what it chooses, until finally that which I wish to see stands out clearly and emerges into sight from its hiding place . . . and as their place is taken they return to their place of storage, ready to emerge again when I want them.[20]

For Augustine, the will ("I") is lord, sending messengers into memory to recover neatly stored, sometimes more deeply interred but still redeemable, always restorable remembrances. Although Krapp, like Augustine, can ("after a delay") retrieve his buried past, it is no longer clear which is master: the will that seeks or the memory that beckons. The easy sway of Augustine's present "I" over stored and malleable memory, its ability to "brush aside" the irrelevant, is no longer the working assumption. Krapp begins by wanting to record the present; he will finally forgo that attempt and allow the luring voice of the past to speak, in the present, instead. The voice of memory will prove stronger than Krapp's own.

Beckett's rememberers, like Augustine's, are often dual beings, split dramatic character—body and mind, voice and ear, Reader and Listener, the perceiving subject and the perceived object. But in Beckett, duality (and, as we shall see, shattered multiplicity) suggests a multiplied cast of characters vying and negotiating for a determination of self. This chasm within being—the impossibility of perceiving the self without turning the self into an object—and thus the impossibility of unity, is a basic trope of remembrance. "Because of this disjunction," writes Linda Ben-Zvi, "all of Beckett's people have the continual sense that they are being watched, if only by themselves."[21] In *Krapp's Last Tape* this duality is turned into a refracting dialogue within an externalized self, and thus made dramatically explicit. In *Not I,* duality is both assumed (Mouth/Auditor) and shown as an insufficient, perhaps a useless model for the dispersed and centerless postmodern consciousness.

Augustine, in his *Confessions,* analyzes the function of memory through a simple example that aptly parallels the mechanistic images of Krapp's memory-machine: the recitation of a psalm. When we recite, Augustine writes, the mind "performs three functions, those of expectation, attention, and memory. The future, which it expects, passes through the present, to which it attends, into the past, which it remembers." As the recitation of the psalm gets on, the expectation grows shorter and the memory grows longer; this is true too, Augustine continues, of every part of the psalm, and of life itself.[22] Augustine's description of the movement of future into past is like the "decantation" of self of which Beckett writes in *Proust:* "The individual is the seat of a constant process of decantation, decantation from the vessel containing the fluid of future time, sluggish, pale and monochrome, to the vessel containing the fluid of past time, agitated and multicoloured by the phenomena of its hours."[23] This same "movement" is given visual form in Krapp. James Olney has suggested that the two spools of Krapp's magnetic tape recorder, in their iconic movement, offer a visual parallel to Augustine's description of time's passage from future into past. Krapp "listens to the narrated episodes of his life pass from the spool of expectation on the left across the head of the tape player, which corresponds to the present narration, to be taken up by the spool of memory on the right—which, when rewound, becomes once again the spool of expectation."[24] Applying Augustine's spatial description of time to Krapp's tapes allows us to easily visualize concepts such as "returning" to the past (rewind), or "seeking" a different memory. It also underscores the basic affinity between memory and theater as fundamentally *present* activities, always dependent upon, and carried out within, the now-time of audience and rememberer.

In *Not I,* memory is less easily compartmentalized, its movement less easily visualized. A disembodied mouth hanging eight feet above stage level is the organ of memory, its externalized form; the "agent" or initiator of recall (such as Krapp), is missing: thus we no longer have an obvious "dialogue." *Krapp* begins in pantomime, in comic gropings that acquaint us with the present Krapp ("characterize" him) before we hear of (and from) the voice of Krapp past. Mouth is found from the first in media res of an already ongoing discourse. She is supplied without context or frame; her mawings begin before she, or we, begin to listen, they continue after. All we will see is red lips endlessly moving, lit by a spot, and downstage left a tall figure, "sex undeterminable," standing in a long, hooded djellaba, facing Mouth, almost unmoving, and silent throughout. Mouth's logorrhea is offered without preamble or explanation. It is not her birthday, as it is Krapp's, this is not a ritual occurrence, a yearly word-letting, as it is in *Krapp,* there is no external, narrative explanation for what we see—aside from what may be gleaned, gradually and at our peril, from Mouth's text, which suggests a sudden and involuntary "coming" of speech to the lips of an old woman at the moment of the body's demise.

Several dualisms and seemingly mechanical repetitions are initially apparent in *Not I.* Mouth and body positioned on stage certainly suggest a mind/body dualism, just as they suggest the division between speaker and auditor in consciousness, parallel to Krapp and his voice-machine. Iconographically, Mouth seems to represent absolute speaker; the second figure, Auditor, so named and physically positioned toward Mouth, would thus seem to image absolute listener. But Auditor does not listen as Krapp listens—choosing the memory ("allowing my mind to pick what it chooses"), judging whether he's interested, returning to a given section. Nor does he (she?) listen as does Listener in *Ohio Impromptu.* Auditor may, philosophically, be a Berkeleyan perceiver objectifying and maintaining the existence of Mouth, but (unlike Berkeley's God) she or he functions as a witness without being an implicit source of what is seen; is, indeed, an affective mediator only for the audience. Unlike Listener in *Ohio,* who intervenes physically through knocks that affect the spoken text, or Krapp who manipulates memory physically through lever and reel, Auditor is totally outside the cognizance, or function, of Mouth, and in no way modifies the workings of memory itself.[25] Auditor comments on Mouth's monologue four times: through four small gestures expressing (so Beckett tells us in his text) "helpless compassion." These gestures are physically directed toward Mouth, but affectively aimed at the audience. Thus Mouth, apparently a speaking and not a listening organ, who would seem to be one half of a dualistic pair—mouth and ear— is, I will claim, actually both, and much more.

Like Krapp's "box," Mouth is also a self-repeater, returning again and again to the same texts. Often the repetitions seem obsessive: but they are never mechanical, never mere spoken recordings. Each repetition is also an addition to and variation of the previous texts, always a "clothed" repetition—to use Gilles Deleuze's distinction between mechanical "naked" repetitions that confirm sameness, and "clothed" repetitions that, through variation, uncover difference.²⁶ Not only is each repetition of key texts ("tiny little thing . . . out before its time . . . godforsaken hole") reworded, each also leads to an additional moment of remembrance. Still, one of the central texts in the play—the text that gives the play its name—is indeed repeated five times with little variation, and underscored through (almost identical yet depleting) gestures made by the otherwise static figure of Auditor. This is the passage that Beckett describes as Mouth's "vehement refusal to relinquish third person" and to which Auditor reacts with "helpless compassion." Five times Mouth rejects the word "I" through the formula: "and she [found herself in the] . . . what? . . . who? . . . no! . . . she!" followed by a pause and (except for the fifth time) a movement by Auditor. This precisely repeated section certainly suggests an unheard dialogue, an inner dualism between the mouth (that narrates), and some further inner voice bringing words—such as the word "I"—that the mouth refuses to say. Thus Enoch Brater, for example, concludes that "Mouth is hell-bent on obliterating any relationship to a questionable past." Brater develops this mimetic image into a figure of duality with the words: "The staging of the play suggests . . . a literally dislocated personality: an old woman listening to herself, yet unable to accept that what she hears, what she says, refers to her."²⁷ Old woman versus inner voice.

But once we begin attending to Mouth's words (not an easy task in performance), we note that the unheard inner voice trying to say "I" is not the only "dislocated" figure that intrudes. Nor is "her" only problem—the only dualism of a "hell-bent" will—a division between the spoken "she" and the proposed "I." Indeed, once we meet the entire inner cast and crew we will have gotten to know voice (speaking), mouth (moving on its own), "she" (wherever she may be located), the unheard inner voice suggesting "I," a possibly additional inner voice intervening periodically in Mouth's narration, brain "raving on its own," and the constant buzzing—but we will have completely lost sight of "I." Mouth tells us of the voice, presumably the voice we are now hearing, which "she" suddenly heard and "did not recognize . . . at first . . . so long since it had sounded." Words "were coming" of their own, voice was speaking of its own volition. The words, which recall a birth and a barely lived life, are ambiguously connected to a "she" who—wherever she may be located—has a hard time hearing or understanding "this steam . . . not catching the half of it . . . not the quarter . . . no idea . . . what she's saying . . . imagine!" (219). Nor can "she" stop mouth, or mouth stop itself. We next learn that "lips . . . cheeks . . . jaws . . . never— . . . what? . . . tongue? . . . yes . . . lips . . . cheeks . . . jaws

. . . tongue . . . never still a second" (220) are also moving on their own. Thus the ear (straining to hear), the lips (moving), the voice (speaking) all seem to be working independently, autonomously, neither understood nor mediated by "she."

In a number of sections of the play we find a seemingly dialogical relationship between Mouth and an inner (unheard) voice that suggests changes to Mouth's monologue. The pattern is constant: each time this occurs Mouth listens, repeats the suggestion, and then self-corrects her speech: "she did not know . . . what position she was in . . . imagine! . . . what position she was in! . . . whether standing . . . or sitting . . . but the brain— . . . what? . . . kneeling? . . . yes . . . whether standing . . . or sitting . . . or kneeling . . . but the brain— . . . what? . . . lying? . . . yes" (217). This inner voice suggesting additional positions to the ones Mouth has already named may be the same inner voice trying to say "I," but we have no way of knowing. In addition to the speaking voice, the occasionally intervening inner voice(s), the self-moving lips and tongue, the "she" straining to hear—there is also the brain, "the whole brain begging . . . something begging in the brain . . . begging the mouth to stop . . . pause a moment . . . if only for a moment . . . and no response . . . as if it hadn't heard." Brain is another important player in this drama, for while it begs Mouth to stop, it is also "raving away on its own . . . trying to make sense of it . . . or make it stop . . . or in the past . . . dragging up the past . . . flashes from all over" (220). Does brain have a memory of its own aside from the memory of voice that is also "dragging up the past"? So it seems; for we now hear of scenes from the past of some life ("walking all her days"), which Mouth claims are occurring in *brain,* not in voice: "the brain . . . flickering away on its own . . . quick grab and on . . . nothing there . . . on to the next . . . *bad as the voice . . . worse* . . . as little sense" (221; emphasis added). Clearly, there are at least two explicit remembering organs here, brain and voice, both of which flicker through the memories of a fragmented and "senseless" past. All the while, even as voice speaks and brain flickers and "she" strains to hear, there is an inner "buzzing"—"dull roar like falls" (221), accompanying all the rest.

Paul Lawley writes that "the whole of the monologue, insofar as it is a denial—'Not I'—is a lie, a refusal to acknowledge the fragmentary nature of the self."[28] But *who,* we must ask, is doing the "refusing"? To assume a potential "acknowledger" who can "acknowledge the fragmentary nature of the self" is to assume the existence of a unifying center of being, an ontological ground everywhere denied in this play. *Not I* invests in every form of fragmentation and splintering, imaging through text, figure, and performance a consciousness inherently multiple, crucially divided against and within itself. This demonstration of splintered being produces far more than a binary opposition of unified I versus fragmented self. Mouth is both cognizant of self-fragmentation (and seemingly gives it some united "form" through the formless, instantly disappearing medium of voice) and herself prisoner to a nonunitary logorrhea that she did not initiate and cannot terminate. Moreover, and increasingly as the play continues, the words that have "come" are contested and denied by, perhaps, additional fragments of self. We find an urge to forget, to erase, to censure and thus change parts of the memory being produced: "think of something else." Mouth strains under the demands of both an involuntary confessional voice and the voice of resistance, refusing to reveal or denying the memories being offered— "what? . . . not that? . . . nothing to do with that? . . . try something else . . . think of something else . . . oh long after . . . sudden flash . . . not that either . . . all right . . . something else again . . . so on" (222). She had all her days, we are told, been "practically speechless . . . *even to herself*" (222; emphasis added). Thus, this sudden internal "conversation" and conflict between parts of being is, in a sense, a moment of self-recognition, a weird version of introspection. But what does she come to recognize? The idea occurs to "her" (mouth? she? brain?) in a "sudden flash" that there may be "something she had to tell . . . how it was . . . how she— . . . what? . . . had been? . . . yes . . . something that would tell how it had been . . . how she had lived" (221). But the attempt to give voice to "how it was" is defeated by the difficulties of how it *is* to remember: the inner fragmentation, the different voices intervening, the strains of recall and, not least, the urge to forget that constitute the activity of remembrance itself. Memory here is not, as Augustine had thought, "a spacious palace, a storehouse" in which "everything is preserved separately, according to its category."[29] Memory, like consciousness, is split and cracked and redoubling, lacking agency or telos, with various and contradictory agendas.

Inner fragmentation is only one of the play's many strategies for signifying dispersal and centerlessness. Another track is through temporal fracturing. The play begins and ends with an ongoing "buzzing" that clearly signifies that we are hearing but a fragment of a monologue that repeats both internally and entirely, dispersing mimetic coherence. The monologue is possibly being spoken out of an immobile, insentient body—"whole body like gone"—after its collapse ("in the field . . . April morning . . . face in the grass"). Yet the words repeatedly refer to a future time, after this event. One of the play's most common verbal patterns, repeated in nine slight variations, is "her first thought was . . . oh long after . . . sudden flash." An additional four (near) repetitions go to the phrases "when suddenly . . .

gradually." How are we to understand this? "Long after . . . sudden flash" implies a time long after the occurrence being related, but well before the narration we are hearing now: that is, it implies a long, ongoing stretch of time. Yet the description of "lips moving" and words "coming" seems to imply that the event being described is coextensive with its description. The physical image of the disembodied mouth reinforces the sense of simultaneity between some incident ("whole body like gone") and the narration. Further, the repetition of the words "suddenly . . . gradually," like "long after . . . sudden flash," creates temporal disorientation through their contradictory senses of time, simultaneously given. This sense of splintered temporality is recaptured in the structure of the play that has both narrative strands—beginning as it does at birth, telling of collapse, recall, memories—and also a collection of inner cycles and repetitions. The ending obviously returns us to the start of the narrative that had itself started before we began to listen: "hit on it in the *end* . . . then *back* . . . *back* in the field . . . April morning . . . face in the grass . . . nothing but the larks . . . *pick it up*" (223; emphasis added). But this section too has been repeated a number of times within the monologue, so that the "return" is not signified as a mechanical repetition of the whole, as in *Play,* but as another cycle within the cycles of "clothed" repetitions and new revelations of the play.

Thus the monologue moves in a number of directions both "suddenly" and "gradually," fusing contradictory senses of temporality, and seeming to evoke unwilled and uncontrollably repeating memories. This fluid simultaneity of times parallels the "profound paradox of memory" that is central to the writings on memory of the modernist philosopher Henri Bergson.[30] In *Matter and Memory,* Bergson differentiates between two types of memory: habit memory and "pure" or spontaneous memory.[31] Habit memory is mechanistic, functional, reflecting a view of time that is serial and consecutive: basically a *spatial* and analytic concept of time, like the image of the movement of Krapp's tape. Pure duration—or pure memory—on the other hand, is intuitive, multidirectional, simultaneous, spontaneous; Bergson speaks of "interpenetration," of flow.[32] Mary Warnock rephrases Bergson's theory through a concise example: learning a Horatian ode by heart employs "habit memory"; recalling the hot summer day when one lay in the field learning the ode by heart is closer to "pure" memory.[33] How can we overlook the radical difference, Bergson writes, "between that which must be built up by repetition and that which is essentially incapable of being repeated?"[34] The former, as in the passage on "recital" (Augustine) cited above, is locked into a spatial image of time, repetition, process. The latter type of memory, key to Bergson's vitalist rejection of dualism, is unanchored in time or space; it is intuitive, simultaneous, lacking in both chronology and image. In Gilles Deleuze's formulation: "The past is 'contemporaneous' with the present that it *has been* . . . The past would never be constituted if it did not coexist with the present whose past it is."[35] In this view, Mouth both exists in her present disembodied form, throbbing on stage, and is equally present in the forms of all the memories that she animates and of which she is constituted. In its idealist version, this view allows for a release from the segmentation and divisions of perception entailed by the corporeality of body (of which Mouth is almost freed), and of the tainted specificity of language (which Mouth almost overcomes through her fragments of speech). Spontaneous memory occurs when the brain's defenses are down, outside the control of consciousness. In its purest form, we would have a "pure intuition of how things are, and were, without the restriction of space, or of time"; in it we would "know ourselves. . . . But, unfortunately, exactly what we know can never be adequately expressed."[36] In Beckett's transformation of Bergsonian "pure" memory, Mouth's "intuition of how things are, and were" remains an interpenetrating chaos of fragments painfully locked within random repetition, incapable of self-knowledge or integration; while for the audience, what Mouth perhaps gets to "know" but cannot express ("nothing with which to express, nothing from which to express")[37] is the complete *absence* of a center of being; that is: essential fragmentation. The merging of past and present, the past as "'*contemporaneous*' with the present that it *has been*" does not create unity in *Not I*, but rather a sense of simultaneity, as in traumatized recall.

Diffusion and fragmentation in *Not I* extend of course beyond the textual to the performative and receptive aspects of the play as well. The textual images are, clearly, preceded and anchored in visual fragmentation—the mouth, the figure, their odd positioning on stage. The fracturing continues through the theater self-referentiality of Mouth's text, which seems to reflect the dramatic production we see—her talk of "this ray or beam . . . always the same spot" (16), for example, mirrors the spotlight in fact aimed at Mouth. The text also encourages us to hear it as reflecting the activity of auditing that the spectator experiences. Not only "she" but the spectator too hears "the buzzing . . . so-called . . . in the ears" and, faced with the speed and fracture of the words, will be "straining to hear . . . to make something of it" (19). The "steady stream," the words "coming," the "mouth alone" on stage, all these, as has been often remarked, reflect metadiscursively on the text we hear, mirror reflexively the physical performance we see, parallel the strain of reception we feel, and still have referential import for the "stories" being told.[38] In addition, this same experience of fragmentation is endured by the actor of Mouth. Billie Whitelaw, who played Mouth in London under Beckett's own direction, was strapped into a chair, head anchored for the spot, body and eyes covered to prevent reflection of the light. Whitelaw speaks of being turned physically into a Mouth, deprived of her other senses—resulting at first in an "out-of-body" experience that is like the extracted mouth we see, inducing hysteria and hallucinations. The speed at which the piece needed to be said gave her jaw-pain, and she had difficulty remembering the text.[39] Thus the actor too experiences fragmentation and memory strain, as does the audience, replicating the experience of the fractured "self" on stage.

Beckett's play of fragments invites us, I think, to "think" intuitively, through the fragmented images themselves, and through the additional fragments produced by text, by voice, by metadiscursive devices, by strategies of reception. Billie Whitelaw tells that she cried when she first read the play, "not understanding one word of it, may I say, intellectually," but intuitively recognizing the mode of Mouth's existence.[40] The nature of Mouth is perhaps not given to rational cognition, to penetration through the will. Every aesthetic decision in the play points to an attempt to create a poetics of dissolution and fragmentation, to be grasped intuitively in something like Bergson's "pure" memory or Proust's "involuntary memory"—but without the consequent Proustian "weaving" of that memory into narrative and thus into restructured meaning.[41] Compared with this, the series of selves in *Krapp* is relatively easy to grasp. The fractured memory of "farewell to love," replayed in three separate fragments, interrupted by additional pieces of Krapp's past, refracted through Krapp's present personality and his own attempts at recording, does finally coalesce into a story and a history that reflect poignantly on Krapp's present loneliness. While *Krapp* may be thought of as a series of distorted and "distilled" selves, *Not I* boggles the imagination in its bottomless, unending production of splinters and fractions resistant to mimetic reconstitution and impervious to closure.

Not I is Beckett's "purest" demonstration of memoried being—devoid of narrative progression or a remembering "self." *Krapp* may already, to quote Steven Connor, consist of a series of mobile utterances creating "a web of mutually enveloping, self-quoting moments, each endlessly displaced from its originating context, and regrafted elsewhere";[42] but the "regrafted" pieces continue to reflect each other (the laugh, the bananas, even the signature loneliness), hinting, even strongly suggesting, some minimal self that survives through time—and thus justifying the material metaphor of a memory "box." In *Not I* we really *cannot* locate a source or place at which an I, a self, resides. Abbott, developing a memoried vocabulary for Beckett's oeuvre, has suggested that the relation between images such as Krapp's tapes and Mouth's "mind" reveals an ongoing process in Beckett's work of what he calls "remembering by *misremembering* in successive works of elements from those that went before," a rewriting of previous works through metamorphosis of elements already used. This dynamic within the works operates to "alter as they recall what went before and are in turn recalled and altered by those to come."[43] *Not I* recalls *Krapp's Last Tape* from the space of a different world, a different zeitgeist, through a changed perspective that reframes the way we look at *Krapp*'s organ of memory and fractured remembrances. With *Not I*—and Beckett's subsequent memory-plays—the mechanisms of memory are rendered forever indeterminate, shifting, plural, incomplete; and that hallucinatory fragment of body, the never-still and thus never "formed" Mouth, becomes a fittingly flighty emblem for postmodern ontological dispersal and centerless being.

Intersubjective Voices from *That Time*

Beckett has remarked that he would never allow *That Time* (1975) to be performed together with *Not I,* since the later play was too clearly "cut out of the same texture as *Not I.*"[44] As in *Not I,* a body fragment evokes a fragmented life, or rather life's fragment. As in the earlier play, the past "comes" through various voices that seem to overtake the visual fragment with spoken memories. But in *That Time* we have even less to look at: instead of a mouth and a figure, we have only a disembodied old white face floating ten feet above stage level, with "long flaring white hair as if seen from above outspread." *That Time* is longer and more static than *Not I,* and Listener's few movements are closer to those of Auditor than to ever-vibrating Mouth. Occasionally, we hear the "slow and regular" breathing of Listener; four times Listener opens then closes his eyes; and twice Beckett inserts pauses: "Silence 10 seconds. Breath audible. After 3 seconds eyes open." As one of the voices resumes, the eyes then again close. These pauses, similar to Auditor's slight movement, divide the play into units and allow the spectator a moment's rest from the incessant and amorphous voices, almost impossible to follow as they tell of three unrelated episodes from different periods of a life. At the end, Listener smiles—"toothless for preference," as Beckett puts it. These are the only movements offered the spectator during the approximately 25 minute performance; everything else is verbal. While it is theatrically significant that, as Beckett put it, "she talks" (Mouth) while "he listens" (Listener),[45] both plays seek to spatialize the interiority of remembrance through a single stage image, and through voice. The differences between the way memory is given and received is what will interest me.

The pose of listening that Beckett assigns to the auditing head directs the audience too toward sound, rather than sight. Memory is both emulated and evoked through voice, and through the repeated and overlapping images described by voices A, B, and C, speaking in three different pitches from three loudspeakers located in three different spaces—that is, three spatial points above the floating face—all separated from any body or source. Speaking in the third person, the voices tell three stories in relay form, describing at least three different places during three different times of year. The sites described are both specific and iconic—a ruin with a "bit of a tower still standing,"[46] a stone in the sun "at the edge of the little wood" (228), a beach, a room, a portrait gallery, a library, a post office. As each tale contains more than one place, and the tales, and thus places, structurally intertwine, visual space as well as ages and time overlap and confound: "that was another place another time that time" (234). As Enoch Brater suggests, evocatively, "Every memory of 'that time' is tied to a memory of 'that space.'" But the connections between them come unhinged in the spectator's mind, as youth and a sun-filled field slip over into old age and dusty interiors without any demarcation—just as the voices themselves move from one unmarked point of theater space to another. Beckett, writes Brater, "makes us see time in terms of space and space in terms of time,"[47] and both float ungrounded and undifferentiated, always virtual, like the floating figure of Listener himself, and thus reproduce neither a specific time nor a specific space—other than the time and space of performance.

On the page, we can see that Beckett's text is not only cut up into three nonconsecutive voices, but also lacks all punctuation or capitalization. There are no sentences, only blocks of unparsed words. This fluid form—unmarked by the signs of beginnings or endings (capitalization, punctuation), of pauses or stress or even the tentative ellipses (. . .) of Mouth's incompletions—suggests and forces an internalization of the text. Missing punctuation—a typical device of postmodern memory-drama from Beckett through Bernhard, Müller, and Parks—suggests the erasure of the temporal progressions and formal shapings that punctuation assures. The blurred distinction between voices, and among the stories, creates a sense of simultaneity and overlap, of voices echoing in memory, of shared and split identities. Viewing the page of *That Time* allows us to understand something difficult to grasp in production: if all the A's, B's, and C's are arranged together, one after the other, the three stories cohere as narrative. Thus, their dissection and interspersals are a deliberate choice to tell the past not consecutively, but simultaneously, as though the thematic division into youth, love, and age were irrelevant for Beckett's purposes. In *Not I,* multiple pasts are signified through the divisions within the absent self, the conflicted inner fragments "dragging up" various pasts and articulated by a captive Mouth. In *That Time,* the coexistence of multiple pasts is more clearly given through the three externally located voices that, while not said to be simultaneous within the text, evoke a sense of temporal coexistence by their very flow. The past is stranded together, we might say, only as a concession to the audience's sense-bound needs, in order to allow reception. This is necessary since, as time-bound humans, we lack the intuitions of Kurt Vonnegut's Tralfamadorians (in *Slaughterhouse Five*), who can "look at the different moments just the way we can look at a stretch of the Rocky Mountains. . . . they can look at any moment that interests them. It is just an illusion we have here on Earth that one moment follows another one, like beads on a string, and that once a moment is gone it is gone forever."[48] *That Time* refutes this linear temporal illusion by refusing to stratify time into a chain of events; it suggests the simultaneity of memory and of being—the past as "'contemporaneous' with the present that it *has been*"[49]—by juxtaposing what cannot be usefully shown as simply overlapping.

If we view these late Beckett plays as offering "models" of postmodern memory tactics, *That Time* presents us with a paradigmatic dramatization of two different, perhaps contradictory, notions: the simultaneity of all pasts within an ever "present" memory; and the gap, or at least ambiguity, between memory and a remembering subject or source. This paradoxical situation implies that "that time" is always an Augustinian "eternal present" existing only in the now of remembrance; and that the place, or site, of memory is both within and outside of a specific remembering "mind." Both of these ideas refute basic dramatic terms such as development and grounding. *That Time* is, in fact, the most unanchored and ungrounded of Beckett's late plays. There is no table (as in *Ohio Impromptu*), no chair (as in *Rockaby*), no ground on which to hop (as in *Footfalls*), nor is there even the figure of an Auditor to suggest the potential fullness of being. The text is unpunctuated and purposely undone, splintered and interleaved beyond mimetic repair, and the fragment floating at a bizarre angle ten feet above stage level is only ambiguously connected to the relayed voices we hear.

The complete separation of voice from body, or from any source, is a new and important element in Beckett's plays. It does, of course, exist in *Krapp's Last Tape,* but there agency is clearly indicated. The connection is apparent between St. Augustine's "will" to recall (Krapp) and the three ages of Krapp stored in the "storage house" of memories (tape recorder), as is the mechanism whereby "will" calls the past forth. In *Eh Joe* too, the camera directs us toward Joe's mind, again clearly indicating the "overvoice's" source within it. The three voices in *That Time,* in their interlaced multidirectionality, might rather remind us of the discontinuous narrative in Beckett's *Play*. But even there, the three "heads" are moved to speech by an outside agent—the spotlight that "provokes" their speech, in turn. Does such agency exist in *That Time?* In a note before the play, Beckett indicates that the text we will hear consists of "moments of one and the same voice A B C," thus informing the reader a priori that one consciousness lays behind the variety of sound. Despite this, and despite Beckett's having written that "Voices A B C are his own coming to him from both sides and above," in other words, that the stories are self-tellings, this is neither apparent in production nor the only conclusion a spectator might reach while listening, with Listener, to the interweave of floating voices. Beckett himself has remarked on the ambiguity of agency in this play. In production, the one indication of a causal link between Listener and the voices is the ceasing/beginning of speech, and the opening/closing of Listener's eyes. According to Beckett, "It is not decided whether he opens his eyes and voice stops for that reason or whether the voice stops and therefore he opens his eyes."[50] This leaves ambiguous precisely the question of Listener's control over the memories, his "calling" them forth, as opposed to their unwilled, and perhaps unconnected, appearance. The conclusion that consciousness calls memory forth is strengthened by Beckett's addition to the stage directions, set out in a letter, that "the light on face is brought up each time the memories flag . . . and faded back to normal as they resume."[51] But the very need for this addition points to the sense of a gap, and perhaps an actual lack of connection, between the figure and the voices.

There is no real reason to connect the floating voices and the static head, other than the fact that these are the only two elements that exist, and their very separation, suggests Connor, "compels us to try to unify the two, without ever offering the prospect of complete success."[52] The effect of their separation is, however, perhaps more valuable then their unification. Through the abstraction of the voices from the body, the "place" of memory is signified as undecidable: both internalized (spoken from "within" Listener, or a subject) and generalized (belonging to a broader communal "memory"). In Maurice Halbwachs's thesis (discussed in chapter 1), personal memory is in any case rooted in collective memory, without which the subject would have no tools or language through which to shape and moor individual versions of a past. Attacking Bergson's idea that all our pasts coexist within the individual mind, Halbwachs emphasized common frame-

to the repetitions of recall. Motion, rather than the fixed posture found in Beckett's other memory-plays, implicates the bodies here in the act of memory itself. *Footfalls* takes repetition—"revolving it all"—as its central action and theme. Pacing, a motion that like stasis is a nonaction, a way of allowing time to pass, becomes the sole choreography and the constant visual stimulant of the play. May paces rhythmically along a prescribed strip, nine steps, a revolve on the tenth, measuring the length of a cell. This length, circumscribed through a spotlight outside of which all is darkness, becomes the narrow length of her world—and of her mind.

> *V:* . . . May. (*Pause. No louder.*) May.
> *M* (*Pacing.*): Yes, Mother.
> *V:* Will you never have done? (*Pause.*) Will you never have done . . . revolving it all?
> *M* (*Halting*): It?
> *V:* It all. (*Pause.*) In your poor mind. (*Pause.*) It all. (*Pause.*) It all.[57]

The "it" that May revolves, just as her body revolves, is the "it" of memory—perhaps re-created as fiction, as a life lived only in its constant retelling and reinvention.

In *Rockaby,* the dressed-up body of an immobile woman moves in the constant and comforting motion of rocking. This motion marks both the passage of time and the movement of the body into timelessness—into death. The chair that dominates the stage is mechanically controlled in order that its movement have an existence separate from the woman (W) who sits in it throughout, rocked and rocking. The similarities between these two plays are immediately apparent. Both focus on obsessively repetitive women, ghostly figures lit through "subdued" or "dim" lighting that from the start suggests figures in memory, traces of a life. In both, prematurely old women with disheveled gray hair—May in a ragged gray wrap, W in a fancy old black evening gown—listen and speak to a voice. In *Footfalls,* the voice (V) is that of the absent Mother, a voice "low and slow" just like May's. In *Rockaby,* the recorded voice (V) is said to be that of W, occasionally joined by W herself. Its hypnotic repetitions remember another "absent" mother, a mother who "in the end went down / down the steep stair / . . . right down / into the old rocker / mother rocker / where mother rocked / all the years / all in black / best black / sat and rocked / rocked / till her end came / in the end came / . . . head fallen / and the rocker rocking."[58] Like the mother, W is also dressed in "best black" and also rocks herself into death. Both women carry and repeat not only the traces of their own pasts, but also the memories and deaths inherited from their mothers, whom they become. Repetition is clearly cyclical and generational in these plays, and what is remembered through the motions of their bodies supersedes the individuality of those bodies. I will briefly focus on the connection between body repetitions, or *em*bodied repetition, and memory in, especially, *Rockaby*.

Rockaby opens with W already sitting in her chair. This is not a figure we can ignore; Beckett stipulates a "black lacy high-necked evening gown," adding that the gown is to be oversewn with "jet sequins to glitter when rocking" (275). W's hat too is to contain "extravagant trimming to catch light when rocking." The glitter, in performance, disperses and reconfigures the outline of the rocking woman, disallowing any constant or unchanging figure, any finalized self. The play opens with W speaking the word "More." After a pause, the chair begins to rock and a voice, signified in the printed text as W's own recorded voice, though not obviously so in production, begins to speak midsentence. The narration we hear is seemingly at the end of its tale—indeed, *Rockaby* is a text full of endings: "till in the end / the day came / in the end came / close of a long day / when she said / to herself / whom else / time she stopped / *time she stopped* / going to and fro" (275). As in *That Time,* most of the text of the play is spoken by a sourceless voice, but this time the figure on stage, W, both joins in sections of the text—notably the repeated line "time she stopped"—and calls for the voice to continue with the word "more," thus indicating a clear link between voice and figure. W's rocking, like May's pacing and the breathing in *That Time,* is a structural means for marking time and dividing up the play. The rocking ceases four times during the performance; and each time the voice too is stilled and only recurs, together with the rock, after W calls out for "more." Once the voice has started, however, its text seems to be fixed and familiar to W, as though this endlessly repeated text had often been repeated before.

The relation between the call for "more" and the reinstated rock and voice once more provokes the question of agency. Beckett told one producer of *Rockaby,* "The woman in no way initiates the rock. The memory initiates the rock."[59] This implies that "memory" precedes the body in motion, is the agent of its activation; it implies too that the mechanical motion of the body is an uncontrollable reaction to the obsessive voice of memory. But the centrality of the rocking body already in place when the play begins, and the eccentricity of the figure seen—overdressed, with wild gray hair, white face, sequins flashing—does not suggest its subordination to memory. Moreover, the repetitions of the body in *Rockaby* not only accompany the repetitions of the text, they also precede it: W is clearly a visual copy of the mother who will be remembered by V. The voice of memory that recalls the mother's death during the play, a death W is now repeating, can only describe what we from the start already see, and what W has physically become. Despite its seeming precedence—in time, and even in Beckett's intentions—the voice of memory is perceived by the viewer as *post factum*.

Rockaby conflates memory and physical incarnation; it also questions the relations between the memory of the body and the memory of the mind. The play's central dilemma is the relation between the image we see—an aged and fading figure, rocking itself into stasis—and the voice we hear, which tells of *another* woman "another like herself / another creature like herself / a little like" (275), who also rocked herself "sat and rocked / rocked / till her end came / in the end came" (280). The problem posed has to do with precedence and agency: is the body that we see *before* we hear the text a repetition *of* the text, or does the text only repeat the already accomplished repetitions written into the mechanisms of the dying body? Beckett plays with these questions both visually and punningly. Textually, the daughter's death is signified as a repetition of the mother's; but visually, the daughter *re*embodies her dead mother from the start, and thus incarnates and becomes her. "[T]ime she went down / down the steep stair," V says in the unpunctuated open-verse lines of the play; "time she went right down / was her own other / own other living soul" (281). What, however, is an "own other"—twice repeated? The only other person W has, seems to be her remembering self. But this "own other" is also signified as her own *(m)other,* whom she becomes in the "otherness" of death. The conflation of the daughter/mother body, and of the voice of self/(m)other (found also in *Footfalls*), implies not only biological repetition and the inevitability of death, but a problematizing of origin and repetition. The past (the mother's voice within her) and the future (the mother's death within her) are "memories" that constitute W, replayed or preplayed by the body—which thus *embodies* memory. The daughter, we might say, both repeats and creates her mother.

This bidirectional repetition is typical of postmodernist art, which, to quote Steven Connor, "is not so much a movement between the fixed polarities of creative originality on the one hand, and plagiarizing imposture on the other, as an attempt to shift and complicate the fixity of each."[60] The most sustained philosophical attack against the hierarchical significances of original/reproduction has been launched by Jacques Derrida, who attempts to force the constant mutual definition and redefinition of these two positions. His attack is based on a repudiation of the assumed value of the source over its reproduction. Repetition, Derrida claims, is both a "trace" and a "presence" that redefines and changes, however slightly, what it imitates.[61]

Thus, each change creates a new "origin" that is, simultaneously, a form of repetition. In *Rockaby,* this redefinition and repetition is aimed backward from the daughter as origin, to the mother she has now become. While the memory may "initiate" the rock, the visual image we see from the start already reproduces the memory we will later hear.

Bodily repetition that evokes a sense of timelessness, and thus of past-ness incorporated in the present, is a theatrical device found in much post-modern theater. Repetitive movements that summon past memories are central to almost any Robert Wilson production—the simultaneous, mechanical smiles of the three identical women at a desk in Wilson's production of Heiner Müller's *Hamletmachine* comes to mind, smiles that recall 1950s television images and a world of inauthentic salesmanship, of libidinal control. We might recall the constant repetitions of set gestures in Wilson's *Einstein on the Beach,* or the single repeated movement of *Deafman Glance.* Pina Bausch's *Tanztheater* is built around the constant repetition of socially conventional gestures, repeating and changing almost imperceptibly, and each time recalling to memory and redefining the world that preceded the gestures and that the movements reembody. Such bodily repetitions, released from contextual or narrative explanation, are also found in Shep-ard's *Action,* or in Müller's *Task,* where the repetitive motion of copulation seems to join past and present in a simultaneous stage image. Bernhard's always obsessive figures spend whole scenes ironing and folding clothes with precisely repeated motions that underlie, or perhaps allow, their obsessive recollections of the past. The automatism of motion that seems so devoid of life, and that in these Beckett plays is so clearly connected with the onset of death, also seems to free, or perhaps compel, the past into coexistence with the "present that it has been" through bodies that contain and recreate the past as present.

Memory, Mourning, *Ohio Impromptu*

Ohio Impromptu (1980) presents us with a riddle. On stage we see two identical men seated at right-angles to each other by a plain table. They are dressed in long black coats, bowed heads propped on their right hands, eyes down. Between them lies one wide-brimmed black hat. In front of Reader (R) is a book from which he reads. Aside from the reading and the pauses, the only other activity in this fifteen-minute play is Listener's (L) occasional knocking on the table, at which Reader stops, then repeats his previous sentence. Both visually and textually, the play thrives on duplications and repetitions that are difficult to sort out. Words such as *retrace, return,* and *redoubled* recur throughout. In addition, the story being read by Reader to Listener reflects the stage picture we see: it too tells of a man reading a story quite like the one we're hearing, to a listening companion. Finally, these mirrorings extend to the very structure of the play in which past and present are conflated, as are text and life.

Memory in *Ohio Impromptu* differs from the previously discussed plays in that it is prompted by an outside loss, the apparent death of the "dear name." The need to obtain what Edgar Allen Poe (in his mourning-poem "The Raven") called "surcease of sorrow" for an unbearable bereavement motivates the story told, as well as the form of its telling. The story Reader reads to Listener tells of "a last attempt to obtain relief" by a man unable to sleep and comforted by a stranger who appears nightly and reads to him. The sleepless man of the story lives in an "Unfamiliar room. Unfamiliar scene"—not unlike the unfamiliar stage before us. He wears a "long black coat" and an "old world Latin Quarter hat"—precisely like the coats worn by the duplicate figures on stage, and like the hat that lies between them. The stranger comes nights—the stage too is dark but for one central light—and repeatedly reads the mourner the same story. In the end he informs the mourner that he has come for the last time. Having finished reading "the sad tale a last time told," the stranger closes the book and (so Reader reads from the volume before him), sits "as though turned to stone."[62] With this, Reader too finishes reading and closes his book. He then sits on stage "Unblinking. Expressionless": as though turned to stone (288). Clearly, the text read mirrors and precedes, thus anticipating and rendering implausible, the situation we see on stage. In fact, the play's central visual and literary device—repetition—finally finds its most disturbing form as a *mise-en-abîme*.

The play opens with the words "Little is left to tell." From the first we are at the end of the tale, with Reader reading from the "last pages" of the book open before him. The "little" that is left is, however, the crucial portion, for it retells the moment of the mourner's potential separation from the memory that haunts him. "In a last attempt to obtain relief," the story begins, the mourner had moved "from where they had been so long together. . . . Out to where nothing ever shared. Back to where nothing ever shared. From this he had once half hoped some measure of relief might flow" (285). But no relief is achieved through distance; the memory of loss moves with him and continues within him. The mourner finds himself invaded (again) by "his old terror of night"—insomnia (286). It is at this point of sleeplessness and despair that the stranger appears, sent by "the dear name—to comfort you," and reads from his "worn volume" until dawn.

Each reading is a repetition, a renewed rehearsal of that same memory of bereavement. Through these repeated readings, the two men "grew to be *as one*" (287; emphasis added). After many such unheralded appearances, the mourner is given the message that the stranger will no longer return. It is this moment of the seeming "ending" to the repeated retellings of his grief, this moment of a possible "surcease of sorrow" that the play, and the story in the play, constantly repeats.

Ohio Impromptu is theatrically canny and self-reflective; it is also endlessly introverted. The posture of the two men—bent, face hidden, eyes lowered, immobile within their long black coats—is an image of complete self-absorption, cutting them off from the audience's view or from the world. The character of the mourner in the story is also described as totally isolated, alone in his small room, or slowly pacing "Day after day. . . . Hour after hour" (286). This breach and introversion is typical, according to Freud, of "profound mourning," which involves "loss of interest in the outside world . . . [and a] *turning away* from any activity that is not connected with thoughts of him [the lost one]. It is easy to see that this inhibition and circumscription of the ego is the expression of an exclusive devotion to mourning." In mourning, the ego is totally tied up with the lost object, invested in what Freud terms *Trauerarbeit*—"mourning-work"—that is, the act of "working through" the trauma of loss by remembering and repeating that loss and the memories of everything connected with the lost one. Through this, the mourner takes the lost object into the self, restructures through repetition all the past moments, and reconstructs his or her own identity in terms of this bereavement. When the work of mourning is completed—when the "sad tale" is indeed a last time told—"the ego becomes free and uninhibited again" and can form new attachments.[63] Through this mourning practice, a traumatic real loss is transformed into a symbolic one that can be managed.

A second, perverted reaction to bereavement, according to Freud, is melancholy. Similarly to mourning, melancholy cuts the ego off from all interests other than rehearsal of the lost one, but in addition involves extreme depression and "self-revilings" brought on by an inability to separate the lost one from the self. "Could he not now turn back?" says Reader. "Acknowledge his error and return to where they were once so long alone together" (286). The melancholic sees the lost one as a mirror of the self ("alone together"); in melancholy, the lost object loses its uniqueness—its name, its history—and is collapsed into the self. Mourning-work, in this case, does not free the libido, and there appears to be no "surcease of sorrow." On the contrary, the melancholic regresses to a total self-involvement, to narcissism in which the "otherness" of the lost object is replaced by endless, painful self-reflection. "In mourning it is the world which has become poor and empty," writes Freud, "in melancholia it is the ego itself."[64] Thus the melancholic looks to the lost past and sees himself.

The parallels between Freud's description of melancholy in his influential 1917 article "Mourning and Melancholia" and Beckett's images in *Ohio Impromptu* are, I think, quite overt. All of the images in *Ohio Impromptu,* textual and visual, reflect one central and self-identical "I," the mourner, whose grief is imaged in narcissistic, regressive terms. The *object* of mourning, on the other hand, is almost completely absent in this text. Beckett is careful never to determine the gender, or indeed even the mode of *being* of the "dear face" or "dear name"—Beckett's ambiguous appellations for the lost object. We know nothing about this object—not even whether it was human; nothing except that it is now a "shade," and thus lost. Unlike Freud's description of "healthy" mourning, in which "each single one of the memories" connected with the departed is "brought up" and relived,[65] here no remembrance of the "dear face" is ever reconstructed. Clearly, the nature of the lost object is displaced in this melancholy text by the effect of the loss on the mourner.

This effect is complicated through the double roles of Reader and Listener, who, despite their identical appearance, reproduce two opposed routes of recall: the involuntary incursion of traumatic memory as repetitive text that, as Cathy Caruth put it, "possesses" the victim of loss,[66] and the critical faculty that tries to control the memory "text" by shaping the form of its enunciation. As the memory is "replayed" by Reader, the listening consciousness critiques the way the text is "remembered" and self-corrects (as does Mouth in *Not I*). Remembrance in *Ohio Impromptu* is shown to be obsessive and, at the same time, subject to the repressive intervention of the will, represented through Listener's "knocking." Beryl and John Fletcher suggest that Listener uses the knock to get Reader to go back a little in his reading—"somewhat like Krapp winding the tape back to hear a section again"—and then to order him to go on.[67] But Krapp rewinds in order to reach the sections he longs to relive; Listener "rewinds," I suggest, in order to gain control over the memory by giving it a certain "shape," a formal and final objectification that might remove the memory from the immediacy of lived experience and thus possibly overcome it.

This attempt to overcome memory by controlling its shape, by turning it into a symbolic practice, recalls Freud's famous example in *Beyond the Pleasure Principle* of the *fort/da* (gone/here) game played by his grandson as a way of mastering his grief over his separation from his mother. By repeat-

edly staging the disappearance of his toys, the boy could control the pleasure of their reappearance and thus, Freud claims, symbolically "practice"
(rehearse) separation and loss. Like Listener, he tries to overcome the pain
of loss by repeating, but also *controlling,* its retelling. The repetitions of
mourning, like the ritual repetitions and formal shapings of theater in classical thought, are meant to be a way to overcome "tragedy" and achieve
cathartic relief (a word much repeated in this short text). But in Beckett's
play of mourning the repetitions fail, relief remains elusive, and the ego's
only "new" attachment at the end of the process is again with the self. This
ambiguity is signified at the end of the play by the tension between closure
and lack of closure. As Enoch Brater has suggested, "The story begins in
the past and ends in a future which foretells the play's conclusion: the con-
gruity is achieved by an audience which tries to make sense out of the
ambiguous relation between treatment and chronicle."[68] This "ambiguous
relation" is in the end impossible to sort out. The "chronicle" will not be
"shaped"; and the "sad tale" is never "a last time told" since the uncontrollable repetitions and self-reflections of melancholy finally engulf every
aspect of the stage.

This is most clearly seen in the final images of the play. The last beautiful paragraph tells, via Reader's reading from the book, of the absolute
silence that follows the stranger's last reading to the mourner of the text.
Both men are oblivious to light or sound, "Buried in who knows what pro-
founds of mind. Of mindlessness. Whither no light can reach. No sound. So
sat on as though turned to stone. The sad tale a last time told" (288). The
nearly final image of the play is thus of petrification and death, of silence,
darkness, perhaps even closure. But Beckett erupts this stasis—first by moving from the inscribed memory (in the book), to its repetition on stage.
Reader too finishes reading and, in a striking gesture, closes his book. Now
the men on stage, imitating those in the tale, sit (for five seconds) bent,
unmoving, silent, as though the ending of the story is simultaneously the
structural closure of the play. But this is not the end—or the closure—
Beckett has in mind. In the last moments of the play, Beckett suddenly
inserts a new gesture that radically shifts the play's imagery. All at once the
two duplicate men "lower their right hands to table, raise their heads and
look at each other. Unblinking. Expressionless" (288; emphasis added). For
the first time in the play, communication via *sound* (reading, knocking) is
replaced by communication via *sight.* The two men enter each other's
eyes—for ten whole seconds, Beckett writes—and thus a sense of commu-
nion, of repair or healing, of recognition and completion might be felt.
They indeed become "as one."

This, however, is not the whole picture; for what the duplicate characters see and what the audience sees them seeing is no more than a replica of themselves. This looking is not a resolution, a closing gesture. Despite the seeming shift in stage imagery, once again we have reflection, introspection, a self-looking; it is a narcissistic repetition that recalls and reinscribes the numerous narcissisms of the play. Rather than open the play out onto the world by, for example, allowing the figures to look out at the audience and thus perhaps signifying, with Freud, the ego becoming "free and uninhibited" again, Beckett stresses through this gaze the play's continuing circulation of reflected grief and of narcissistic interiority, its *lack* of closure.

This final gesture, which both changes the stage reality and repeats it, has an additional resonance. For the first time in the play, the audience gets to see the actors' faces. Yet, frustratingly, those faces remain turned away from the audience, locked in their own gaze, implying a rejection of the outside world (the audience) *by* the melancholic, as well as by Beckett. *Ohio Impromptu,* indeed, consistently "excludes" the witness of the spectator, who is less implicated or "factored into" this play than into any of Beckett's other memory-plays. The spectator is never addressed, implied, faced, or acknowledged. No gesture mediates between the viewer and the text (such as Auditor's "compassionate" gestures in *Not I*), no floating voices implicitly include the spectators among its listeners (as do the voices in *That Time*), no eyes ever face outward toward the auditorium. The bent posture and shaded face shun all intrusion and keep the spectator forever at bay. The final image, with the two duplicate "I"s locked into each others eyes "as one" in the silence and immobility of the stage, becomes a wrenching expression of the isolation and introversion of melancholic mourning, and of its obliviousness to any exterior (spectatorial) gaze. Frozen into introspection "as though turned to stone," this self-looking offers no way out of the "sad tale"—nor does it offer the spectator any way *in*. Rejected, forced to witness a pain they can never alleviate, the spectator is cast in the role of that "world" from which, according to Freud, the mourner forever "turns away."

In *Ohio Impromptu,* memory achieves its most portentous image of interiority. In a few brief pages, through one penetrating image, using one speaking voice on a darkened stage: Beckett portrays the nature of the unending memory of grief. Memory as mourning and melancholy is central to many of the plays I discuss in the following chapters, and to the sense of "loss" and epigonism common to postmodern theater. Müller places this "loss" at the heart of *The Foundling,* as does Bernhard, more obliquely, in *Eve of Retirement.* Suzan-Lori Parks, especially in *The Death of the Last Black*

Man in the Whole Entire World, mourns the obliteration of a black American memory; while Sam Shepard's *Action* mourns the passing of a world grounded in historical, memoried identity. All of these plays expand Beckett's self-circulation, transforming the subjectivity of grief into a broader historical, and collective, context. An interesting intermediary example of a performance that combines Beckett's minimal and introverted stage image of grief with the theme of historical and collective mourning can be found in Hans-Jürgen Syberberg's six-hour mono-movie *Die Nacht* (*The Night*). Through a recyling of past texts, through temporal conflation and repetitions, this postmodern German film director laments the "end" not of a relationship—but of a world. *The Night* (1984) takes place (like Shepard's *Action*) in the future, after the passing of the West. On screen we see only a single actress, Edith Cleaver, in one unchanging, darkened room that, not unlike Hamm's room in *Endgame,* appears to be the last lodging of a destroyed civilization. For six hours she speaks a multivoiced monologue: considered by Syberberg to be an "oratorio" for one voice. Unlike Syberberg's earlier style in such controversial movies as *Hitler: A Film from Germany* (1977)—with its visual extravaganza and the dense overlap of texts, voices, and discourses—in *The Night* Syberberg mourns through a single, theatrical voice the passing of "Europe." His memorial text is constructed from mixed and repeated fragments of Western literature and philosophy that relate, not an individual tale of loss, but a story shared—culturally and historically—by Syberberg's target audience. Interminably long, the monologue's length seems an attempt to hold onto the memory of a disappearing culture. What Syberberg does through extension (of screen-time and text) and the complex collage of cultural voices, Beckett does through concentration (of stage-time and text) and the complex circulations of inner-directed images. The important difference between these two memory texts is that while Syberberg mourns "Europe" and the passing of history, Beckett *simply mourns* and thus becomes paradigmatic for an open-ended postmodern rendering of memory into the idiom of mourning and melancholy.

In the following chapters, Beckett's abstracted postures of memory will find more concretely situated forms. The act of remembrance will no longer lack an "object" and be inner directed; indeed, it will have a surplus of objects—historical, cultural, collective.

Chapter 3

Heiner Müller's Landscapes of Memory

Our work is raising the dead; the theater troupe is recruited from ghosts
. . . the set a travel guide through the landscapes beyond death.
                              —Heiner Müller, "Raising the Dead"

In Heiner Müller we have a playwright clearly associated with memory and remembrance; "a classical writer against forgetting," as he has been called,[1] Müller's "Theater der Erinnerung" (Theater of Memory)[2] refuses to allow the dead their peace. Unlike Beckett, Müller's "memories" are not only about remembering, but about the memories themselves: he invokes the concrete political and cultural world of Europe, the figures and events that have shaped its people, the transgressions and oppressions of European, and particularly German, history. Before *die Wende* (the political "turn" of 1989) Müller held the anomalous position of a writer, thinker, and practitioner of theater at home in both East and West, who used a postmodern theater aesthetic to recover the repressions and betrayals of German, and especially East German, history, and who occupied that chasm between the "two German capitals Berlin" whose "shared and not shared history" he saw, and portrayed, as "piled up by the latest earthquake as a borderline between two continents."[3] Walter Benjamin's image of the "piled up" ruins of history is particularly apt for Müller's theater, which explores both the massive traces left by a ruinous past upon the collective memory and the continued eruptions of that past in the present. For Müller, as for Benjamin, the complexity of the past and the fracture of its memory-load remained a lifelong preoccupation—a preoccupation that came to represent, for both writers, nothing less than a "literary signature."[4]

Routinely referred to as "Brecht's heir," Müller both continued and subverted Brecht's aesthetic and political projects. His numerous plays (almost sixty theater texts that range from scraps of scenes to long and difficult works) are usually divided into three styles, which loosely correspond to three periods.[5] Many of his early works (of the 1950s and 1960s) have a local, German Democratic Republic (GDR) orientation; influenced by Brecht, they are styled as quasi–socialist realism within a Marxist theoretical context. It was during this period that Müller began to question the didacticism of the socialist model he had appropriated and to turn against the dialectical formalism that underlies it. Müller reacted in such plays as *Philoctetes* (*Philoktet*, 1964) and *The Horatian* (*Der Horatier*, 1968) against the constricting dialectical view of history—a view that subsumes, and tames, the past within an edifice that inevitably predicts a reformed future. He also reacted against the aesthetic counterpart of this model as found in the parables and didactic theater of Brecht. From the early 1970s, with *Germania Death in Berlin* (*Germania Tod in Berlin*, 1971) Müller leaped out of the confinements of Brecht's direct influence toward a new form that he later called the "synthetic fragment," a kind of assemblage play constructed from diverse parts. His 1970s plays—for example *Germania, The Battle* (*Die Schlacht*, 1974), *Gundling's Life Frederick of Prussia Lessing's Sleep Dream Scream* (*Leben Gundlings Friedrich von Preussen Lessings Schlaf Traum Schrei*, 1976)—draw from a broader palate than the early work, using more history, especially German historical material. Rejecting his former aesthetic and theoretical positions, Müller introduced extravagant, Artaudian "total theater" effects into his texts,[6] putting into practice a dramaturgy of "flooding" or inundating the audience. This was aimed at the paradoxical project of both involving and overwhelming the viewer, offering too many simultaneous options to too much stimuli and thus defeating any easy position-taking.

With *The Task* (*Der Auftrag*, 1979), perhaps already with *Hamletmachine* (1977), a new phase begins in Müller's dramaturgy—and it is this phase that will be my main focus. A new seriousness informs these later plays; the exorbitant theatrical devices are for the most part replaced by complex lyrical tactics and deconstructive imagery. Collective memory speaks in a collage of voices from a postideological stance that reaches out, thematically, beyond German history, beyond Europe, to a universal history—or, as some will claim, to an "end of history."[7] The theme of failure—the failure of Enlightenment Europe, of revolution, of socialism, of the intellectual, of the unified self—is given through a series of memory moments that both bemoan the forgotten past ("FORGOTTEN AND FORGOTTEN AND FORGOTTEN")[8] and combat that amnesia. These plays have been called "Bewußtseinslandschaften"[9]—landscapes of consciousness—and they do indeed move inward, presenting a less gestural and more expressly stream-of-memory dramaturgy. Through fragment and obsessive image, these theater texts recall a no longer grounded past: a past that floats, uprooted, within the collective memory, as a place of (fragmented) collective identity. Conventional stage instructions all but disappear, blocks of text often go unattributed, the speaker is implicit—a collective and shared speaker. Times and places become fluid and overlapping. It is during this period that Müller began his ongoing and successful work with Robert Wilson. Indeed, stimulated by the texts' formal openness, by the fluidity and overlap of time and place, plays such as *Hamletmachine, The Task, Quartet (Quartett,* 1981), *Despoiled Shore Medeamaterial Landscape with Argonauts (Verkommenes Ufer Medeamaterial Landschaft mit Argonauten,* 1982), *Explosion of a Memory/Description of a Picture (Bildbeschreibung,* 1984), *Volokolamsk Highway (Wolokolamsker Chausee,* 1984–87), among others, received often wildly different productions—a circumstance of which Müller approved. In the decade before his death, productions of Müller's plays, including his own productions, were ubiquitous in Germany, as were the reviews, critiques, and academic studies dedicated to his work. Müller became the first playwright to have an entire Frankfurt "Experimenta" festival (seventeen days) dedicated to him. Thus, write his bibliographers Ingo Schmidt and Florian Vaßen, Müller managed in his lifetime to become an "always self-skeptical—Institution."[10]

Müller's two major (political and personal) traumas were German fascism and East German communism. Born 1929 to a working class family in Saxony, Müller saw his father, a minor social democratic functionary, beaten and taken away by Nazi SA agents in 1933; he was himself drafted at sixteen into the German Labor Force and sent to the front in 1945, where he witnessed the ending of the war. Due to the division of Germany he became an East German, a socialist soon critical of the socialist state (his father crossed over to the West). Müller's career has been a dialogue with, and against, the political and ideological forces that defined and constricted him as well as with their historical antecedents.

In *The Foundling (Der Findling,* 1987), for example, the narrator-son remembers his father's body: broken first by the Nazis in the camps (genitals crushed) and then by the Party in East Berlin (back broken). The fractured voices and fragmented forms of Müller's plays recall the interleaved memories of these ruinous pasts, often written onto the same bodies. But Müller's memory extends beyond these two defining moments. His "history collages"—such as *The Battle, Germania, Gundling's Life*—overwhelm the reader/audience with reconfigured images and voices ranging from the Nibelungs to Stalin, showing the rise of Hitler (who literally gives birth to the Third Reich through a sexual union with the pregnant Goebbels) as part and product of an entrenched and ongoing mentality of brutalization and excess. The question simply put is: what is the meaning of all these particles of Western culture strewn across Müller's "landscapes beyond death"? How

Tshingis Aitmatov's description of slave "maintenance" through torture and memory erasure. By this time Müller had already supplied Wilson with many texts for his diverse projects,[15] and during all of these, the two men worked closely together. But Wilson's request for a theater-piece on memory/torture seemed to meet with failure on Müller's part, and Müller responded with a letter initially intended (he claims) to explain *why* he had failed. This letter developed into a fervent defense of the need to remember—"There is no revolution without a memory," Müller wrote—and a warning against individual and collective forgetting. The letter ends, paradoxically, with Müller's request that Wilson "[a]ccept this letter as an expression of my desire to be present in your work."[16]

As with all of Müller's later writing, this letter is a collage of strikingly vivid transmuted images organized around a central stimulus. The stimulus here is Aitmatov's horrific description of Mongolian torture that served "to turn captives into slaves, tools without a memory." The technology described is graphic: the head of the shackled captive is shaved and tightly covered with "the skin of a freshly slaughtered camel's neck" that, when exposed to the sun, cakes and contracts into a tight helmet, forcing the captive's regrowing hair "to grow backward into the scalp: the tortured prisoner lost his memory within five days—if he survived them—and was, after this operation, a laborer who didn't cause trouble, a Mankurt." The violence of this horrific technology, and its totally dehumanizing effect—"An early design of total utilization of labor, until its transformation into raw material in the concentration camps"—seemed to stun Müller. "I couldn't represent this event—the disintegration of thinking, the extinction of memory—only describe it," he writes. Müller's conclusion—"There is no revolution without a memory"—is expanded through a series of dream images; it is then complicated through a description of Tintoretto's *Miracle of Marcus,* and is finally historicized through Müller's closing remarks: "Written as the crow flies between the two German capitals Berlin, separated by the chasm of their shared and not shared history, piled up by the latest earthquake as a borderline between two continents."[17]

What is interesting is the reasons Müller gives for his "failure" to turn this historical text into a theatrical one. He writes of his despair at being able to produce a text "which could serve as a gravitational center" for Wilson's *DD&D II*—"a creation that more than any of your earlier works consists of its own explosion." Müller seems to be claiming that a subject of such seriousness—"a text which willy-nilly means something"—would get lost in Wilson's choreography of centerless detonation. In one of his dream descriptions, Müller images Wilson as cut off from the political voices of the impending cataclysm, as "harnessed in a spacious steel construction" and wearing headphones that render him unreachable to the calls or sirens of disaster. "I find what he does important," Müller told an interviewer about Wilson; "but I would never do it that way . . . If we want to make theater here in Europe, we need a theater with text, a theater with history, and for Wilson that doesn't exist."[18] In his letter, Müller describes a nightmare of "the end of libraries" in which "putrid paper, decomposed letters"—such as this letter he is writing?—are seen sunk in the mud: a further image for the destruction of historical memory. Worst, Müller writes of his fear that the significance of the Aitmatov text on "the extinction of memory" would, like the books in his dream, be "silenced . . . when confronted with the cen-trifugal force of your images." Wilson, with his "coyote-like laughter," is pictured here as the innocent, unhistoried American: "America is the most subjective, the most innocent nation in the Western world," Müller said, in conversation. "There isn't a nation in Europe that didn't experience the Holocaust. This makes a difference in the subconscious."[19]

Thus Müller's reluctance seems to translate as a fear that the historical resonance of a text on memory would be "silenced," its multiple connota-tions lost, in Wilson's hands. Yet, and here we strike on a pattern that will recur in Müller's memory-theater, he ends his letter with a plea to become, through this very letter, part of Wilson's "explosion." Wilson's "use" of Müller's text further develops this doubleness by both mixing Müller's text with other very different texts in his production—and thus silencing it ide-ologically, as Müller had feared—and also reprinting the letter in its entirety, as a supplement to the program notes for *DD&D II*, thus allowing his plea for remembrance to speak for itself, unencumbered. The contradictions implicit in Müller's position are typical of an intellectual who always thinks in political terms, but who, as an artist ever wary of cliché, finds in contra-diction (or "slipperiness") the underlying fund of his imagination.

This letter/theater text raises another question of central importance in Müller's theater: the breakdown of generic distinctions. Within Müller's theater we find texts that, formally at least, seem to be prose pieces, or poems, or letters, as well as plays with more conventional speakers, setting, and stage instructions. Indeed, some of his "plays"—or theater texts—appear both in theater anthologies and in his poem collections, and, as noted, texts are often reused and reconfigured for completely different con-texts. Thus, a written piece only receives its generic definition through its *use*—a very postmodern circumstance. A poem that is anthologized in a book of poetry, however visual its imagery, remains a poem, whereas once it is inserted into a collection of plays, or performed on a stage, its generic

definition multiplies. Carl Weber hypothesizes that Müller's "experimentation with structure and genre isn't done so much to arrive at the most fitting
form for a given content—a rather traditional approach—but to capture
several of the many angles by which the content may be viewed."[20] Such is
Müller's *A Letter to Robert Wilson*. Ostensibly a letter, its "plea" to become
a text for theater, and Wilson's use of the text *in* his theater, renders it a theatrical text open to, and a stimulus for, scenic interpretation. Its additional
inclusion in Wilson's program notes transforms the text into an essay on
memory and on the dangers that "centrifugal images"—such as Wilson's
own—pose to the effect of remembrance.

Müller's handling of the "task" of writing a text on memory for an
unmemoried theater (Wilson's) parallels his uses of memory in his own theater. On the one hand, memory is encased and spotlighted, equated with
revolution and the very condition for liberty. Throughout Müller's work,
the viewers' memory is engaged through specific historical and cultural references, through lyrical voice and obsessive repetition—to become a
provocation against forgetting. On the other hand, these memory-units
appear in Müller's own postmodern texts as displaced, fragmented, and
flooded in form. The formal structure shatters context and continuity, rip-
ping the past out of its situation, mixing it with other pasts, and in the
process dissolving it as grounded "history." The past floats and invades the
viewer's consciousness in the multiple and ahistorical forms of traumatized
memory. Müller is aware of this paradox of the simultaneous invocation and
explosion of the past through postmodern aesthetics, but his use of this aesthetic has a political aim. As he wrote in a 1978 lecture for the MLA in New
York, "I cannot keep politics out of the question of post-modernism."[21] In
an interview, Müller was asked how he accounted for the disparity between
his often grotesque theatre texts, and a rational leftist political position. He
answered that politics and art are not parallel activities. "When an idea is
translated into an image," he said, "either the image comes out crooked, or
the idea is exploded. I prefer the explosion. . . . The only thing that an art-
work can do is to awaken longing for a different type of world. And this
longing is revolutionary."[22] Despite the evasiveness of this answer, Müller's
nonchronological, noncausal evocations of history, his serious attempts to
place the present beside the distortions and betrayals of the past, recall Walter Benjamin's attack on teleological history and his explosive desire "to
blast open the continuum of history."[23] For Benjamin, the task of the historian was to read the past in a way that would return to memory, and thus to
history, moments potentially meaningful, and transformational, for the present. Such a reading cracks open the progression of homogenous (chrono-

logical) history, and through the openings, marginalized, oppressed, forgotten voices can "redeem" memories written out of the victor's linear tale. Thus for Benjamin, as for Müller, linearity, a Hegelian historical progression, is repudiated in favor of a memoried methodologically. Memory, that "dialogue with the dead" out of which the future arises, is for Müller an ideological principle. After all, as he half-seriously put it, the dead are "in the overwhelming majority when compared to the living."[24]

Fragments, Floodings, Memory Devices

During the 1970s, Müller developed a dramatic structure called the "synthetic fragment" that became his signature form of work. This construction refuses the idea of textual "integrity" and instead sees each work as both text and pretext for further texts, creating reusable modular writings. Ideologically, this approach renders Müller's oeuvre as coextensive and simultaneous, rather than as a chronological—time-bound—creation. Moreover, it is an approach impregnated by a view of memory as coexistent with the present, a view that his collage texts as finished plays further encourage. The "synthetic fragment" is an always tentative collaborative form composed not only of Müller's own earlier literary texts, but also, intertextually, of parts and particles from such diverse cultural artifacts as myth, autobiography, dreams, literary paraphrase, quotation, and self-citation, "a composite," writes Carl Weber, "that challenges the reader's knowledge and imagination."[25] One of the objectives of this splintered method is to achieve what Weber termed Müller's quest for the Western collective memory.[26] The flood of uprooted images found in these amalgamations stress process, the process of reception and interpretation, thus, according to Müller, turning the audience into a coproducer of meaning and memory.[27]

Germania Death in Berlin (1971) and The Battle (1974) are examples of this method. They are history collages that, while focused more on de-rigging history than on exploring memory, already contain some of the aesthetic devices and exploded forms of Müller's later memory-theater. In Germania, one of Müller's most popular and often produced plays, we have a compilation of "performance texts" that he wrote between 1956 and 1971, linked by a theme rather than a narrative line. The nightmare of history—German, Prussian history—found throughout, begins on a Berlin street in 1918 and moves simultaneously forward and backward: from the Roman conquests to the East German strikes of 1953; from war scenes to a cancer ward in which we meet Georg Hauptmann's reactionary figure, old-man Hilse (from The Weavers), here "the eternal bricklayer" who speaks to a women he takes for Rosa Luxemburg about socialism. The play presents scenes from German myth, literature, and history, scrambled and set in a variety of genres. In scene 3, "Hommage à Stalin 1," we get a grotesque version of the battle of Stalingrad featuring Napoleon, Caesar, and the Nibelungs, who sit on mounds of corpses, drink beer from skulls, masturbate, and hack each other to pieces. Scene 5, titled "The Holy Family," takes place in the *Führerbunker* where Goebbels gives birth to Hitler's child—a Thalidomide wolf—while Germania (*das Volk*) plays midwife, and the three Magi, bearing gifts of torture, witness the event. Frederick II appears in one of the scenes as a vampire; in another, a skull salesman (a former historian) in postwar East Germany offers an eighteenth-century (Enlightenment) skull as a decorative piece to a prostitute. The wild mélange of images is presented in styles veering from realism to circus spectacle to Grand Guignol. Their visual acuteness seems a direct application of the counsel of classical mnemonics "to set up images of a kind that can adhere longest in the memory . . . images that are not many or vague, but doing something" (*Ad Herennium*).[28] Centered on such images, as well as on excremental language, Müller stratifies the cataclysms of German history *horizontally,* turning Germany's *lieux de mémoire* into a scenic potpourri of jumbled hallucinations. This is an imagistic theater whose contextless events seem to suffer from, and to critique, what Pierre Bourdieu has termed "genesis amnesia": a form of commodification that cuts the (consumer) item off from its own history.[29] Such commodification, Müller seems to be saying, has overtaken the contemporary imagination for which history has become a huge stockpile of cartoonish icons. The Nibelungs as commodity (consumed as an icon for a mythic/barbaric past), set beside other such historical conquerors—Napoleon, Caesar—turns all of history into a series of disruptions perceived functionally but denuded of both historical process (the conditions of their evolution) and of origin (genesis), and thus denuded too of political affect.

A similar, though more realistic, mixture is available in the five scenes, or miniplays, of *The Battle*—written between 1951 to 1974 and conceived as an "answer" to Brecht's "scenes from daily life" in his *Fear and Misery in the Third Reich (Furcht und Elend des Dritten Reiches,* itself written between 1935 and 1938). Christopher Innes calls *The Battle* the psychological dimension of *Germania,*[30] featuring the "people" rather than the myths. With a greater degree of restraint than in *Germania,* Müller gives us Gestapo torturers, starving German soldiers who shoot and eat a comrade at Stalingrad, people caught between the outgoing SS and the incoming Russian soldiers, eager to betray each other in order to survive. "Everyday Fascism," from the

Night of the Long Knives in 1934 to war's end in 1945, is imaged in the cruel and knowing detail missing from Brecht's earlier account of the same period, reflecting a subsequent German collective subconscious, and what Innes terms an "expressionistic replay of the national past."[31] Parallel to the play's dramas of historical and personal betrayal, Müller portrays the deep craving to forget—to extinguish those who tie us to memory and guilt. This desire for freedom from witness and trace motivates, for example, scene 3, the ironically titled "A Middle Class Wedding" in which a man declares that he and his family must "follow our Führer's great example" and kill themselves, rather than succumb to the enemy who will soon arrive. The wife and daughter object fiercely; nonetheless, the man ties, gags, and shoots them both. He has less success, however, in killing himself. At this moment of failure, Hitler steps out of a *Führer* portrait hanging on the wall. The man tries to hide his gun, pretending innocence and ignorance, like Adam in Eden. Hitler wags his finger at the man's failure, for "The Führer is dead, to live is treachery." In the end, the man's very Brechtian solution is to turn Hitler's picture to the wall—"Hitler disappears"—and to exit with the words, "Where there was an end, there will be a beginning. / He who is strong is strongest when alone."[32] Clearly, the nuptials that the husband has chosen are devoid of past or memory, Führer or family. He has chosen the famous *Stunde Null* (*Zero Hour*) solution. This short play is a recycling of a story written by Müller in 1956, entitled "The Iron Cross." In that story, Hitler's picture is replaced by the Iron Cross of war. The husband draws his wife and daughter far away from their home, shoots them on a deserted path outside of town, and runs. At the last moment he remembers to throw away the gun—as well as his Iron Cross. Thus Müller links personal and ideological violence; he also links personal and ideological amnesia.[33]

The same compulsion to forget is found in section 4, titled "Butcher and Wife," of *The Battle,* a miniplay composed of five separate, almost filmic, units. Here, a butcher has joined the Nazi SA in order to improve his business opportunities at home and is sent with his troops to find and kill an American pilot shot down in their woods. The subscene "Storm Troopers Marching" takes place in the always-mythic German woods. The stage directions tell us that from offstage come "the sounds of German fascism: Speeches Heil-shouts Beerhall-brawls Crystal Night War."[34] This concise list of eight run-on words (five in the German), unpunctuated or otherwise semiotically differentiated, give the equivalent of a history of German fascism from the early 1920s to the 1940s and is meant to evoke the voice and feel of growing fascist fervor through an audial *Rausch*. Each loaded word is

filled with raw historical memory, and each evokes sounds and images that
have been endlessly reproduced in radio, film, and video, and thus immediately evoke a world. Choreographed into this "audial history," Müller has
the storm troopers physically march across the stage, speaking "random"
lines that together create another audial quilt, ranging from the banal to the
horrific:

> *Storm Troopers:* . . . Till the very end at the machine gun / I can't do it
> / The letter arrived yesterday / Did you say the Eastern front is looking
> pretty bad / . . . But not a word to my wife / Did you hear this one: a
> Jew goes to the cathouse. Says the madam: you can't go up now,
> Goebbels is upstairs. Says the Jew / 'Toon Halt / He has had it / Rip
> his guts out / Off with his pumpkin / He's half charred / A nigger
> maybe / Jews the lot of 'em.[35]

These lines supply the "collective voice" of internalized fascism as opposed
to the official offstage voices of enforced fascism. Audial simultaneity—the
collage of voices and sounds that erupt as out of a submerged past and provoke in the audience subliminal memory responses—will be of great
importance in Müller's later plays, such as *Landscape with Argonauts, The
Task,* or *The Foundling,* where multiple voices often appear undifferentiated, split and shared within one collective text. The audience for whom
Müller wrote this play would have easily recognized these voices and the
mentality they re-create; through this, they would, perhaps, also have
understood the characters' desire to forget. The scene ends with the
"groans of the wounded pilot" who is then "butchered" by the butcher
and sold for pork. The need to forget is the overt theme of the playlet's last
scene, in which the will to erase the visceral images of memory is victori-
ous—and again murderous. In a long verse-line monologue, far more
introverted than the previous scenes, the wife recalls how her husband, on
the eve of the Russians' arrival, left their bed and went to the river to
drown himself. She tells how, despite inner conflicts, she set out at first to
stop him —"Why do you run / Turn back Stop now Slow down What
will be will be / You didn't do in that American / A volunteer or not, he
was the killer"—but finally, after long hesitation, while struggling to pull
him from the water, she pushes him under instead. "It was him or me."
Thus the wife frees herself of both her guilty husband, and of her own connection to that past.[36] Like the murderer husband of scene 3, a new beginning means, in the end, extinguishing the past.

　　Helen Fehervary has argued that Müller's collage plays—especially
Germania and *The Battle*—are constructed through what she terms an "aes-

thetics of entanglement," which she then contrasts with Brecht's (in *Fear and Misery*) "aesthetics of enlightenment."[37] Müller rejects the ideal of *Aufklärung* (Enlightenment/making clear) and opts instead for density, inundating the reader/viewer with "piled up" remnants from the explosion of teleological history. This frees the viewer from what Müller has called Brecht's dramaturgy of A-B-C, of development and didacticism, and forces an active "unraveling" of the entangled (theatrical and historical) texts. Entanglement complicates the process of thinking and tears across rationality, a conscious goal of Müller's theater. "Es geht, glaube ich, nur noch mit Überschwemmungen" [I think we can proceed now only through flooding (or inundation)] Müller has said—a statement much quoted by critics because it really hits a nerve. "You have to pack more into a play than the viewer can carry," runs Müller's postmodern argument, to present "multiple views . . . simultaneously"—so that choosing "what to carry first" becomes both necessary and difficult.[38] The spectator, packed with more than she or he can carry, bombarded with sounds and images, is confronted with the explosion of an irreparable past. Müller's postmodern aesthetics of simultaneity, overloading, fragment, and flooding acts as a form of shock, imitating, perhaps, the psychoanalytical effects of the "trauma" of history, a subject that underlies most of Müller's writings. "In order to get rid of the nightmare of history," Müller said in interview, "you first have to acknowledge its existence. You have to know about history"—otherwise it might return "the old-fashioned way, as a nightmare, Hamlet's ghost."[39] Freud's description of trauma as "excitations from outside which are powerful enough to break through the protective shield (*Reizschutz*)" and thus cause the mental apparatus to be "flooded with large amounts of stimulus"[40] is imitated in Müller's theater of excessive, contradictory input. This stimuli, in typical postmodern fashion, draws on symbolic (historical, cultural) material common to his specific collective audience and is aimed at their collective memories. The task of "binding" or "mastering" the stimuli, that which in Aristotelian theater is achieved through catharsis, is left open, possibly unachievable, certainly dependent on the coproductive work of his audience.

Forgetting *The Task*

The Task (*Der Auftrag*, 1979), subtitled *Memory of a Revolution* (*Erinnerung an eine Revolution*), is one of Müller's most sophisticated longer plays. Aimed at his audiences' collective memory, it is structured as an act of anamnesis arising from "fragments embedded in fragments"[41]—and is thus extremely difficult to summarize. Müller based his play on a real historical episode and on its retelling in another text: Anna Seghers's short story "Das Licht auf dem Galgen" ("The Light on the Gallows"), from her cycle *Caribbean Tales*. This story is fractured by Müller, presented in a plurality of theatrical styles, extended to the twentieth century, and compounded with additional fragments of text. Thus, *The Task,* like his previous plays, has a collage structure, although this time "the deviation from some dramaturgical norm is especially extreme," Müller claims, "since so many historical periods are mixed."[42] While there *are* actions, even highly dramatic acts of betrayal and despair, the logic of *The Task* is one of transformation, analogy, simultaneity, overlap. Both thematically and in its radical juxtapositions of opposed theater languages, *The Task* is an intertextual meditation on the failure of revolution as the failure of memory.

The text begins in post-Revolutionary France with an unattributed block of prose, signifying a voice reading a letter: "Galloudec to Antoine. I am writing this letter on my deathbed." This is the letter that the Sailor has been entrusted to give to Antoine—he who had sent Galloudec (a French peasant), Sasportas (a black ex-slave), and Debuisson (an intellectual) on the "task" of exporting revolution from France to the slaves of Jamaica. The letter is an important, almost iconic figure in the play. Old by the time it arrives, it has wandered with the Sailor from Cuba, where the "Spanish detained us," to Trinidad, where the English detained him, through the streets of London, where the Sailor was robbed but the letter survived, to Paris—where the Sailor followed every clue until he tracked down the concealed Antoine. The letter, Galloudec's testament, is the Sailor's task, a task so important that Galloudec had him learn the letter by heart "in case it got lost."[43] By the time the letter arrives, both revolutions have failed—Bonaparte has replaced the Directorate in Paris, and Debuisson has betrayed the revolution in Jamaica. By delivering the letter, this witness to death and betrayal, the Sailor passes the task of memory on to Antoine. By reading the letter, the history of an almost forgotten past is reopened, and with this reopening, memory (and theater) is let loose.

The initial structure of the play recalls Brecht's "learning play" *The Measures Taken (Die Massnahme,* 1930). Both begin with a message that must be delivered to the head(s) of a revolutionary cell—Brecht's "control chorus" or Müller's "taskmaster" Antoine. Both are structured around recall and the reenactment of a failed revolutionary past. In both plays, agitators arrive in a prerevolutionary country, put on masks, try to fulfill their "mission," and fail. These similarities are conscious and others follow; but their meanings are purposely undermined in *The Task.* Brecht's "learning play" was an optimistic, rational tool in the service of revolutionary education.

His parable of the ideological murder of a comrade who endangered the mission is complex and elicits debate, but it is clearly weighted on the side of disciplined ideology as opposed to the weakness of individual compassion. Müller's play is neither optimistic nor a rational didactic tool. On the contrary, it shows the collapse of (revolutionary) reason in the face of subjectivity and personal desire, and *demonstrates* that collapse through a dramatic structure that veers like traumatic memory through time and style. Finally, Müller offers no "control chorus"—other than the audience—who, at the end of the historical reenactment, might (or not) pass judgment.

Remembrance and oblivion form the thematic frame of *The Task*. Although not narratively cohesive, the play's beginning and ending reflect each other through a repetition of physical gestures (two acts of copulation) and an echoing of verbal texts. Beginning with the mournful return of memory, and history, through the unwanted letter, the play ends with a passionate act of oblivion embraced. Throughout, we find myriad levels of betrayal that echo other cruelties and deaths without any clear teleological goal. Müller has explained that he sought to instill ambiguity into *The Task*, to blur its contours "perhaps through a diffuse movement that cannot be fixed into a clear perspective or intention."[44] It is through this crucial blurring that the rational reenactment of an ideological murder (as found in Brecht's play), and its didactic moral, are subverted and converted into a "diffuse" shimmering of simultaneous or interlaced historical and personal betrayals—all funneled through the master betrayal of memory. The entire opening scene of this short, dense play is an attempt to get Antoine to accept responsibility for the letter and the history he refuses to remember. The Sailor breaks through Antoine's willed oblivion by detailing the death throes of Galloudec. "[H]e howled and that was the pain. It came in waves. And it took long enough—until he was through with dying. . . . First, they cut off one of his legs up to the knee, then the rest of it." Black Sasportas was hanged at Port Royal, at the gallows on a cliff. "When they're dead they're cut down to drop into the sea below. The sharks take care of the rest" (86). These horrors erode Antoine's facade, and he reveals himself: "I am the Antoine you've been looking for." He also admits that, far from being an unknown, he *is* History, a leader of the Revolution—who slaughtered the peasants at Vendée "for the Republic," who saw the Gironde "tremble" before him; he was there "when the people stormed the Bastille" and "when the head of the last of the Bourbons dropped into the basket" (86). Now, with the Revolution a failure and terror in the streets he, like his emissaries, has dropped out of history. Hiding and frightened, he only wants to forget. "Go. Go away. Get lost," he says to the suddenly intruding ghosts of Galloudec and Sasportas. "You tell them, woman. Tell them they should go away, I don't want to see them anymore. Are you still here. Your letter has arrived, Galloudec. This is it" (87). Galloudec's letter, like Müller's letter to Wilson (discussed above), explains the writer's failure to produce a "text"—here the text of revolution—and instead evokes, or restores, the tasks of memory.

This short prologue section of the play, the first half of a "frame" story whose closing half never occurs, at least not in the same form, shows the forced reentry into consciousness, into memory, and thus into historical memory, of an episode that had been relegated to oblivion. Müller took the basic elements of his fabula from Seghers's short story, itself based on a true though little known incident that occurred in 1798–99, the year Napoleon dissolved the Directorate in Paris. In Seghers's story, Jean Sasportas is a Spanish Jew and Revolutionary enthusiast, not a black ex-slave. Müller chose to emphasize race and the third world. Galloudec was a sailor, not a Breton peasant. Müller chose to emphasize class. Only the traitor Debuisson is the same in both versions: intellectual, physician, son of slave-owners. Seghers tells the tale through the memory of the sailor Malbec, who appears in the frame story. Müller retains the same beginning but refuses the closure and universalized "meaning" offered by Seghers. Instead of an ending in which the narrator ties remembrance and self-sacrifice to revolutionary action, Müller closes with a voice like that of his Angel of Despair, telling of Debuisson's betrayal.

In discussing this play, commentators grope for terms of scenic division: the words *scene* or *act* recur. But Müller inserts no such divisions into the text. Anne Ubersfeld's idea of a *troué* text, gapped and waiting to be filled through stage interpretation,[45] is valuable here. Only by inserting production values (as I discuss below) into this extraordinarily dense and scenically unmarked text can we begin to "read" the numerous sharp transitions and transformations that turn the play into both an individual and a collective act of recall and recrimination. After the Sailor leaves, for example, Müller instills one of those "diffuse movements" that make his play so difficult and rich. Antoine, letter in hand, confronts his "ghosts," denying responsibility—"What do you want of me. Am I responsible for your stump. And for your rope. Shall I cut off one of my legs" (87)—throwing food at his "dead," at the ghosts of the two men he had almost succeeded in forgetting. At this point, the Woman calls Antoine to bed. They copulate, and as the body loses itself in the *Rausch* of desire, another "diffuse" figure appears: the "Angel of Despair." "Who are you" Antoine's (disembodied, perhaps subconscious) voice asks. Her answer, piped in from above her ambivalent body, is central to the play:

> I am the Angel of Despair. With my hands I dispense ecstasy [*Rausch*], numbness, *oblivion,* the lust and the torment of bodies. My language is silence, my song the scream. Terror dwells in the shadows of my wings. . . . I am the knife with which the dead man cracks open his coffin. I am the one who will be. My flight is the rebellion, my sky the abyss of tomorrow. (87; emphasis added)

Following these words, again without explanation or stage instruction, the scene switches to Jamaica and again a prose block, unattributed, narrates, "We had arrived in Jamaica, three emissaries of the French assembly." This might be Galloudec's voice, the voice of the letter. It is, however, also the first voice we hear after the Angel brings Antoine, in the "lust and the torment" of his copulating body, the fullness of memory (the "cracking" open of the coffin of the dead), and the promise of oblivion. Indeed, the entire play (subtitled *Memory of a Revolution*) might be seen as a moment of remembrance before the onset of total forgetting. These three elements—the memoried letter, release from rational control through sexual desire, and the visit of the Angel of Despair—initiate a multilayered text in which Antoine finds himself, as one critic put it, before "the court of his memory."[46] Akiko Teraoka has argued convincingly that in the scenes that follow, Antoine recalls his own betrayals through his parallel figure, Debuisson, that he *is* in fact Debuisson—that other white intellectual who, at the end of the play, will be given the gift of oblivion.[47] The connection between these two men is imaged textually and structurally within the play and is strengthened by Müller and Ginka Tscholakowa's decision, in their joint 1980 production of *The Task* at the Berliner Volksbühne, to use the same actor for both characters. This is however *not* to say that we enter a "flashback" sequence. Neither scenically nor structurally is there any stratification of time in this play; all times and levels coexist. Nor can Antoine be strictly seen as the (single) source for the "Memory of a Revolution" and betrayal that occupies most of the rest of the text. Müller's open structure and porous collage discourages any psychological reading. Not only are some of the ensuing texts outside Antoine's compass of knowledge, but the transformation of the characters, the unattributed texts, the interflowing structure and generic jumble, and especially the prophecy of the Angel all encourage us to see the memory as belonging to, and aimed at, a larger collective.[48] Müller's emphasis on audience coproduction is clearly called upon here.

It is difficult to speak of angels without thinking of Walter Benjamin's "Angelus Novus"—nor would it be wise, since Benjamin's angel clearly underlies Müller's. The Angel of Despair is a rewriting—or an "overpainting," to use Müller's own term[49]—of Müller's previous prose fragment "The Luckless Angel" ("Der glücklose Engel"),[50] which overpaints Benjamin's ninth thesis on the philosophy of history,[51] which itself is a word-painting of Paul Klee's drawing *Angelus Novus*. In Benjamin's famous image, the helpless spectator of history, the angel, has his face permanently turned toward the past, which the present is in any case always becoming. Unlike Müller's Hamlet, who has "the ruins of Europe" behind him, this angel—"eyes staring, mouth open"—watches as the ruins of history, the "pile of debris," accumulate before him. The important passage for us here is Benjamin's description of human, as opposed to "angelic," perceptions of that past: "Where we perceive a chain of events, he sees one single catastrophe which keeps piling wreckage upon wreckage and hurls it in front of his feet." Benjamin opposes a historicist view of historical time—developmental, causal, linear, "a chain of events"—to a composite view in which all times coexist within the eyes of the angelic viewer. The linear view is rational and predictive, based on the belief that historical time unfolds, and "historical knowledge can be projected into the future"[52]—that is, it can be learned from and implemented, an idea that Brecht embraced. Benjamin's angel stares into the collective pasts always from the position of the *present,* Benjamin's *Jetztzeit.* For Benjamin, the past is a formless potential that is chosen and reclaimed by the needs of the present. History does not precede us; it comes into being only through us: through the act of memory that recalls and inscribes/narrates it.

Using these terms, Antoine becomes a complex witness to the historical failures of which he was part, and which he had hoped to forget. His "human" memory had recounted the revolution in historicist terms as "a chain of events"—"I was there when the people stormed the Bastille. I was there when the head of the last of the Bourbons dropped into the basket." But with the sudden and unexplained appearance of the Angel of Despair, Antoine experiences the past not as a logical progression, a chain of events, but in its entirety: as an undifferentiated pile of wreckage of pasts and present, from the Enlightenment through the elevator-ride to the future revolutions of the third world. Müller's collage of fragments, and his wide net of textual and visual triggers, evoke a noncommensurate "pile" of failed revolutions and historical betrayals narrated through the "present" mind (or collective memory) of Antoine, Müller, and the (always implied) East German audience who have lived through their own failed National Socialist and

Socialist revolutions. Müller's staring Angel, like Benjamin's, is a passive witness with no power to intervene or act. And indeed, neither the Angel nor Antoine will be seen to "act" again after this scene; neither will be mentioned again in Müller's text after they initiate the flood of memory. "The angel would like to stay, awaken the dead, and make whole what has been smashed," Benjamin writes. "But a storm is blowing from Paradise. . . . This storm is what we call progress." Müller's Angel cannot stay either, but she can, however briefly, awaken the dead and force Antoine, and us, to recall the failures and betrayals that lay suppressed in the collective memory of Müller's audience, memories that will, in the play's final images of reason's surrender, sink back into the oblivion of "progress."

These memories—the awakened "dead"—are now dramatized in four sections between the frame of Antoine's remembering and the final section of Debuisson's forgetting. Each of the four sections is written in a totally different style. The first section, close to Brecht's *The Measures Taken,* shows "Debuisson Galloudec Sasportas" in Jamaica, where it is "our task to stir up a rebellion of the slaves against the rule of the British Crown in the name of the Republic of France" (87). Through realistic dialogue we watch the three assume their "masks," the false identities that will allow them to prepare the uprising by pretending to be monarchists in the service of the slave-owner Debuisson. The black Sasportas, in a land of black slaves and white masters, suffers most from the restraint and duplicity required by their roles. "I know your role is the most difficult to play," Galloudec says to him. "It's written all over your body" (89). This ideological section ends with the arrival of "a gigantic Negro," a slave from Debuisson's plantation, come to carry Debuisson home on his back. This slave, Debuisson explains, "is deaf and mute, a thing between man and dog." He looks at black Sasportas with contempt, seeing in him only the slave. Like Aitmatov's tortured captives, speechless and submissive after the "memory operation" they undergo, this deaf-mute slave too is imaged as identityless, a machine, a "Mankurt."

The scene now switches, or rather transforms, to Debuisson's rich estate, and the idiom becomes that of theatrical spectacle, the "Theater of the Revolution" played out in the language of Genet, of Peter Weiss's *Marat/Sade,* through the metaphor of a Grand Guignol play-within-a-play. Themes of revolutionary "roles" and ideological conflict are translated into violent and excremental theatrical images. FirstLove (ErsteLiebe) sits on a throne and welcomes home the prodigal son, Debuisson, returned from "playing" at Revolution. Slaves undress and costume "Debuisson Galloudec Sasportas" as Slaveholder, Overseer, Slave (91) who must "act out" their "natural" position within the antirevolutionary hierarchy. Through

his 1990 Hannover production of *The Task,* overcame both the metaphysical and the static elements of this monologue by dramatizing the collective
nature of these anxieties and memories. Using a chorus of seven young men
and women, all identically dressed in pants, tie, and glasses, he created a collective "I" speaking in overlapping voices, or in groups, producing a choric
and rhythmically echoing effect.[56] And indeed, through this fragment,
Müller stretches and "echoes" the historical context of the play, speeds time
up, and allows the anachronistic images already written into the play to resonate more easily. Debuisson had spoken of the "clouded skies of Europe
muddied by the smoke of conflagrations and the bloody stench of the new
philosophy" (88), an image more immediately apt for the twentieth-century
history of Germany, brought to the forefront in the elevator fragment, than
for eighteenth-century France. These contemporary images multiply in the
play's subsequent debate scene, which precedes and anticipates Debuisson's
final fall into denial and oblivion.

The last section of the play is an ideological discussion between the
intellectual/aristocrat Debuisson, for whom revolution was an option, not a
necessity, and the black ex-slave, Sasportas. Unlike the travesty of the Dan-
ton/Robespierre debate, this one is serious and transhistorical. Debuisson
hands Sasportas and Galloudec a paper telling of the Revolution's failure in
Paris, of Napoleon and the Eighteenth Brumaire, and thus of the end of
their task. "The General Bonaparte has dissolved the Directorate. . . . France
is called Napoleon. The world will be what it was, a home for masters and
slaves" (96). Sasportas and Galloudec refuse to allow the vagaries of rule to
divert them from their cause—unlike Debuisson, who has already reverted
to the comforts of his class and race, to his aristocratic "body." In the following discussion, past and future interweave freely. "We're carrying other
corpses on our back now," Debuisson warns Sasportas; "the dead victims of
terror, pyramids of death," which has initiated "a future that already has
become the past" (98–99). Black Sasportas, whose revolution has yet to
begin, prophesies that the repressed, those passed over by the "theater of the
white revolution," will find their own power in the memory of their dead.
"When the living can no longer fight, the dead will," he warns (100). The
scene ends with Debuisson begging Sasportas and Galloudec to kill him
"before I betray you." He fears the treason of his desires—"I am afraid, Sasportas, of the shame to be happy in this world." But his surrender to those
desires—the betrayal of the white intellectual—has already begun.

This betrayal is textualized in the final moments of the play as an act of
seduction that gestures toward and implicates the audience as well. *The
Task*'s final block of text has the same unattributed status as that which

opened the play, but this time it is a third-person voice, sharing with us the "end" of this tale of failed revolution and seducing us into identification. In Dimiter Gotscheff's 1992 post-Wall production of the play in Cologne, the Angel of Despair figure read both Galloudec's opening letter and the closing betrayal speech. This established a coherence and metaphysical overvoice nowhere available in the written text, linking personal and ideological infidelity and creating a didacticism foreign to Müller's play. The ending of *The Task* is the contrary of didactic, and it is vital to a reading of memory. In its lyrical and darkly sensual voice of desire the final texts tells us of Debuisson's seduction into "happiness" by "the temptation . . . of his first love who was Treason"—a seduction into subjectivity through which history is replaced by the lust of the body, the lust of oblivion.

> Treason danced. Debuisson pressed his hands against his eyes. He heard his heart beating the rhythm of the dance steps. They grew faster with his heartbeat. Debuisson felt his eyelids twitching against his palms. . . . [Treason] her hands placed on her hips or, by this time, grabbing her crotch, her vulva probably quivering already with lust, looked with swimming eyes at him, Debuisson, who just now was pushing his eyes into their sockets with his fists, afraid of his hunger for the shame of happiness. . . . He opened his eyes. Treason smiling showed her breasts and silently spread her legs wide open, her beauty hit Debuisson like an axe. He forgot the storm of the Bastille, the Hungermarch of the Eighty-thousand, the end of the Gironde, their Last Supper, a corpse at the banquet, Saint Just, the Black Angel, Danton, the Voice of the Revolution, Marat hunched over the dagger, Robespierre's broken jaw, his scream when the executioner ripped off the bandage, his last pitying look at the exultant mob. Debuisson clutched at the last memory that hadn't left him yet . . . rubbed the sand from his eyes, covered his ears against the song of the crickets. Then Treason threw herself upon him like a heaven, the bliss of the labia a dawn. (100–101)

In this speech, Debuisson's surrender to desire and life is textualized in the Deleuzian language of *délire* that both enacts Debuisson's final betrayal and acts upon the audience/reader as a seduction. This text of desire freezes the intellectuals—Debuisson, Antoine, both "fallen" from failed political action into self-abnegation and "the bliss of the labia"—into their own betrayals. But if "desire is revolutionary in its essence," as Deleuze and Guattari claim, and if it is transsubjective and liberating, perhaps the betrayal of oblivion is also a route to freedom from the past.[57] The unbearable weight of that past was already imaged by Müller in his 1958 fragment, "The Luckless Angel." There, Müller's Angel is actually buried under the raining debris of the past that is "washed up *behind* him," not in front as in Benjamin's essay. It is the *future* that "piles up before him," torturing his body as it "presses his eyes in their sockets, bursts his eyeballs like a stone, turns his words round into a mouth gag, chokes him with his own breath."[58] Clearly, Debuisson in the final monologue, resembles this luckless angel. Both are frozen, crushed, blinded. Both have their eyes "pushed" into their sockets as they succumb, almost against their will, to the oblivion that frees them from the enormous weight of the past, but also from any future.

The ending of *The Task* is ambivalent and contradictory. We hear a list of events from the horrors of the French Revolution—which Antoine/Debuisson will soon forget. This list *reminds* us of the historical past being forgotten: the Bastille, the Hungermarch, the Gironde, Saint-Just, Danton, Marat, Robespierre; and contrasts that "sexless revolution" to the language of "bliss" that seduces Debuisson into betrayal. The lyrical last monologue thus sets the audience up between the alluring language of personal desire and dissolved consciousness, and the knowledge of the betrayal this submission signifies. The play's ending also (subtly) ties Debuisson's betrayal—his "copulation" with Treason—to Antoine's opening search for release and oblivion through the memoryless ecstasy of his body, his original copulation with the Woman/Angel. That Angel—the Angel of Despair—had promised release *from* despair (and history), at the price of forgetting. Her promise to Antoine of "ecstasy, numbness, oblivion, the lust and the torment of bodies" has now been fulfilled, and "the bliss of the labia" has replaced memory. The final voice, with its fierce, ravishing images, its schizophrenic attraction and repulsion—words that "become physical and affect the body immediately . . . act directly on the body, penetrating and bruising it," as Gilles Deleuze put it[59]—acts also upon the body of the audience like a longing for release from the burden of history, like a mourning for the insupportable "nightmares" of history—as the voice of the body replaces the voices of history.

Structurally, we might say that Müller's *Memory of a Revolution* traces an act of anamnesis carried out by the masters/survivors—like Brecht's three revolutionary executioners. But remembering does not have an ethical or didactic function here (within the play): Antoine remembers in order to forget. And it is this search for oblivion that is itself signified as both treason and salvation; for while forgetting allows "happ[iness] in this world," as Debuisson says, it is only the privileged survivors of history—neither peasant nor black slave—who can afford to forget. The Sasportases and Galloudecs, who sent their memory of betrayal and torture into the world in Galloudec's opening letter, are left waiting in the wings. The final delirious voice of oblivion, available only to the intellectual Debuisson, is contrasted to the voice of Galloudec's letter of memory, which traversed time and history in order, like a Benjaminian historian, to "blast open the continuum of history" with its already forgotten tale. It is a tale we, the audience, have relived; it is also a memory better "forgotten" by those for whom revolution has become too much of a burden. Memory and forgetting are thus entangled in this play without the moralistic intervention of a "control chorus" who can pass final judgment on their meaning. The openness—but also the passionate advocacy of imagery in the service of both memory and forgetting—allows this play to become a vehicle for complex audience responses, and for directorial interpretations that implicate other pasts, also perhaps best remembered and forgotten, as we will see below.

The Task: A Memoried Production

Müller claimed that the French Revolution interested him both "as a revolutionary model that had an especially large arsenal of theatrical forms," and as an event that had become "the only model for revolutions in Europe."[60] In both of these respects—as a model for theatrical experimentation and as a model for political intervention—Eduard Erne's 1990 production of *The Task* at the Frankfurt "Experimenta 6—Heiner Müller" is remarkable. The important Frankfurt avant-garde theater festival was dedicated that year, for the first time ever, to the works of only one author: Heiner Müller. It lasted seventeen days and offered over ninety events—theater, radio, video, exhibits, lectures, debates, even concerts—all by or about Müller. Within this abundance, Erne's *The Task* has been called "*the* event of the 'Experimenta 6.'"[61] It was remarkable in that it took the play's subtitle seriously, almost literally, and produced a one-time performance that stretched to its fullest the audiences' own "memory of a revolution."

Erne organized a scenic "reading" of the play—not a staged production. Nor was it a theatrical reading. His focus was not on the rendition of the text—but rather on those he got to render it: three famous (or infamous) ex-revolutionaries/terrorists, and one former high functionary of the East German government. The aristocratic intellectual turned revolutionary turned traitor, Debuisson, was read by Daniel Cohn-Bendit, the legendary leader of the May '68 student uprising in Paris. Cohn-Bendit had long since returned to Germany and become politically involved; at the time of the production he was the Frankfurt city councillor for multicultural affairs. Cohn-Bendit, the most internationally famous of the group, was a controversial figure on the Left as many saw his involvement in establishment politics—however radical his views—as a betrayal of his original revolutionary aims. Galloudec, the peasant revolutionary who died for the cause, was read by the famous Extra-Parliamentary Opposition and Red Army Faction (RAF) member and lawyer, Horst Mahler. Mahler was one of the central theoreticians of the 1970s student movement in Germany, and acting attorney for such important and notorious terrorist leaders as Rudi Dutschke, Fritz Teufel, and Andreas Baader. In 1975 he was accused of aiding terrorist causes and imprisoned. The RAF subsequently kidnapped the chairman of the Berlin Christian Democratic Party in order to secure Mahler's (and six other members') release from prison. Mahler refused to participate in this action and did not join the other released prisoners in escaping to South Yemen. Later, after his release from prison, Mahler publicly confessed and critiqued his role in the RAF, and in 1990 was again active as a lawyer.[62] The ex-slave Sasportas was read by the ex-RAF member Christof Wackernagel, who had spent ten years (1977–87) in prison for terrorist activities and was in 1990 a freelance writer.

The biggest surprise of the event was the reader of the politically potent elevator monologue: Erne had gotten former East German Central Committee and Politburo member Günter Schabowski, one of the top officials of the party and state apparatus, to read the long monologue. His reading had been previously recorded on video and was preceded by an interview in which Schabowski discussed the elevator of the Central Committee building—reserved only for the "bigwigs and their bodyguards." His reading of Müller's text about the employee who can't find the floor where his boss awaits him with a "task" he never receives turned this icon of East German political power and corruption into a cog like any other, always in thrall of someone *even* higher up. This meeting between a completely metaphorical text—a dream text, a Kafkaesque excursion into personal anxiety and cerebral fear of powers-that-be and powers-to-be (Peru)—and a very real political figure, himself feared and unreachable, added layers of complexity to Müller's already complex play.

The context of this theater reading—a shared and remembered past—is what created the sensation and gave depth to the event. The German audience, acquainted with the French Revolution and its failures, was also assumed to know the histories and records of these four famous readers—and the "revolutions" at which *they* had failed (and if they didn't, they could read about them in the abundant festival pamphlets and media coverage). Nor did the readers appear as "actors"; they were there as themselves, as political personalities and living witnesses to Germany's "revolutionary" past—West and East. Erne's experiment depended on the audience's capacity to filter a literary text through a historical memory, thus allowing

Müller's text to reverberate anew. A truly postmodern *mise-en-abîme* effect was achieved by remembering the former radical Cohn-Bendit, now part of the establishment, as he "remembers" Debuisson's betrayal as remembered in Antoine's memory; or by recalling the history of the once-radical and idealistic lawyer Mahler—whose faith in the student revolution had been betrayed by the extremism of members of his own party—through the words of the betrayed Galloudec. Erne added to this built-in layering of memory an additional shimmer of conscious artifice: a frame for these readings was created by surrounding the stage with screens and monitors. Before the readings began, a young boy stepped on stage and read the title and sub-title of the play out of a thick volume, resembling a child's book of fairy tales—which the past obviously was, for him. He then went to a computer and flashed images quoting films ranging from *Blond Venus* to *The Battleship Potemkin* on the monitors, producing a virtual reality that could then be contrasted with this "virtual" history. He represented, writes the critic Marianne Streisand, "a new generation . . . for whom even the *memory* of the revolution belongs to the distant past."[63]

Embodied Memory: *The Foundling*

In Müller's quasi-autobiographical play *The Foundling,* the past returns as highly concentrated layers of memory, as an act of mourning by a "foundling" son self-exiled from East to West Berlin. Centered on the broken body of the son's stepfather, and on the ideologies that tortured and disciplined it, *The Foundling* is a bitter elegy to the terrors of German history as translated into the flesh of its victims/perpetrators. The fractured voices and fragmented form of the play, its repetitions, regressions, and refusal of narrative cohesion or closure, replicate the interlaced memories of these traumatic pasts.

The Foundling (Der Findling, 1987) is based on motifs from Heinrich von Kleist's 1811 short story of the same name. It is a self-standing play directed by Müller himself in a production that serves as an interpretation of his text (as I discuss, below). But it is also the last part of a cycle of five performance texts written between 1984 and 1987, each originally published and performed separately. The complete cycle, titled *Volokolamsk Highway,* was first performed in 1988 at the Theater de Bobigny, Paris, and later that year in Cologne. All five texts are written in open-verse form as dramatic poems that, to quote Carl Weber, "read like inner monologues, or better: a 'stream-of-memory' in which a person recalls, or dreams of, moments of extreme crisis and awesome responsibility."[64] The thread common to all the plays is their thematization of various aspects of German/Russian relations from 1941 to 1987. Parts 1 and 2 of the cycle, *Russian Gambit* and *Forest Near Moscow*, retell incidents between the Red Army and the Germans during the 1941 battle for Moscow. Part 3, *The Duel*, remembers, through a battle of wills, the 1953 East German workers' strike and insurrection, crushed by Russian troops. Part 4, *Centaurs*, is a nightmare text remembered in the mind of the chief police officer of an East Berlin precinct. While not actually based on Kafka, the subtitle—*A Horror Tale from the Saxonian of Gregor Samsa*—points to the theme of transformation and disintegration. In part 5, the most lyrical of the five texts, Müller "sums up" and elegizes this past, exposing the wounds of memory cut into the bodies of a father and his stepson by the last fifty years of German history.

The texts' historical intertexts are complicated by additional literary ones: parts 1 and 2 use Alexander Bek's book, for which the entire cycle is named; part 3 uses a motif from Anna Seghers, who had also supplied the characters for *The Task*; part 4 is inspired by Kafka, and part 5 by Kleist. Thus, these plays tap into shared—and specific—collective memories through the mediation of cultural contexts as well as common history. Though the play was written for a knowing East German audience, Müller would have had little hope, in 1987, of their becoming the actual audience for viewing it in production. All five pieces contain specters and miseries from the past that cling to the rotting state of the present—a view that an East German reader/spectator would have understood, and that would have (and did) preclude the play's performance in East Berlin. Through dense references to historical moments and daily life, and through irrational memory triggers, Müller sought to encourage his reader/spectator to remember through the memories of his speakers, a world (the German Democratic Republic) that was, in fact, about to become "history."

The Foundling is the most contemporary of the five monologues. It speaks in the voice of a dissident son who, in a collage of remembered moments, recalls the betrayals of his crushed and politically orthodox (step)father—tortured first by the Nazis and later by his own Communist Party—betrayals that led to the son's imprisonment:

> He sat across from me during visiting hours
> All my five years at Bautzen penitentiary
> He preached IN MARXANDENGELSTONGUES
> About his workers' paradise . . .
> And in five years I never said a word
> Not a syllable during his visiting hours
> . . . And his back

Was more bent still every time he left
To his hell that was his paradise[65]

The play is not easy to follow. Speaking always in the voice of the present, of Benjamin's *Jetztzeit*, the voice moves backward from West Berlin to the son's five-year imprisonment at Bautzen, to the father's betrayal of the son some years before that (1968), to the Party's betrayal of the father seven years earlier, to Stalin's myriad betrayals and death further in the past; behind it all looms the memory of the Nazi terror and the concentration camps. These time periods are not systematically layered in the play; they jar against each other and intermingle, structured like the structures of memory itself. Temporal conflation and the rhetorical compounding of multiple acts of betrayal render the story—the specific "fabula"—not quite clear. Rather than subjugate memory to the formal structures of narrative linearity, Müller again opted to instill ambiguity through that "diffuse movement" (discussed above) which challenges the rational solutions of historical chronology through the unruly obsessions of memory, and the struggles with repression.[66]

The play's verse-line monologue form is unmarked by punctuation or diacritical signs, and the speeches are attributable only by means of context. Deprived of semiotic guidance, the reader is forced to "find" the voice, to uncover the speaker, to establish emphases. This difficulty creates a sense of simultaneity, of voices submerged and intertwined in memory rather than speaking in realistic space. And indeed, the voices of father and son merge and rip against each other within the voice of the present rememberer, creating interlinked and contradictory scenes of memory.

Take off your coat You're soaked through
Put my jacket on It fits you Doesn't it
I don't think your jacket fits
I gathered you up out of the ruins
A bundle of misery

(69–70)

This density is further complicated by the various time periods returned to in memory, again braided into each other. Further, an additional voice, seemingly not under the control of the "rememberer," intervenes with growing frequency, speaking the recurring words (always in capitals) "FORGOTTEN AND FORGOTTEN AND FORGOTTEN." This subconscious cry tears through the play—directed at memory itself and, perhaps, at the audience's collective amnesia of their so recent past. Before *die Wende*—the political "turn" of 1989—this play was considered in the GDR not only as a provocation, but as an ideological blasphemy.[67]

The voice of remembrance begins in the GDR's infamous political prison, Bautzen, to which the son had been sent "During an unforgotten summernight / Of Nineteensixtyeight Year of the Tanks," having been arrested for protesting against the Soviet invasion of Czechoslovakia.[68] Having served his five-year sentence, he resettled in West Berlin, formally leaving his home in the East ("With Are you sure Do you know what you're doing / Here you have housing work security / There the person counts for nothing only capital" [67]). The son remembers through shifting voices the failures and betrayals that brought him to this unhappy end in a political system he despises no less than the failed Socialism for which he mourns and from which he has escaped. For him West Berlin is a

> Halfcity of old and new widows
> Corpses in cellars and money in the bank
> Corpses with stars-of-David In brown In armygray. . . .
> Smoke from the chimney Dust from the carpet-bombings
> Monument in Plötzensee on butcher hooks
> The plaque disappeared from Landwehr canal
>
> (68)

The Nazi and capitalist past and present of West Germany are evoked in specific shorthand images—meant for a "knowing" audience. They recall loaded moments of German history: the ever-present "hidden" past ("in cellars"); the dead Jews, Nazis, soldiers; Auschwitz ("chimney"); the carpet bombings of German cities; the anti-Hitler resistance hung from butcher hooks (in "Plötzensee" prison); the no longer commemorated murders of Communist leaders Rosa Luxemburg and Karl Liebknecht ("Landwehr canal," where they were thrown after being shot). These images underlie, and serve as the background for, the perversions of his father and of the GDR; they also target an audience whose identity is composed of, or against, these same historical memories.

The father, now a high Party functionary, is the central figure of this tragic elegy. While in a concentration camp under the Nazis, he had his genitals smashed by a German guard. After the war he found the boy, an abandoned infant, in the rubble of Germany and adopted the "foundling" son as the child he himself could never have. "I wouldn't want to know who your father was / Maybe the Nazi who smashed / My genitals at roll call in the camp/ And no children for me Only you" (70). The monologue's central scene of betrayal takes place on a wet night in 1968 when the

narrator, soaked through, arrives at his father's house after illegally distribut-
ing handbills protesting the Russian invasion of Prague—"With tank tracks
you have written your cause / On the bodies of OUR PEOPLE" (69)—looking for protection from the police. The father, bitter and frightened,
answers the doorbell: "I only saw his shadow The light at his back" (68).
With this image of his shadowy father framed in the doorway, Müller
obliquely quotes from another of his earlier texts, his autobiographical
prose-piece, "The Father" (written 1958). In interviews, Müller often
referred to this childhood memory as "the first scene of my theater": a
memory of guilt and betrayal inflicted by history, which haunts much of his
writing. On January 31, 1933, at four in the morning, Nazi brownshirts
arrested and beat his father (a functionary in the Social Democratic Party
during the Weimar Republic) in their house. Müller, four years old, saw it
all through a crack in his bedroom door. Before they took him away, the
father came to see the child—"My father stood in the door, behind him the
strangers, big, in brown uniforms. . . . The light was in my father's back, I
couldn't see his face. I heard him softly call my name. I didn't answer and
lay very still. Then my father said: He's asleep. The door was closed. I heard
how they led him away."[69] "That's my guilt," Müller told an interviewer;
"I pretended I was asleep. This really is the first scene of my theater."[70] This
betrayal—the choice of silence, of denial—is for Müller a personal trauma
that underlies the broader historical amnesias and repressions of the play.

   The intersecting of public history and private memory, of public and
private betrayals, is at the heart of Müller's text. The father in *The Foundling,*
called by the son "Comrade Father," is a complex figure whose social formation through the discipline of first Nazi and then Socialist terror has rendered him both shadowy and morally impotent. He has internalized the
lessons of obedience and appears in the text as a broken but unquestioning
representative of ideological dogma and historical forgetting. "How do you
talk with an editorial," the son says of the father; "And how do you hug a
Party platform." The conflict between father and son centers on the father's
total appropriation by the Party line—"Comrade Father Who is not my
father / How often have I wished you were my father / And not the Comrade who adopted me / My enemy in every proxy-war" (69). Like the
racked and tortured Winston in Orwell's *Nineteen-Eighty-Four,* the father
has come to identify fully with the terror of the state. "I'm not just anyone,"
he tells the son who comes to him that rainy night: "Even if I wanted to I
can't pretend / Not to myself and not to the Party / That I didn't hear your
confession." "Confession" is used here in the Stalinist sense; thus
the father/son standing that night in their living room, become a kind of

unseen dying mother "in whose breasts cancer had made its home" (71). She is twice remembered in this short text, in two contradictory scenes that add to the narrative difficulty of the play, but also supply a metaphoric underpinning. "Speak quietly next door my wife is dying / Have you finally noticed When was she ever alive" (70). Cancer, that "historical" disease that eats away at so many of Müller's characters (and that finally put an end to his own life), lurks, in its too great concreteness, as the metaphor behind the memories of bodily destruction. "Her cancer you can call it comrade" (71), the son accuses his father. This is not the first time that cancer has figured in Müller's plays. "We're of the same Party, I and my cancer," says dying old Hilse in *Germania Death in Berlin*. "I am not well," Hilse tells the Young Bricklayer, "But I'm only one half / Of me, the cancer ate the other half. / And if you ask the cancer, he is fine."[75] Cancer eats at Ophelia's breast (*Hamletmachine*); Merteuil, after killing Valmont, remains alone in a postapocalyptic world, embracing her cancer (*Quartet*). It is especially women and the old, the sexually repressed and powerless who are eaten away by that metaphor-bearing disease in Müller's plays. Susan Sontag (who wrote a book *against* the transformation of cancer into metaphor), shows that one strand of the cancer "mythology" is the supposed connection between cancer and inner "repression"—the repression of "violent feelings," or violent memories. Wilhelm Reich actually defined cancer as "a disease following emotional resignation—a bio-energetic shrinking, a giving up of hope."[76] The insidiousness of cancer, eating the body away from within, producing a slowly disintegrating ruin, lends itself almost too easily to metaphoric use for repression, corruption, and moral decay. In *The Foundling,* Müller connects the political amnesia and ideological betrayals of Communism and of his father with the personal tragedy wrought by "comrade" cancer.

The doubleness of cancer (the personal pain, the public metaphor) is twice remembered by the son in scenes that offer a good example of how Müller subverts narrative logic through memory devices and creates complexity by conflating the historical and the personal. The memory of the cancerous mother is tied to memories of Stalin, conquest, and the death of the friend at the Wall. It is at this point in the text that the words "FORGOTTEN AND FORGOTTEN AND FORGOTTEN" first appear.

FORGOTTEN AND FORGOTTEN AND FORGOTTEN
The Thaelmann Song The Partisans of Amur . . .
The red neckcloth wet from Stalin's funeral
And the torn blue-shirt for the dead friend

   ... FORGOTTEN Kronstadt Budapest and Prague
   Where the ghost of Communism haunts
(72)

The mother is set within the context of political resistance ("The Thaelmann Song The Partisans of Amur") and concomitant political betrayal
("Kronstadt Budapest and Prague"—all overrun by Soviet tanks). These
political contexts invade one of the most painful sections of the text, the
son's last memory of his dying mother. In the narrator's first version of that
memory, he recalls how he naively cried at Stalin's death—"The red neckcloth my umbilical cord / Heavy with my tears fifteen years ago / When
Stalin died." Crying again, at Stalin's and his father's betrayals ("Kronstadt
Budapest and Prague"), he entered the side room "where the woman /
Who was and wasn't my mother lay dying" (71), took off his clothes and lay
his head on her cancerous breasts. A bit further on we read a more restrained
version of that same memory:

> The red neckcloth wet from Stalin's funeral
> And the torn blue-shirt for the dead friend
> Who fell at the Wall Stalin's memorial
> For Rosa Luxemburg
> ... FORGOTTEN AND FORGOTTEN AND FORGOTTEN
> ... I didn't cry I had no tears
> I didn't go into the side-room where the woman was dying
> I stood in my mud-tracks on the carpet
>
> (72)

These contradictory scenes are simultaneous in memory, braided as
metaphor in order to expand the "scene of memory" into a broader scene
of ideological betrayal. In his own 1991 production of the play, Müller used
more than one actor for the son figure, thus allowing "him" to enter and
not to enter the mother's room, both generalizing and multiplying the son,
as does the text here. In that same production (the *Mauser* project, discussed
below), Müller rendered the importance of the broader betrayal—Stalin and
Socialist ideology—*explicit* by splicing into *The Foundling* a text written
especially for that production: *Heracles 13*. Heracles, whose thirteenth labor
consists of freeing Thebes from its own people, represents the murderous
Stalin for whom the son had filled a red neckcloth with tears. The cancerous mother and the memories of Stalin are both embraced and not
embraced by the bitter and betrayed son; and both are discursively linked to
the memory of the father's betrayals within a "cancerous" history.

signifies history. *Heracles 13,* a short piece based on the messenger's report at the end of Euripides' play and written 1991 specifically for this production, was piped in over loudspeakers halfway through *The Foundling.*

Mauser, Müller's "answer" to Brecht's *The Measures Taken* (an earlier and more overt reaction to Brecht's famous *Lehrstück* than what we find in *The Task*), is a dialogue between the chorus (the Party or the Revolution) and two revolutionaries who have failed in their mission, one through empathy and weakness, the other through excessive brutality (the revolution had turned him into a cold killing machine). Both revolutionaries must now learn to accept their own deaths. *Quartet,* which Müller sees as a "companion piece" to *Mauser,* is based on Choderlos de Laclos's anonymously published (1782, written earlier) epistolary novel of seduction and betrayal within the pre-Revolutionary decadent French aristocracy. The lascivious novel has four central characters: the Marquise de Merteuil and the Vicomte de Valmont are the cynical schemers who plot to abuse the innocent Madame Tourvel, and a virtuous spouse. Their cruel and empty sexual games end in an orgy of sadomasochistic destruction. Müller redoubles the perversions of the original by having two actors—representing Merteuil and Valmont—play all four roles, switching roles back and forth, slipping in and out of genders in a Genet-type theater of sexual/political degeneration directed inward. For Müller, *Mauser* and *Quartet* belong together:[83] "In the one we have terror and violence in the political field, in the other terror and violence in the most intimate human relations." Moreover, "*Quartet* takes place before the French Revolution, *Mauser* after the October Revolution, during the Civil War. Both revolutions are now put clearly into relation to each other."[84] To complicate matters further, Müller sets *Quartet* in "Timespace: Drawing room before the French Revolution / Air raid shelter after World War III." The lines connecting apocalypse and Enlightenment failure are clearly drawn.

Thus, the *Mauser* project presents us with texts written between 1970 and 1991, referring to historical periods from right before the French Revolution to right after the third world war, ranging from the epic voice of Communism's Revolutionary beginnings (*Mauser*) to the personal voice of its failure in the GDR (*The Foundling*); with texts as concrete as the Son's memories of Nazi and Communist torture, and as abstract as Heracles' battle with the unending "forest" of revolutionary history on his way to fight the Hydra. As part of the production, Müller produced a fifty-page program book stressing the place and importance of "memory" in this tapestry of his own work. Among other material, a quote from another Müller letter/text, called "Raising the Dead" (1986), appears on the title page: "Our work is raising the dead; the theater troupe is recruited from ghosts . . . the set a travel guide through the landscapes beyond death, where causalities have been given leave from the cancer of resurrection."[85] The production, which split critics, raised "the dead" of European history and its historical struggles; but it was positioned within the specific struggle over East German history and the memory of the GDR that unification threatened to engulf. Thus, although the production tapped into a broad cultural bank of European artifacts, these were shaped as a summation, as well as an act of mourning, for the failures of East Germany—after its demise. It was important to Müller that this summation be undertaken by a German who had lived through the forty-year experiment of its Socialist state, who could appraise "the experience of these battles of resistance and conformity, and compromises . . . and the experience of the failure."[86] It was equally important that this ideological experiment not be simply forgotten or buried under the weight of unification. As such, the *Mauser* project had a political memory agenda. In addition, the production mapped twenty years of Müller's own dramatic output, charting his repeated attempts to transform cultural and personal materials (from the tragedies of Euripides to his own father's biography) into writings that rouse, and reveal, a collective memory.

The more than four-hour production took place on one unchanging stage. Müller's staging was "heavy and static, a calculated kind of 'Wilsonian' statuary performed at varying speeds with echoed and miked voices resounding," as one critic wrote.[87] The unchanging set was designed by the acclaimed Greek sculptor Jannis Kounellis. At center stage he put a tall metal column, a smokestack, "somewhere between a gun barrel and an oven-flue";[88] while around this "giant phallic chimney" he placed tracks on which coal carts were occasionally pushed. Above the stage, Kounellis suspended a row of meat hooks on which the greatcoats of the slaughtered would be hung at the end of *Mauser*.[89] "Kounellis's set suggests the space of historical memory at once as factory, mine, and slaughter house," wrote John Rouse.[90] It is hard to imagine a German audience who would not have connected Kounellis's smokestack/train-tracks/slaughterhouse images with the memory of the concentration camps, and especially of Auschwitz. This visual "memory" was verbally reinforced in the text of *The Foundling* and recurs transformed in the curtain of dripping blood against which *Quartet* was played. Thus, the still-present memory of the very recent past became an ever-present stage image, against which the cold logic of passionless Enlightenment desire (*Quartet*), the heartless killing-machines who murder in the name of ideology (*Mauser*), the terror of the woods/history, and the anger and loss of the foundling son were all played out.

Two other stage images added to this memory fund: as the play began, a guillotine could be seen in the background, through a doorway. This guillotine, another slaughter-machine of European history, feeds into the images of *Quartet* and the entire discourse on Enlightenment reason/ Enlightenment terror (also found in *The Task*). An additional image central to the production was "performed" before the play began: stagehands opened a trapdoor near the smokestack and pulled out of a pit old cupboards and closets from various historical periods. These furnishings finally filled the stage, barely allowing room to act. The clutter (of history) pushed the actors onto the area just above the proscenium between two long Louis XIV tables placed at either side of the stage. The tables and closets, together with the images of train-tracks, smokestack, guillotine, and meat hooks, recall Hamlet's opening line in Müller's *Hamletmachine:* "I stood at the shore and talked with the surf BLABLA, *the ruins of Europe behind me*" (emphasis added). It is these same "ruins" of a suicidal Hamlet and of Müller's weighed-down "Luckless Angel"—these end-of-millennium fragments of the failures of modern Europe—that were refracted through the collage of plays Müller presents.[91]

The production began with the prologue, *Heracles 2,* a "metaphor for the passage through history: the enemy is not hiding behind the Forest, the enemy is the forest."[92] This ideological fragment is directed against the mechanization of revolution. Heracles is caught and entangled within the forest of a history (Communist history) that could not stop struggling against the enemy, and so finally *became* that enemy. Revolution had become its own foe. Müller presented this collective struggle through a splitting and multiplying of the Heracles figure. Five men and women in greatcoats represented, collectively, the Heracles of the text. They walked across the stage pushing a cart carrying a coffin on which five busts of (a split and multiplied) Lenin rested. The Heracles group spoke Müller's text in an equally nonunified manner, rejecting—in typical Müller fashion—the idea of a unified subject. The actor Hermann Beyer began. His voice, miked, was refracted from speakers placed in the house, rather than from his lips. Soon his words were echoed by a woman following him, adding to the vocal resoundings and repetitions.[93] This opening device, the separation of sound from source (lips), and its echoing within the space of the audience (reminiscent of Beckett's vocal/visual image in *That Time*), was used repeatedly in the production and served to abstract and generalize the central component of Müller's production: the text. It also emulated the echoing of words in thought and memory, stressing the collective nature of the text over contextualized meaning.

The staging of *Mauser* was far more static. Written in blank verse for a chorus and two speakers, A and B, Müller again shared the text among various actors. His chorus was two old men in whiteface and greatcoats, sitting behind the two tables at forestage and staring coldly ahead. These "Party functionaries" held copies of Müller's text that they read alternately, together, or repeating each other's words. As each page came to an end, they tore it out it unison, crumbled it, and let it drop to the stage floor. Obviously a "page" of history, a text of memory, a part of the performance was symbolically and concretely discarded. Figures A and B were shared among six actors. Paranoid lines such as "You know what we know" circulated from one speaker to another, repeated over and over. Little movement occurred on stage. "It is rather the text that moves," writes Rouse, "decomposed and recomposed through echoing and repetition."[94]

After the "execution machine" of *Mauser* came the "desiring machine" of *Quartet*. Positioned midway through the evening and breaking with the stasis and echoing that characterized the other stagings, *Quartet* was played on the forestage, behind which hung "a widely-spaced curtain of blood, dripping into buckets placed along the curtain line,"[95] and with Kounellis's set plunged into darkness. The text was performed in modern costume, fast, funny, cold, impersonal, dispensing with eighteenth-century costume or wig, internalizing the postapocalyptic bunker, turning the fractures of history and the failures of Enlightenment discourse into a contemporary discourse on other failed revolutions (such as Socialism and Nazism).

The final play of this production, *The Foundling,* reverted to the static staging of *Mauser,* played at and between the two forestage tables against the backdrop of Kounellis's history fragments. The text of the play is devoid of attributed speeches, but its "story" does suggest two "characters" or dramatic positions: father and stepson. In Müller's production, the father was played by four men at the forestage tables—the same tables occupied by the Party functionaries in *Mauser*. The son was shared by two women and three men, one in a wheelchair. In *Mauser,* the positions of tribunal and accused, while all part of the same perverted revolutionary logic, were clearly demarcated. In *The Foundling,* the splitting of subjectivity imitated the "single" voice of the memory text and turned the father/son positions into the collective voice of an historical tragedy within which both are actors. The text again moved through miked and echoing techniques, broadening the collective voices even further to imply as well the voice of the audience. The echoing also took up the echoes and repetitions already written into the script, so that the incessantly repeated "FORGOTTEN AND FORGOTTEN AND FORGOTTEN" both arose out of and engulfed the text.

Partway through *The Foundling,* Müller intercut *Heracles 13,* a new four-page text reprinted in the program, whose placement in the production served a clear ideological purpose. It tells of Heracles' thirteenth labor, as reported by the messenger in Euripides' *Heracles:* liberating Thebes from the Thebans by killing his own wife and family. This theme would have already been familiar to a Müller audience from scene three of *The Battle,* where a German man kills his family in imitation of the Führer, but fails to kill himself (discussed above). Here, however, the cruel text was turned into a grotesque comment on the murderous mechanism of Stalinism (and all revolutionary violence) that finally always turns inward. This new play underlined and made more politically specific the personal/ideological betrayal motifs of the play within which it was situated, *The Foundling.* Müller had the text of *Heracles 13* piped in through loudspeakers, again disconnecting text from source, during which the father repeatedly whacked his children over the head with a huge volume of Stalin's collected works. But instead of dying, the children kept jumping back up, like jack-in-the-boxes, refusing to be erased—and thus denying closure to this revolutionary violence or its memory.

In the *Mauser* project, Müller combated forgetting by assembling what Eric Santner has termed the "stranded objects" of history into an aggregate that performed the "task" of forcing his audience to reencounter and thus remember its own traumatic history.[96] Müller collected the consequence of Nazism, of Communism's rule and failure in East Germany, of the failures of the Socialist dream and the Enlightenment dream, and shaped these through past and present texts from his own memory-theater into a memoried summation of an era, as well as of his own work. Thus was a traumatic past remembered and repeated, "brought up" as fragments and "worked through" in a theatrical gesture reminiscent of Freud's *Trauerarbeit.* Freud's "working through" the trauma of loss is aimed at *restructuring* traumatic moments through their repetition and "insertion" (integration) into the (private or collective) self. For Freud, the repetition functions to reconstruct the mourner's identity in terms of the loss. That is, mourning—and a theater that induces and imitates mourning—allow for the past to find a "place" within the identity of the remembering community. When the work of mourning is completed, Freud promises, "the ego becomes free and uninhibited again" and can form new attachments.[97] The object of mourning—or loss—in Müller's hands is aimed at a collective subject and a collective past; a past, moreover, being contested in the political realm of 1991 "reunified" Berlin. In his theatrical collage, Müller insists that his (especially East German) audience remember the past of their now demised

Socialist state, remember the Western history and culture of which it was born, and remember, as well, its betrayals. Müller replays repressed psychic wounds left by (specifically East) German history, and struggles with them *through* the struggles among his various texts, and between the texts and his target audience. If, as he wrote to Wilson, "There is no revolution without a memory," then the memory of Germany's failed revolutions must be acknowledged, brought up to the surface and integrated into the national psyche before any future revolution can take place. Otherwise the past might return "the old-fashioned way, as a nightmare, as Hamlet's ghost,"[98] forever inciting us to "remember me" and never allowing release from the failures of the past.

Chapter 4

Sam Shepard and the Anxiety of Erasure

From his earliest plays, the short theater-sketches *Rock Garden* and *Cowboys* (1964), Sam Shepard has struggled with the instabilities of memory, personal as well as cultural. Unlike either Müller or Beckett, memory is imaged in Shepard not through its obdurate returns, but through anxieties of loss and displacement, through the perils of transformation and amnesia. The ceaseless internal recall of Beckett's later figures, the relentless evocations of historical pasts in Müller, are replaced in Shepard's plays by signs of absence: by empty spaces, fading traces, and the instant commodification of the past into transient pop images or depthless consumer clichés. A theater of *lack,* of lacunae and stunted "actions" (as we see in his ironically titled play *Action*), is constructed out of the debris of a pop culture whose signature characteristic is its unhistoried immediacy. Despite its vivid imagistic surface, this lack and loss is not without a concomitant yearning to remember and return. Indeed, Shepard's plays betray a permanent tension between memory and forgetting, and my interest will lie precisely in his theatricalizations of this tension. I will ask about the floating icons from an ungrounded cultural past that surface in Shepard's plays. I will also ask about the connections between an unmemoried past and Shepard's recurrent science-fiction fantasies of a destroyed future—his obsession with apocalypse and epigonism. Finally, I will try to uncover the mechanisms of forgetting and erasure in Shepard's plays, and the connection between these and postmodern anxiety.

Shepard's oeuvre is in a constant state of self-transformation and cannot be treated as a uniform whole. Commonly divided into roughly three periods and styles, his work moves from the explosive fragments of his early experimental plays, through a period of longer "pop culture" plays, to a more fully integrated thematic and structural quasi-realism. Articulations of memory and the anxiety of loss appear throughout his work, but also undergo permutations. In the early short plays, anxiety is deeply personal, imagistic, preconscious, given through uncontrollable bodies—sexual

orgasm (*Rock Garden*), bleeding and bug-infested skin (*Red Cross, 1966*)—
and through wildly long monologues. These plays "have the random at
their heart" and release "anarchy and poetry," to quote C. W. E. Bigsby.[1]
They also already display Shepard's preoccupation with the unsustainable
mythology of the West (*Cowboys* and *Cowboys #2, 1967*), with amnesia (*La
Turista, 1967*—Kent's sleeping sickness), and with apocalypse (*Icarus's
Mother, 1965*). In the longer "middle-period" plays, cultural memory (or its
loss) supplements personal anxiety. The plays of this period, writes Deborah
Geis, "reveal an apparent infatuation with the contemporary mythology
that the American collective unconscious has populated with images of
cowboys, gangsters and detectives, movie stars and rock stars, and even
creatures from outer space."[2] But these myths are already undermined and
drained through Shepard's postmodern strategies of dislocation and temporal conflation. Bringing to the fore collective anxieties of late 1960s/early
1970s America, these plays display dread of nuclear destruction, antigovern-
ment paranoia, a profound sense of cultural rootlessness. It is here—in *The
Tooth of Crime* and *Action,* for example—that an erased past and apocalyptic
forgetting become prominent themes. Both of these latter plays were written during Shepard's early 1970s sojourn in London, far away from the
America both plays try to comprehend. *Action* is a puzzling postapocalyptic
play whose textual surface seems completely divorced from any embodied
theatricality. *The Tooth of Crime,* considered by many to be Shepard's finest
play, is also his most voluptuously embodied, his most aggressively *performed*
play. Theatrically opposed, these two very different dramas are Shepard's
most interesting representations of unmemoried states of being (both are
discussed below). Beginning with *Curse of the Starving Class* (1977), we find
a new striving for mythic resonance and integration, and a formal switch—
and ideological backtracking—to a modified realism. *Buried Child* (1978)
and *Fool for Love* (1982) are obsessed with the past, *A Lie of the Mind* (1985)
is overtly about amnesia; but these late plays abandon, for the most part, a
postmodern dramatic aesthetic, and I will thus discuss them only briefly.

    Shepard's theater is remarkable for its visual and verbal abundance.
Heaping onto his stages and pages incarnations of America's pop imagination, Shepard provides overly familiar fragments from the image library of
an American cultural memory. In his prefamily plays, images of the mythic
West, the fantasized world of Hollywood, the mock-security of Eisenhower's America, images drawn from the science-fiction and Western
movie industry of the 1950s, images that "suddenly spring up in living
technicolor" within the memory and imagination of the writer,[3] as Shepard put it, proliferate and coexist. "You see the territory he travels in," says

the doctor in *Geography of a Horse Dreamer* of Cody, the Shepardian artist-figure, "He's perfectly capable of living in several worlds at the same time. This is his genius."[4] But the images found in this "territory" are breakaway images weirdly stranded in incoherent worlds, cut loose from context or history. Displaced and lost—like the characters in *Action* who have lost their place in the book they constantly try, but fail, to read—the past is alluded to through images of absence, or through splintered and transmuting pop icons that erupt on stage as though emerging from within a collective psychic wound. More insistently than almost any other contemporary playwright, Shepard's floating images exemplify the anxiety of "ungroundedness," or what David DeRose has called "a world unfixed."[5] His characters constantly transform, perform, speak in "voices." Parallel actions and generic shiftings undermine any possibility of stability, even within a theatrical code. This postmodern rejection of essence and foundation, of "metaconcepts," or what Jean–François Lyotard calls "master narratives," supplies the frame of Shepard's imagistic plays. The past appears as a picture book of lost signifiers in which disembodied wild Indians attack mock-cowboy figures among the car-honks of an urban setting (*Cowboys #2*), or mythical character such as Mae West and Captain Kidd get conjured up by rock singers who move from scene to scene without finding a "place" for their unmemoried icons (*Mad Dog Blues,* 1971). Shepard's underlying sense of history seems to consist of precisely such disturbingly unrooted and free-floating fragments. For Shepard, writes Bigsby, "the discontinuities, *the absences,* the incompletions of personal and public existence are a primary fact."[6] Within these incompletions, the absence of a rooted past is the foremost incitement toward the images of erasure and fragment that define his postmodern landscape of anxiety.

Torn out of context and out of emotional identity, the past invades Shepard's plays either as random, depleted reference, or as displaced two-dimensional image. *Chicago* (1965), for example, begins with the unmotivated, and unexplained, recitation of the Gettysburg Address; Lincoln is suddenly invoked, though not remembered, in *Action;* Doc and Sonny wear clothing "from Civil War times"—for no reason, with no explanation—in act 2 of *La Turista;* Kennedy's assassination is arbitrarily referred to in *The Unseen Hand* (1969); Nixon, Wallace, Humphrey, and their political campaigns suddenly surface in *Operation Sidewinder* (1970). These references tie the stage events to the traces of an American history that would be easily recognized by Shepard's audience; but the relevance of that history is lost. Parallel to this, visual icons gleaned from an American cultural memory appear in forms that are forever prepackaged and commodified—Marlboro cowboys in jeans and hat, comic-book spacemen in orange tights, cliché cheerleaders from a "simpler" time. History, through which identity is rooted in collective memory over time, is unavailable in Shepard's plays except as a mediated replacement-image or parodic icon. The value of the past—that which Adam Smith termed its "use value," its unique ability to fulfill some human need or desire (as identity or ideal)—has transformed in Shepard's world into what Karl Marx called its "exchange value," its *function* as a sellable image, as a commodity. Commodification is a process by which ideas or figures are cut off from their own history, especially the history of their evolution, resulting in reification and, worse, the freezing of complex ideas into easily grasped images. The poster image of the jeans/boots/hatted cowboy, for example, becomes a replacement for the history of American westward expansion, and for the ideas of freedom, lawlessness, and an originary bond with the land. The replacement-image is then manipulated to create instant identification with a product (cigarettes, for example), and thus to evoke consumer desire. Late capitalist society, according to Fredric Jameson, has made such instant commodification inevitable: exchange value in our society, Jameson writes, "has been generalized to the point at which the very *memory* of use-value is effaced."[7] In this context, the past radiates no intrinsic worth, no root in a collective identity. It becomes a mere function of market operations and, as such, can fulfill no emotional need.

In one of his more famous utterances, Shepard said of America that "you don't have any connection with the past, with what history means"; all that remains is "this emotional thing that goes a long way back, which creates a certain kind of chaos, a kind of terror."[8] The chaos and terror engendered through the replacement of history by commodity, and the ensuing erasure of a rooted memory, is made unusually explicit in Shepard's early, angst-ridden *Icarus's Mother* (1965). Inspired by an actual Fourth of July celebration that Shepard experienced as void of all significance aside from the fireworks' spectacle that had by now replaced the event being marked,[9] it shows a group of young people waiting for an annual (though unexplained) firework display. What they get instead is an apocalyptic off-stage plane-crash. The fantastic explosion, whose reverberations engulf the entire world, is presented in these terms: "This is the nineteenth wonder of the Western, international world brought to you by Nabisco Cracker Corporation for the preservation of historians to come and for historians to go by."[10] The eruption of light and flame is indicated as a corporate event: world's end as promotional campaign. The historian, rather than bringing signification to this commemoration of the birth of the nation, is marked as already appropriated, sponsored by the same corporate capitalism whose tool and agent she or he becomes. Commodification, a hallmark of post-modern society, an essential part of Jameson's ever-quoted "cultural logic of late capitalism," is a staple in Shepard's theater. What will concern me, and what vitally concerns Shepard as well, is how the commodification of the past has voided America of authentic, rooted memory. The erasure of a rooted past gives rise in Shepard's plays, as well, to anxieties of an erased future.

Shepard's situation is a paradoxical one. A product of postmodern America and of postindustrial capitalism, his dramatic language reflects this world in conflated, ungrounded, open, and constantly shifting images that grant stylistic freedom and allow imaginative release. At the same time, Shepard cannot escape a concomitant angst and longing in the face of this foundationless world, anxieties expressed through images of claustrophobia and the desire for escape. An aspect closely connected with this paradox is his presentation of identity, private and public. Shepard's characters are caught in the bind of seeking postmodern release from culturally induced determinations of personality—and are thus constantly transforming. At the same time, they have the modernist need to find sustenance in a memoried past, often expressed in long monologic fables, or through nostalgic imaginings of the past. Shepard's transmutational strategy, through which his figures continuously slip out of identity, is evident from his earliest plays, as well as in his early change of names[11]—and probably has a psychological root in his biography. He has said as much in interview: "[Y]ou have this personality, and somehow feel locked into it, jailed by all of your cultural influences and your psychological ones from your family, and all that. And somehow I feel that that isn't the whole of it, you know, that there's another possibility."[12] The need to reinvent the self is thus an urgent reaction to the formulating forces of societal pressure and tradition, viewed by Shepard as prisons to be struggled against. Among those forces is also memory. "That's not me at all," says Shooter when Jeep reminds him of his previous fear of water: "That's entirely the wrong image" (*Action*).[13] "That isn't me! That never was me!" says Dodge when reminded of the pictures of his youth: "This is me. Right here. This is it. The whole shootin' match" (*Buried Child*).[14] On the other hand, and simultaneously, there is the anxiety of a culture that is too loose, too unstructured and unformulated. In that same interview, Shepard speaks of the influence on his plays of "that particular sort of temporary society that you find in Southern California where nothing is permanent, where everything could be knocked down and it wouldn't be missed, and the feeling of impermanence that comes from that—that you don't belong to any particular culture."[15] Having escaped from the prison of personality, Shepard's characters find themselves stranded in the fluidity of a culture where nothing endures and too little is rooted or remembered. Freed from the past's determination, they find themselves marooned in postapocalyptic worlds, in postmodern "unfixity," or, with the later quasi-realistic plays, locked into their longing for a return to nourishing roots. The "true West" may exist only as a Hollywood filmscript, only as a textualized commodity, but the longing for rootedness and authentic recall—even if no longer available—remains. This is the emotional subtext of many of Shepard's early and middle-period plays and can be seen as the modernist seed of a postmodern dramaturgy—and as one of the reasons for the ongoing debate as to Shepard's (shifting) place between modernism and postmodernism.[16] Up until his 1977 "turn" toward family and modified realism, Shepard situated his vision of America between erased past and exploded future, within a chaotic, depthless, anxiety-ridden present. Characters who appear constantly displaced and eternally inventing themselves, also expose the unhistoried and disinherited center of America's selfhood.

Two-Way Memory: Temporal Conflation

> "That's the effect of living backwards," the Queen said. . . . "one's
>   memory works both ways."
> "I'm sure *mine* only works one way," Alice remarked. "I can't
>   remember things before they happen."
> "It's a poor sort of memory that only works backwards," the Queen
>   remarked.
>   —Lewis Carroll, *Through the Looking-Glass*

Lewis Carroll's passage on memory that "works both ways" begins with the Queen's offer that Alice be paid two pence and "jam every other day" for her services. "The rule is," the Queen says, "jam tomorrow and jam yesterday, but never jam today." While this bit of sophistry leaves Alice confused, and jamless, it suggests a view of time (Queen: "today isn't any *other* day, you know") in which the present is always an empty center between the disappointments of the past and the promise of the future: a view dramatized—or rather, inverted—in some of Shepard's early and middle-period plays. Shepard's procedure for presenting America in those plays is to revive a "lacking" past and join it to an equally unavailable future. Both coexist on the stage and are conflated through their style of presentation via a visual and verbal rhetoric drawn from the film, music, and theater resources of the popular, ahistorical imagination. Thus, although yesterday and tomorrow seem to appear on stage, they are recycled and "remembered" in terms that vitiate them both, rendering all time as the product of a mediated pop imagination. This meeting between past and future appears, for example, in *Operation Sidewinder,* where ancient Hopi Indians meet flying saucers. But the question of how American memory—and forgetting—is illuminated through this strategy of "two-way memory" finds paradigmatic expression in Shepard's *The Unseen Hand* (1969), which is both an early version of themes more fully developed in *The Tooth of Crime* and an almost programmatic fusion of past and future within the junkyard of a flat and frighteningly empty present.

The Unseen Hand features an imagistic, comic-book set of characters and situations that mask the serious nature of its critique. Set on the off-ramp of a freeway, near the emblematic hick-town of Azusa ("Everything from 'A' to 'Z' in the USA: Azusa"),[17] Shepard places at the center of the play a battered '51 Chevrolet convertible, stripped, bashed, and surrounded by "garbage, tin cans, cardboard boxes, Coca-Cola bottles and other junk" (3): the discards of consumer America. This unvarying central image is sensually supplemented through the constantly repeating noise of big diesel trucks whooshing by, accompanied by the double-eyed illumination of headlights that cut across the stage. The ominous sound of commerce roaring on, and the transient, homeless headlight image so well known from B movies, are poignantly permanent elements in a play full of transformations. On this highway/junkyard, the run-down cowboy figure Blue Morphan, 120 years old and himself a remnant from a discarded world, lives in the wrecked Chevy and inside the memories of his lost West. Blue's identity is clearly established from the start: like all Shepard's cowboys, he wears the trademark jeans, boots, and hat and speaks in a musical Western idiom. The play opens with a long monologue in which Blue recalls his "prime," when he and his dead brothers Cisco and Sycamore, the Morphan Brothers gang, made history. "Hadn't a been fer the old hooch here I'd a been in history books by now. Probably am anyhow, under a different name" (5). As soon as Blue's identity is established, another figure appears—Willie "the space freak," dressed in "super future clothes," orange, black, and vinyl, with a half-hood covering the back of his head, and the mark of a black handprint burned into his hairless skull. Willie is as easy to decipher visually as was Blue. Dressed in the comic-book outfit of space invaders, he evokes the entire mythology of sci-fi movies, of cartoon extraterrestrials—just as Blue's figure assumes the audience's acquaintance with the semiology and ethos of cinema Westerns and American folklore. Thus, two-dimensional icons of past and future meet among the ruins of present-day America.

Blue's opening monologue is the first half of a paranoid/nostalgic frame that compares a simpler past of self-reliant "free agents" and "real" people ("The people people"), to the intangible "silent, secret" workings of contemporary power structures. His long, rambling speech is directed at an invisible listener on the debris-filled stage, that is, directed at the audience. The monologue culminates with Blue telling his imaginary interlocutor (who, like most of Shepard's original audience, would have been "too young to remember") of his cowboy prime, his historic acts, and of a "lost" past (4–5). As if by magic, this evocation of a lost and unremembered past brings unto the stage the extraterrestrial Willie, representing a destroyed and hopeless future. Willie has in fact come because the future *does* seem to remember Blue and his brothers. Willie has traveled "through two galaxies" to seek the aid of Blue and his mythic brothers in freeing his race of slaves— half humans, half baboons—from the power of the Silent Ones and their telepathic mind-control. Two things are clear: the future needs the past in order to regain a spirit of freedom lost to totalitarian ("silent, secret") governments; and the strength of that past—now lacking—is what Willie calls its concrete "reality."

> *Willie:* If you came into Nogoland blazing your six-guns they wouldn't
> have any idea how to deal with you. All their technology and magic
> would be a total loss. You would be too real for their experience. (8)

The future Willie describes is one of severe control and abstraction. The rulers "have lost all touch with human emotion. They exist in almost a purely telepathic intellectual state" (8). Through these powers, they control the thoughts of the slave class, squeezing down on the minds of thought criminals—the hand on Willie's skull is the visual sign of their invisible (abstract) manipulations. In contrast, Blue and his brothers are imagined by Willie to be fiercely concrete men, capable of nonmediated action. Indeed, when the two dead brothers are revived through Willie's mental powers, they arrive with rifles, revolvers, and pistols ready for use: "Like old times. A showdown" (20). Unlike the future (which sounds very much like the present), the past is imaged as immediate and vital, perhaps even authentic; and this renders the past, despite its decayed and parodic portrayal, as a site of longing.

The cosmic battle between the concrete six-shooters and the ethereal Silent Ones, between past and future, never takes place. Instead, a third element is introduced, a character as stereotyped as are both the cowboy and the space freak but drawn from a different subset of Americana: the Kid, a high-school cheerleader with pants down and legs bleeding who has just been whipped by a rival gang of youth. The Kid represents a contemporary—that is, a 1950s and 1960s—America. He transforms during the play from a cowering sissy into a potential guerrilla-war leader, and finally into the voice of a patriotic apple-pie ethos that would have sounded parodic and dated in 1969, the era of student protests and the Vietnam War. It is this final transformation that leads to Willie's release from the Hand.[18] The Kid slips in and out of roles mainly through a shifting monologic voice, a form of verbal ventriloquism that allows Shepard to evoke small stations of political reality, and instability, while refusing to give any priority. As a terrorist, the Kid's belief that "freedom and revolution are inextricably bound up" evokes the political ideology of leftist radicals who were active and vocal at the time. His emphasis on "a war of the masses, a war of the people" (25) connects the Kid's (rhetorical) struggle to Willie's imprisoned masses on the planet of Nogoland. The Kid's next transformation is to turn against the cowboy brothers as "a bunch a' subversives" themselves whom, he claims, want to take over his utopian Azusa. This speech is spoken to rock-and-roll chords, becoming a talk-song tribute to "my home," small-town America with its "drive-in movies and the bowling alleys and the football games and the drag races . . . and the freeway and the pool hall and the Bank of America and the post office and the Presbyterian church and the laundromat and the liquor store and the miniature golf course" (27–28)—thus invoking an Eisenhower era rhetoric of patriotic faith and innocence that is the opposite extreme to his previous radicalism. Although neither speech is specifically historical, both are specifically reminiscent of—contradictory and coexisting—American ideologies, adding to the confusion of stances already represented by Willie's world of tyranny and the cowboy brothers' outlaw world of boundless freedom.

Transformation occurs on many levels of *The Unseen Hand*. Ideologies are always tentative, overlapping, coexistent. Age and time are reversible. Willie turns Blue from an ancient codger into a thirty-year-old (in preparation for the battle). Sycamore, at the end of the play, "becomes older and older just with his body," physically becoming the Blue he replaces in the beat-up Chevy. Through these physical changes, time is collapsed and rendered meaningless; future and past interchange. The play's physical idiom is also constantly transmuting: Blue and Cisco switch from staid cowboys into performers turning somersaults on stage and singing "Rock around the Clock." Willie, half-paralyzed and convulsive during much of the play, begins "an elated dance" when he discovers the "secret" of mental freedom. Joined by Cisco, both frolic while Day-Glo painted Ping-Pong balls fall in glowing streams of color from the sky, bouncing on the stage, caught and thrown up in the air in a bit of Broadway extravaganza quite contrary to the original style of the play. All of these transforming figures—past cowboys, present cheerleaders, future mutants—despite the radically different worlds they typically represent, despite the markedly different genres from which they have been wrenched, do not, as David DeRose suggests, finally remain "stranded without a cultural or social framework, a master narrative, that would give meaning to their lives."[19] On the contrary. In the end, all coexist as ahistorical showtime performers covered by confetti, pop-culture figures who belong to—and emanate from—the spectacle (and "framework") of America's culture industry. These media-generated images are presented as part of a media-formed collective cultural consciousness against whose "unseen hand" Shepard is in fact protesting.

This is not to say that Shepard has succumbed to Jean Baudrillard's pessimistic thesis that reality has been undone in America by a culture of technological and media simulations that mask reality, and then mask its absence through commodified image replacements.[20] Baudrillard's vision of America as an unending "precession of simulacra" is resisted through Shepard's reflexive representations of mythic icons *as* performers (here, and also in *Tooth of Crime*), a reflexivity that "unmasks" the media images by exposing their appropriation and bespeaks a critical stance toward their commodification. Criticism is also implicit in Shepard's framing device, the opening and closing memory monologues spoken by the two interchangeable cowboy figures. Overt "framing" is an unusual move for Shepard; its effect (ironizing, distancing) is not. In *The Unseen Hand,* Shepard undermines and ironizes the prepackaged image of his own pastiche figures by positioning them within the hull of memory. At the same time, the authenticity of that hull remains equivocal. Blue and Sycamore, ancient and deluded, begin and end the play with speeches that reach back into a diction and imagery recognizable from matinee Westerns—to a time when one road routed through the West ("Follow the Union Pacific till ya' come to Fish Creek"), and anyone could direct you to the house of Blue Morphan ("Just ask any old body fer old Blue. They'll tell ya" [4]). Their cowboy speech is long-winded, slow-paced, sometimes sentimental, revealing nostalgia for a time when the fragmented discards of Shepard's present landscape cohered into a full world as well as revealing an awareness of the theatrical posturings of their longings. This doubleness, a longing for a lost fullness that carries nostalgic undertones, together with an awareness of how the present landscape has shaped even those longings, recurs in many Shepard plays. I would agree with George Stambolian that "Shepard has a real love for the popular myths of our culture and a genuine nostalgia for some lost age of innocence when life was simpler in America. He also knows that this world may never have existed . . . and that our memory and imagination may well be based on lies."[21] Michael Vanden Heuvel expanded this doubleness to cover two sides of Shepard's dramaturgy, text and performance. Writing on the double nature of consciousness in Shepard's plays, Vanden Heuvel proposes that it is predicated on the affinity

> between consciousness conceived on the one hand as derived from transformations and transcendence (the *jouissance* of indeterminacy, and the escape from the burdens of memory . . .), and, on the other hand, consciousness structured around psychological integrity, a nostalgia for lost grace, the burden of memory, and a claustrophobic sense of closure.[22]

The transformative *jouissance* of the play's pastiche center would, in these terms, be contrasted to the nostalgia and memoried reach into a lost "utopian" past provided by the monologic frame. It is, however, a nostalgia devoid of any illusion that the lost past might be revived or restored— even if only as narrative. By framing the highway-intersection of America's present through the monologues of its cowboy visitors, Shepard critiques the melange at the play's (and America's) center; but this is not a critique that believes in its own efficacy. Spoken by decrepit remnants of the West housed within the gutted Chevy and surrounded by mounds of waste, the voice of the frame cowboys sounds irrelevant and out of touch, like the replay of an old B movie. The weakness of that voice—and of most of Shepard's displaced cowboys, as I will discuss below—is an acknowledgment of the irrevocable eclipse of America's originary mythology and a self-ironizing gesture by Shepard toward his own nostalgia. The play ends with an ancient Sycamore curled up in the back of the Chevy, defeated, admitting to having no desires left other than "to live out my life with a little peace and quiet." He has succumbed to the depleted reality within which he is housed and can, at most, produce a didacticism that would encourage us to slow down and "take stock a' things," to figure out the next move, to "make sure they're yer own moves and not someone else's" (32). No longer capable of anything more than the mouthing of cliché sentiments, the concrete gunslinger himself finally vanishes into the ruins of America's discards.

"Yearning for a New History": Cowboys and Indians

The historical cowboys, Shepard has said, were young rebels "about 16 or 17, who decided they didn't want to have anything to do with the East Coast, with that way of life, and took on this immense country, and didn't have any real rules."[23] These historical rebels, however, rarely figure in Shepard's plays. The nineteenth-century migration of restless youth from the settled East Coast cities out onto the lawless frontier is, in fact, reversed in many of the plays; Shepard's cowboys reappear ensconced and entrapped within the very environment they had historically escaped. The images of the West created by Shepard from *Cowboys* (1964) up to *The Sad Lament of Pecos Bill on the Eve of Killing His Wife* (1976), have less to do with the historical figures he so admires than with their mediated returns in the American imagination. These cowboys are largely rooted in the pop culture of 1950s American cinema, literature, and music, all deep influences and resources for Shepard. DeRose identifies the 1950s with the advent of a postmodern consciousness in America. It was a time, he writes, "when media-generated myths grew to such proportions and with such speed that they lost all connection to the reality from which they once sprang. They became hollow simulacra infiltrating all aspects of America's cultural identity, but no longer capable of sustaining its inhabitants."[24] Although the mediated image of the mythic West is the one most apparent in Shepard, the lure of the absent "true" West—the *pre*-mediated mythic dimension— underlies his representations, creating constant semiotic conflict: the West is signified as both absent and hidden, as both irretrievable and an irrationally erupting source. There are moments in Shepard's plays when the West breaks out of its tinsel-town image to return in a flash of "authentic" dust-clogged clothes and double-barreled violence—in the form of Cody's brothers in *Geography of a Horse Dreamer,* for example. But despite this occasional revival, the "true West" figures lack the strength to imagine a whole past and thus to re-create a real world. They always fade and are usually replaced by textualized and unmemoried postmodern images.

This ambiguity is already apparent in Shepard's earliest play, *Cowboys,* in which the West infiltrates the imagination of two young urbanites with the strength of emanations from a collective memory. *Cowboys* has no published edition; Shepard rewrote it three years later, and this version was published as *Cowboys #2* (1967). Both versions document a state of mind and are clearly rooted in Shepard's own move from a small western town to the menace of New York City. In *Cowboys #2,* the memory and unavailability of the West are enacted by two young men, dressed in black, on a nearly empty stage. In a series of shifting improvisational scenes, Chet and Stu act out their empty urban existence by enacting/inventing the roles of Clem and Mel, two old-timer cowboys stranded in the Indian-infested deserts of the classical West. Kenneth Chubb, who originally directed the play, wrote that *Cowboys #2* is about two men "remembering not only their own pasts, but also a collective past. Whether any of it is true doesn't matter; what matters is that it is a part of our experience"[25]—at least our culturally mediated experience. The two men watch approaching clouds, discuss the need for rain, fantasize a night among the stars of the prairie, find themselves stranded without water, under the hot desert sun. The young men move in and out of their cowboy roles, both accepting themselves as role-players and becoming the roles they play. Throughout the play, the sound of a single—desert—cricket can be heard, along with voices and noises from the urban street. Audial input is used to arouse a sensual sense of a missing reality—the sound of rain, then the sound of horses and of yelling Indians. As the imaginary Indians shoot at them, Chet and Stu "make gun noises," pretending to return fire. Stu gets shot in the arm and Chet pretends to clean the wound with water from an imaginary river. During the simulated battle, the honking of urban car horns is heard in the distance, joined by the increasing audial onslaught of horses galloping and Indians shouting, reverberating like the soundtrack of a Western. The urban desert of the American present is thus juxtaposed to the memory traces of a dangerous past. But while the stage arrangement seems to imply that the urban apartment is the play's "reality," and the cowboy/Indian text is imaginary, this dichotomy is lifted toward the end of the play. Stu (as Mel), shot by an Indian arrow, "dies," refusing to be revived by Chet, who, reverting to his role as a young man, begs him to get up. "Stu, this isn't funny," he says in his "normal voice" (153). Chet drags Stu downstage, becoming a panic-filled old cowboy as the lights grow brighter, imitating the merciless sun of so many cowboy movies, and vultures circle overhead. Chet, no longer "acting," tries to protect Stu/Mel from the sun and the birds while the noise of car-honks grows in volume. Looking toward the audience, he says, "This ain't funny! This ain't no joke, you shitty birds! What do ya think this is TV or somethin'? I ain't gettin' et by no vultures" (153). As his panic peaks at the confusion between the commodified images of a TV imagination and the too real incursion of those images into his life, the contemporary actor and the true West conflate.

In the original 1964 play, *Cowboys,* the New York audience was shot at and came in for verbal abuse by the displaced cowboys whose myths were dying on this urban stage. "Their battle with Indian marauders becomes a battle against urban America and its sprawling suburban masses," writes DeRose, "expressing a panicked response to a postmodern America in which their personal myths have no meaning and in which they cannot function."[26] In *Cowboys #2,* this initial, immature gesture is replaced by a comment on representation itself. At the very end of the play, as Stu lies dying and Chet tries to fight off the birds, two additional young men—this time formally dressed in business suits—enter the stage "with scripts in their hand" and begin to read aloud the play we have just seen, from the beginning, in monotone. These self-controlled young men read the West not through their sinews, but with dispassionate alienation, as an irrelevant, fictive "text." With them, we get another "version" of the lost West— tamed, removed from agency, turned into a harmless part of the "corporate" stock of sellable images that has come to represent America.

Cowboys are almost always a site of loss and erasure for Shepard. The memory of a real westward migration and the meaning of that optimistic act seem to have been so thoroughly diluted by the clichés of a media-nurtured culture that there is no way to even protest those images without appropriating them. In Shepard's plays we meet the parasitic outgrowth of a mediated imagination: "old-timers," matinee cowboys, a rock star who has built his (fake) image on a cowboy ethos (*The Tooth of Crime*). Each of these manifestations is, at the same time, a site of longing for the "true West" that, even in Shepard's play by that name, is once again inscribed as a filmscript. Shepard is often personally identified with the cowboy image, a perception encouraged by his biography, by photo spreads of him in popular magazines, with horse and Western hat, and by plays such as *Cowboy Mouth* and *Geography of a Horse Dreamer* whose roots are clearly autobiographical. Shepard speaks of his attachment to the landscape of the West in nearly mythic terms. He has said, for example, that the American West feels "much more ancient than the East . . . primordial."

> It has to do with the relationship between the land and the people—between the human being and the ground. I think that's typically western and much more attractive than this tight little forest civilization that happened back East. It's much more physical and emotional to me. . . . I just feel like I'll never get over the fact of being from the West.[27]

But the primordial land that promises depth and roots has been populated by the American imagination with dime-store cowboys and mediated travesties. In his collection of prose sketches, *Hawk Moon,* Shepard gives a mov-

ing portrayal of the Hollywood cowboy's betrayal of his originary landscape
and its history:

> The cowboy dressed in fringe with buckskin gloves, silk bandana, pale clown
> white make-up, lipstick, eyes thickly made up and a ten-gallon hat, holds the
> reins of his horse decked out in silver studs. The cowboy squints under hot
> spotlights. The gaffers all giggle. The cowboy sweats but there's nowhere for
> the sweat to go. He sinks to his knees and screams: "Forgive me, Utah! For-
> give me!"[28]

This faux cowboy, ubiquitous and rarely challenged, has betrayed Utah and
the West by replacing it—and thus *dis*placing it—within the collective
memory. This is the cowboy that is spoofed in *La Turista,* where the transformation from sunburned vacationer to matinee cowboy takes place,
tellingly, in a bathroom. He appears in parodic fashion in *Forensic and the
Navigators* (1967), where two young writers, dressed as a cowboy and as an
Indian, elaborate a bourgeois dream of rebellion—which leads to sweeping
destruction instead of the rebuilding of the West. Shepard presents the past
always at a commodified, mediated remove: the past as filmscript (*True
West*), the past as a construct determined by style and discourse (*Tooth of
Crime*), the past as comic strip (*Mad Dog Blues, The Unseen Hand*). As in the
Hollywood he critiques (*Angel City,* 1976), the past is always reduced to a
popular cultural form, or else—in the later poetic-realistic plays—imbued
with mystical longing.

Philip French writes in *Westerns* that "the one thing the Western is
always about is America rewriting and reinterpreting her own past."[29] Many
postmodern American writers—E. L. Doctorow, John Barth, Thomas
Berger—have been attracted to this genre as a form that allows the rewriting and ironizing of earlier myths of America's past, and of their formulation
of its "history." Shepard, however, does *not* write Westerns. Nor is he seriously concerned with the past as history. Rather, he seeks to display the erasure of a collective identity through the total commodification of a mythic
memory. For Shepard, the term *myth* has, in its American context, come to
mean denatured "fantasies" about the past that no longer "connect with
anything." As he has said, the original purpose of myth "had to do with
being able to trace ourselves back through time":

> Myth served as a story in which people could connect themselves in time to
> the past. And thereby connect to the present and the future. . . . It was so pow-
> erful and so strong that it acted as a thread in culture. And that's been
> destroyed. . . . All we have is fantasies about it . . . [that] speak to some lame
> notions about the past. But they don't connect with anything.

Where peoples once had "a connecting river" they now have only "a fragmented river." All contemporary efforts to create myth will fail, says Shepard, since it must "be connected to ancient stuff" in order to succeed—"or
else it will come apart."³⁰ The loss of rootedness and of a tradition of ritual
transmission is a fact of contemporary life that is signified by Shepard
through images of absence and distortion, through pastiche and overabundance (as in *The Unseen Hand*) or through emptiness and stasis (as in *Action*).
The loss of this mythic "connectedness" is, however, also theatricalized
through moments of grief and peril. In such moments, America's pioneer
past is shown to be a real, though absent, source of hope. In *Tooth of Crime,*
for example, Crow's one moment of weakness occurs when Hoss reverts to
a Western idiom. In *True West,* Austin breaks down in face of Lee's seemingly "intimate" acquaintance with the desert. In *The Unseen Hand,* the
three cowboy brothers are presented as the only hope against the mental
constriction with which the future threatens us. In each of these, the past is
the venerated resource. But, in each, the past turns out to be weak, the
potency of the cowboy an illusion, a site of *lack*.

 The closest Shepard comes to reproducing a "real" Western image is in
Geography of a Horse Dreamer. Geography presents Shepard's typical "cowboy"-artist, Cody—named for Buffalo Bill. Cody has been kidnapped from
the soil of his authentic imagination and forced to manufacture diminished
and diminishing "dreams" that will profit a group of gangsters. This allegory
of the distortion of artistic talent by commercial demands belongs to Shepard's plays on the process of artistic creation—along with *Angel City,* or *Suicide in B-Flat*. But here a miraculous release from the dangers and depletions
of commerce arrives in the form of the West. Written while Shepard was
living in London at the beginning of the 1970s, the play's sense of dislocation—lost "geography"—is doubly signified as the loss of the West and of
America. The peril posed by that loss is so powerful that only a fierce act of
imagination and of deep memory (Cody's, Shepard's) can avert disaster.
Geography of a Horse Dreamer, subtitled *A Mystery in Two Acts,* ends with
Cody's life on the brink as the doctor prepares to remove the "dreamer's
bone" from the back of his neck. Injected with tranquilizers, Cody invokes
the sacred Wakan, the Indian god whose spirit fills the white buffalo, while
the doctor begins to operate. Suddenly, as though erupting out of a suppressed genre, or an exploding subconscious, Cody's two brothers, Jasper
and Jason, burst onto the stage firing shotguns so powerful their blast throws
the gangsters "clear across the room." These mighty apparitions are
described in unusual detail: "They're both about six-foot-five and weigh
250 lbs each. They wear Wyoming cowboy gear, with dust covering them

from head to foot," Shepard writes. The shotguns they carry are detailed as "double-barreled twelve-gauge," and they wear additional "side guns on their waists." Shepard makes it perfectly clear that these dust-filled, double-barreled figures are not his usual run of fake cowboys. "Their costumes," he stipulates, "should be well used and authentic without looking like dime-store cowboys" (129). These "true" emanations from the West, called up in a moment of spiritual longing so strong that it overcomes geography and dramatic consistency, possess momentary connections to a real frontier of identity, and thus to magic transformational powers. They are incursions from the same concrete West that Willie, in *The Unseen Hand,* believed could overcome technology and abstraction through its "reality." The battle that never takes place in *The Unseen Hand* is performed here as larger than life. It not only shatters the genre of the play and allows for another of Shepard's orgasmic endings, it also repeats images of "authenticity" found in earlier plays, where spiritual validity refuses to be represented as commodified or turned into theatrical travesty. Such images surface in the Indian witchdoctor and his son in *La Turista*—who perform rituals of revival "as though they have nothing to do with the play and just happen to be there,"[31] and, more problematically, in the Hopi Indians of *Operation Sidewinder.* But white, mythico-American cowboys are rarely allowed such "authenticity" without a concomitant questioning of its validity. The ethos of the West has been too completely eroded. "Authenticity," for what it's worth, is reserved for the "outsider" figures of American mythology, those who are usually defeated in the popular imagination: the Indians.

Indians appear less frequently in Shepard's plays than cowboys, and their representation is very different. The most conventional use of Indians is found in *Cowboys #2,* where even the disembodied sound of galloping invaders suffices to evoke in a media-savvy audience an automatic danger alert. When the disinherited Indian is physically revived in *Operation Sidewinder,* it is less as a movie cliché than as a spiritual alternative to the technology and material culture that supplanted, and destroyed, the West. This use of the "spiritual native" is already found, briefly and thus less problematically, in Shepard's earlier *La Turista,* in the Indian witchdoctor who not only performs strange and prescientific rites over the dying Kent, but also refuses to be appropriated by the theatrical frame into which he has stumbled. In both *La Turista* and *Operation Sidewinder,* Shepard pits the grotesque representation of a flat and violent contemporary world against an "authentic" and spiritually driven ancient culture that, Shepard seems to imply, was wiped out of real memory and authentic existence by the injuries of American history. The Indians, for Shepard, were not only a "rooted" people, they also expressed themselves through cultural forms of connectedness. They "were connected to the ancestors . . . through myth, through prayer, through ritual, through—dance, music, all of those forms that lead people into a river of myth. And there was a connecting river, not a fragmented river."[32] These romanticized figures represent a form of continuity no longer available in America, indeed destroyed *by* America, and now revived—in a nostalgic and appropriating gesture, by Shepard.

Operation Sidewinder (1970) is structured through a wild series of paranoid scenes and songs that sketch a collage of America in the late 1960s. It contains a computer built in the shape of a snake, evil military officers and a mad scientist, a desert that recalls a lost Eden, a group of black revolutionaries who plan to conquer the country with drugs. Into this national amalgam—these "fragments and refuse of American history," to quote Leonard Wilcox[33]—Shepard injects an Indian tribe that gains possession of the computer and transforms it into a spiritually potent snake-god, thus transforming technology into religious iconography. The play's central character, Young Man, begins the play as a gun-running, drug-shooting murderer and ends up inducted into the spiritual world of the Hopi Indians. Through his participation in the ritual that ends the play, he is transformed and will be "saved" from the apocalypse, the "great war" in which "materialistic matters will be destroyed by spiritual beings."[34]

Young Man's America is a rootless, violent, unhistoried, and hopeless place—"Depressed. Despaired. Running out of gas" (225). When asked by Honey, the sexy blond "Eve" he finds in the desert encoiled by the snake, "Where are you from?" his answer is a cultural pastiche of homelessness: "I am from the planet Crypton. No I am from the Hollywood Hills. No. I am from Freak City. . . . I am truly an American." Having no origin other than the endless consumption that is America—"I devour the planet. I'm an earth eater" (228)—Young Man is a comic-book version of spiritual displacement and despair. In the song that follows his autobiographical portrait—significantly titled "Alien Song"—we find the following verse:

> I couldn't go back where I came from
> 'Cause that would just bring me back here
> And this is the place I was born, bred, and raised
> And it doesn't seem like I was ever here.
>
> (229)

For everyone in this play except the Indians, writes John Lahr, "the only experience of America is loss";[35] and only those who find a way out of the spiritual aridity of America can avoid destruction.

As opposed to the blankness of the unknown "place I was born," with its void of memory or spiritual connection, we have the rooted—though (or because) exploited and historically suffering—Hopi Indians. The Hopis and their shaman Spider Lady, have abundant memory. They remember their exploitation—"For too long now you have been used by the white man's cavalry. . . . You have tracked down your own kind for the white man's money," Spider Lady says. They remember their legends—of the severed Snake and the splitting and splintering of their people. They understand their goal—to withstand the coming apocalypse, "the end of the Fourth World and the preparation for the Fifth" (234–35)—through spiritual preparation and strength. Wilcox calls this play a "postmodern allegory" of lost origins; it is Shepard's search "for the lost frontier of America" with its biblical Eden of spiritual wholeness and mythic integration.[36] This search leads him to apocalyptic conclusions; the destruction of the West is identified with the "snake" of technology, materialism, and commodification, which can only be overcome through a return to "spirituality," or through the Armageddon that closes the play.

This Armageddon takes place alongside a ritual dance, described by Shepard in great detail. The Hopi snake-dance is to be performed, he writes, as an *actual* ritual practice, with full costume, real chanting and dancing, in clear distinction to the earlier parodies in the play: "Everything about the dance is spiritual and sincere and should not be cartooned" (251). As they dance, soldiers, sent to retrieve the snake as computer, fire into the circle; but the Hopi's spiritual powers protect them. Finally, an apocalyptic flash marks the fulfillment of the Spider Lady's prophecy of imminent world's-end. Extraterrestrials arrive in a streak of blue light, beaming up to salvation only those—the chanting Indians and their converts—who are spiritually connected to the land and its peoples; those whose memory of themselves and their ancestors is drawn from a "river of myth." *Operation Sidewinder* marks a clear shift in Shepard's work from the early plays, where anxieties are found mainly within the central character(s), to his later, more culturally positioned plays, where unease is often a result of cultural and historical factors. This transitional play, overwrought with cultural references and personal dread, attempts an allegorical representation of America through the war between its present materialism (embodied in the military and young countercultural radicals) and its lost spirituality (as imaged in the Hopi Indians and their shaman Spider Lady). Somewhat programmatically, the "authentic" connectedness of the Indians and their ritual performance, is offered by Shepard as a way out of the theater of materialism and violence that are present-day America. Salvation seems to lie in a return to a "simpler" past.

Operation Sidewinder is not really a successful play; in terms of its memory agenda it is in fact a disturbing play. Whereas Shepard's other middle-period plays maintain a productive, and often illuminating, tension between postmodern fragment and the traces of a modernist longing for wholeness or origin, *Operation Sidewinder* tips over into an uncritical nostalgia, "a curious mixture of sentimentality and condescension" in its portrayal of Native Americans, to quote Bigsby.[37] This nostalgia for a rooted spirituality that may well never have existed is directed, rather unfortunately, at the victims of American history—to whom Shepard ascribes an essential identity that removes them from their own history and reduces them to an expression of his longings. It is of this play that John Lahr wrote of Shepard's "yearning for a new history,"[38] of his reversion to the defunct myths, the repressed voices, and the forgotten oppressions of the American past. But rather than expose the experience/consciousness of those whose voices and oppressions have been "forgotten" as does, for example, Suzan-Lori Parks in *The Death of the Last Black Man in the Whole Entire World,* or show the memoried wounds left by these oppressions as does, for example, Heiner Müller in *The Foundling,* Shepard uses the oppressed to create a sentimental dream of redemption. Drawing from the underside of American history—the painful memory of the destruction of America's native population, which forms a subtext to their spiritual superiority—Shepard connects this via the spaceship to a vision of "rebirth" in the future. In *The Unseen Hand,* written the same year as *Operation Sidewinder,* incursions from an irretrievable past (the cowboy brothers) and a fantastic future merge in order to *critique* America's "missing middle," its sterile, facile, and memoryless present. In *Operation Sidewinder,* the past (pre-white America) is uncritically restored, valorized, voided of its own history and held up as a salvationist ideal or, as Bigsby put it, as "an image of the holistic grail" that Shepard sought.[39] The extended ritual at the end of the play—a device used by Shepard to undercut the theatrical frame within which it takes place—and the portrayal of a life-giving spiritual essence in the very peoples American history has destroyed, results in a mythical confusion Shepard is otherwise careful to criticize. Rather than probe and dissect the myths of America, Shepard propagates his own cliché version, resulting in an appropriation of the Hopis history and in a simplistic binary contest between America's past and present.

A similar—yet very differently inflected—mythic "restoration" of the past can be found in one of Shepard's most unusual plays, his Bunyanesque operetta *The Sad Lament of Pecos Bill on the Eve of Killing his Wife* (1976).[40] This is the only play in which Shepard allows himself to explicitly mourn the passing of the myth of the West—this time through the figure of the cowboy—while undercutting sentimentality through the play's distancing balladic form, its folkloric use of fantastic imagery, and by critically tying the death of the West to the materialism of a commercialized culture. *Sad Lament* was written for the San Francisco Opera's bicentennial project. The commemorative frame within which it was to appear, an event marking two hundred years of nationhood, gives a particular edge to Shepard's choice of hero, and to the play's "lament"—and ultimate Brechtian moralizing—on the loss and trivializing of a once potent mythology. Set within a western landscape (signified through the lighting and the openness "in all directions" of the stage), *Sad Lament* is a musical duet between the extravagantly dressed mythic cowboy who settled the West—"dug the mighty Rio Grande / All by hand / All by hand," and his wife Slue Foot Sue, bucked by a bronco on her wedding day until she "cracked the sky / And was forced to duck the moon." Sue is dragged on stage laying on the back of a giant catfish, dead and dressed in white. In a series of tall-tale songs and poetic repetitions that consciously draw on American folkloric elements, the couple retell how Bill "dug out the Badlands" and was acclaimed and famed and "proclaimed throughout the land." At the same time, Bill and Slue Foot Sue lament the contemporary death of their myth—"My legend and time and my myth is forgot." Pecos Bill, larger than life, "bigger than mountains / I'm bigger than time / I'm written in history pages," can't accept the fact of his disappearance from current American memory, "Not even leavin a trace / Not even leavin a trace." The recurring refrain of this short piece—the couple's joint "lament"—asks the audience bluntly:

> Then why is we both dying
> On this land
> Why is we forsaken
> Lost and shamed, forgotten
> Why is we both rotten
> In the memories of man
> In the memories of man
> In the memories of man

The play ends with Bill entreating the audience to think of what they now have instead of a memoried past: "while you go shopping / And watching TV / You can ponder my vanishing shape." Thus Shepard, in celebration of two hundred years of American history, revives the mythic dimension of a past that, he has claimed, is lost to us both as a memoried past and as a productive myth, tying the erasure of memory and mythic cohesion with the commercialization of the American imagination. Through his "sad tale a last time told,"[41] and through the fantastic and celebratory representation of that past, Shepard had perhaps hoped to reverse the losses already incurred. But what happens to an artist when every attempt at authentic recall throws up already commodified, tainted, emptied images of a pasteboard past, creating a suspect history that becomes both an extension and an indictment of the present it can no longer explain? Such a state of affairs may well lead to thoughts about the future, to science fiction, and finally to apocalyptic memories. Carlos Fuentes called this paradoxical mnemonic situation "remembering the future, inventing the past."[42] This situation is brought onto the stage in Shepard's most specific, and polemical, confrontation between future and past, between a world that has rejected memory, and a longing for an irretrievable past, in *The Tooth of Crime*.

"Fence Me with the Present": *The Tooth of Crime*

The Tooth of Crime (1972) has been convincingly discussed by Leonard Wilcox as a postmodern play that thematizes the confrontation between modernism and postmodernism.[43] From the point of view of this book, its interest lies in the way that opposition is inscribed in the play as a conflict between a memoried consciousness and postmodern amnesia, between images of a rooted selfhood and the rule of the shifting image. Written in 1974, while Shepard was living and working in London—thus allowing him a distanced perspective on the cultural sources of America—*The Tooth of Crime* contains many of the themes found in the earlier plays, but more stringently structured into a binary battle, with classical overtones of the fall of the old "king" and the rise of the new. Hoss is a cross between Elvis Presley and a Western gunfighter. He has a fifties manner and a style that combines a modernist faith in art with a traditionalist belief in the sustenance of the past—especially the myths of a no-longer-available West. Past his prime, an establishment figure ruled by managers and markets, Hoss senses that his time as king of the charts, Star Marker, top gun of the violent "turf" of the pop music industry, will soon be over. He is presented as emotionally complex, nostalgic, and out of touch. Crow, the contender for Hoss's title, is a Gypsy Marker and renegade, an outlandish, high-heeled, gum-chewing punk-invader wearing a silver swastika and shark's tooth earring, whose futuristic style and "unheard of" language represent a new departure. He is cold, clear-sighted, detached from any past and ideologically devoid of memory. These two singers represent the styles and discourses—musical, ethical, ideological, aesthetic—of two worldviews, and of past and future.

Often referred to as a "style battle," *Tooth of Crime* is a strangely potent Foucauldian study of identity as formed by the discourse of a period.[44]

Act 1 sets up Hoss's past and memories within the futuristic world he inhabits. Act 2 is dominated by the unhistoried image flashes of Crow, whom Shepard described as a "totally lethal human with no way or reason for tracing how he got that way. He just appeared. . . . He speaks in an unheard-of tongue."[45] Crow has neither a past nor a psychology. He is paradigmatically postmodern, a "blank" screen without the burden of heritage, a "master adapter," whose "image is [his] survival kit."[46] Crow floats, all surface, on the discontinuous discourses of an evolving futuristic idiom not meant for communication, but for action. He will, of course, win the battle. The inevitability of Hoss's defeat is understood from the start; it is a structural inevitability, planted within the mythic situation that the play repeats: the fall of age before youth, of past before future. Hoss's defeat by Crow is the ultimate routing of tradition by a postmodern generation of culture "outlaws" unfettered by ideology, roots, biography, or cultural memory. Unlike *The Unseen Hand,* the future in this play has not come to learn from the past, to capture an immediacy or directness lost in a world of abstraction and mediation. The romantic notion that the past can be harnessed to change the present is avoided in *Tooth.* While Shepard probably identifies with Hoss rather than Crow, and while an audience would find it easier to understand Hoss's language, Crow's verbal inventiveness and physical energy are overwhelming and seductive. He is Shepard's most fully imagined embodiment of a postmodern ethic and style.

Unusually for Shepard, Hoss draws on a coherent and recognizable cultural past. In act 1, while waiting for the Gypsy Marker who has been "sussed" by Eyes, he builds up his courage by placing himself within his own formative influences through ongoing reminiscence. He remembers his early battles as a "sideways killer," a "warrior" filled with "blind fucking courage" (22) and fears that this is his last chance to reach "gold." "I'm gettin' old. I can't do a Lee Marvin in the late sixties. I can't pull that number off" (12). Tamed and managed, admitting that he has become "too old fashioned," Hoss dreams of going against the "codes" of his own industry, like "the big ones. Dylan, Jagger, Townsend. All them cats broke codes" (10). The repeated namings of real cultural icons from the world of music and film, is Shepard's shortcut device for placing both Hoss and later Crow within a firm cultural context. The two major contexts evoked are the music industry of the fifties and the sixties—"You remember the El Monte Legion Stadium?" Hoss asks his manager, Becky, "Ripple Wine? . . . The

Coasters?" (27)—and the mediated mythology of the West. The West holds
a privileged place in this play. According to Shepard, *The Tooth of Crime* "is
built like *High Noon,* like a machine Western. It's gotta work with all its
insides hanging out."[47] This contradictory sentiment seems to imply that the
play imitates the mechanism of the Western voided of its moral center—
similar to Heiner Müller's *Hamletmachine* in which the characters of Shakespeare's *Hamlet* appear but in a world where doubt and tragic necessity have
become irrelevancies, as has heroic status. "I was Hamlet," reads the play's
first line; "here's another illusion to add to your confusion" goes the refrain
of *Tooth*'s first song: both figures begin by denying the authenticity of the
world they are in. Thus Shepard does not claim to have created a Western
in this "machine" version; but he does want to achieve the sense of heightened battle between two forces, "head to head till one's dead" (49). "You
gotta believe, Hoss," Becky says. In what? "Power. That's all there is. The
power of the machine. The Killer Machine" that is (or was) Hoss himself
(27). It is this "power" that will pass on to Crow—despite the opposition of
their views and styles. Just as the possibility of tragic form and rooted identity is lost to "Hamlet" in Müller's postmodern world, so too, Hoss as cowboy and *Tooth* as Western point to their own lack, to what they can no
longer be. It is Shepard's point that the West has become irretrievable in a
world of lost essences, that it has eroded into one more style among many.
But the *longing* for that lost world—a feature Hoss has and Crow doesn't—
can be real.

Hoss is named for the West, as is his sidekick and driver, Cheyenne.
"Cheyenne knows the West," Hoss says. "Born and raised like me"
(22–23). Crow immediately recognizes the cowboy image in Hoss and calls
him "Leathers" throughout. Hoss, who claims "The West is mine" (20),
describes himself early on in the song "Cold Killer" as associated with desert
vistas and cowboy gear, with "snakes in my pocket and a razor in my boot,"
with "silver studs" and "black kid gloves . . . whiplash magic and a rat-
tlesnake tongue" (13). In one passage of the play, Hoss questions Doc, his
dope supplier, as to the ethics of Gypsy "kills." Doc answers with the story
of another renegade, Doc Carter, "the 'Spirit Gun of the West'" who lived
in the shadow of William F. Cody. As he tells the story of Buffalo Bill, the
"fella pallin' it up with the Indians," and of the "true" West, he shoots dope
into Hoss to give him courage for the battle. The inauthenticity of Hoss's
borrowed Western imagery becomes even clearer during an initial conversation between Hoss and Crow. Trying to intimidate Crow, Hoss puts on a
series of "voices." The first is a "kind of cowboy-Western image" that, for
the only time in the play, makes Crow uncomfortable. "A pup like you,"

Hoss says to Crow. "Up in Utah we'd use yer kind fer skunk bait and throw away the skunk."

> *Hoss:* So you gambled your measly grubstake for a showdown with the champ. Ain't that pathetic. I said that before and I'll say it again. Pathetic.
> (*Crow is getting nervous. He feels he's losing the match . . .*)
> You young guns comin' up outa' prairie stock and readin' dime novels over breakfast. Drippin' hot chocolate down yer zipper. Pathetic . . . We'd drag you through the street fer a nickel. Naw. Wouldn't even waste the horse. Just break yer legs and leave ya' fer dog meat.

Crow suggests to Hoss, "Better shift it now, Leathers" (47). Hoss indeed shifts "to a 1920s gangster style" and with that shift loses the only power he might have had over Crow, without even knowing it. "Crow begins to feel more confident now that he's got Hoss to switch," Shepard writes. Crow, having recognized Hoss's strategic, rather than authentic, use of the West, later says, "I'll play flat out to the myth" that Hoss has adopted as his own, but that no longer carries the potency of authentic memory. Hoss, who for years has lived (like the later Elvis Presley) shielded from the world by a select coterie of mediators, is out of touch and isolated. He lives mainly in his memories and in the clichés of the past for which he longs. His alienation from the present becomes clear when he threatens to quit the "game" completely and return to New York, or go to the country to join the cowboys and ranches. "Ain't there any farmers left, ranches, cowboys, open space? Nobody just livin' their life?" he asks. Becky is forced to tell him that he "ain't playin' with a full deck, Hoss. All that's gone. That's old time boogie." The world Hoss no longer knows is a world controlled by the "packs" who are controlled by the gangs: "The gangs and the Low Riders. They're controlled by cross syndicates. The next step is the Keepers" (29). Indeed, it is these two worlds—the no longer existing world of "ranches, cowboys, open space" on the one hand, and futuristic packs and lowriders on the other, of historical memory and nostalgia for a grounded social order, as opposed to an unmemoried faith in "now"—which will do battle in act 2, through Hoss and Crow.[48]

In the three-round "style battle" of act 2—imaged as a boxing bout, with a referee, a scoreboard, and cheerleaders—Crow uses Hoss's past, or the narratives of the past with which Hoss identifies, in order to deconstruct the identity Hoss has constructed. Crow's round 1 attack on Hoss's youth uses well-known motifs of 1950s rock music, the history of the young unloved "shame kid": "the kid with a lisp. The dumb kid. The loser. The runt. The mutt. The shame kid" (53). His seething narrative of masturbation, incarceration, humiliation is indifferent to Hoss's protests that the narrated past is fabricated—"Never did happen!" Indignant at Crow's incursion into his discursive territory, Hoss protests, "History don't cut it. History's in the pocket" (54). But history is not a closed chapter for the postmodern Crow; it is a collection of materials to be used and deployed at will. The referee marks Crow the winner of the round for his brilliant performance and "clean body punches." This, and Hoss's complaint that Crow is all "flash and intensity . . . a fuckin' fish man. Nothin' but flash. No heart," underline Crow's power as a performer and the irrelevance of what Hoss terms "honest pool" in this game. "He was pickin' at a past that ain't even there. Fantasy marks. . . . How can you give points to a liar?" "I don't," answers the referee, "I give 'em to the winner" (56). Crow's powerful moves against Hoss draw on elements immediately recognizable—from song and film—as cultural components of the world of Hoss's past. Thus, Crow's verbal recreation of Hoss's past "against the grain" of Hoss's own self-image remains within the discourse of that image, achieving what Amos Funkenstein has called a "counterhistory." Counterhistories, according to Funkenstein, are a polemical genre of history whose method consists of "the systematic exploitation of the adversary's most trusted sources against their grain" with the aim of distorting the opponent's self image, "his identity, through the deconstruction of his memory."[49] The power of such narratives is their intimate appropriation of the cultural territory they destroy, territory of already written histories. Here, Crow's inversion of Hoss's sources serves to destabilize Hoss's own version. In addition, whether true or not, Crow's rendition of Hoss's life is emotionally effective.

Round 2 of the match gives Hoss the upper hand. His tactic is to insist on playing without the mediation of microphone or music, to play "naked," along some basic existential ground that he considers his own terrain. "You should be past roots on this scale, Leathers," Crow says. "Very retrograde" (57). Hoss's appeal to "roots" is interesting. Rather than pick up Crow's tactics and attack him or his discursive past—of which Hoss knows nothing—he explores the "authentic" past of music, the past Crow lacks. Hoss returns to the origins of American rock music, becoming the living incantation of its roots in jazz and the blues. Drawing on an essentialist vocabulary of origins and a memoried past, he attacks Crow's emptiness—"you miss the origins, milk face." Hoss regresses, embodies the past. His diction modulates into that of the black man's South, evoking music borne of the black slave's "moan," putting on "voices." Crow is untouched by this display and counters, "I'm in a different time. . . . Bring it to now."

Hoss: You'd like a free ride on a black man's back.
Crow: I got no guilt to conjure! (59)

Hoss develops an entire narrative around the birth of the blues, placing himself firmly within that line. His failure will finally result from the inauthenticity of his stance as a spokesman for the sufferings of the past, as a voice of conscience and memoried empathy. "Somethin's funny. Somethin's outa' whack here," the referee says of Hoss's new persona. His skewed aspect is made clear by Crow in the third and final round of their match, in which he claims that Hoss's identification with the past, his seemingly authentic memories of the pain-filled origins of music are only a pose, a performance of pilfered styles, a putting on of "voices." Hoss indeed begins the round by "talking like an ancient delta blues singer," incarnating the past vocally like "a menacing ancient spirit. Like a voodoo man." His body even changes; Shepard tells us that he "grow[s] physically older" (57–58). This appropriation of a performative stance is a new element for Hoss and may account for Crow's aggressive reaction. Michael Vanden Heuvel has identified the worlds of memory and erasure in Shepard's plays, with, respectively, strategies of textuality as opposed to the flights of performance.[50] He suggests that the need to recover memory and history is given through Shepard's stress on textuality, in the figure of Hoss, for example, while the erasure of the past is equated with performance strategies, as in the figure of Crow, whose language is a performance of style rather than content. In this section, Hoss places himself between the "authenticity" of, for example, the Indian witchdoctor and his son in *La Turista* and the playfulness of the performance artist. He "puts on" the past and claims it as his own.

This pose it attacked by Crow in round 3, in which Crow goes after Hoss's cultural sources. He accuses Hoss of being a collage version of the musical influences available in his youth, no more "authentic" than Crow himself, only given to a different set of terms and sounds. In a powerful offensive, he counters Hoss's claim to being part of a rooted tradition by labeling his style a tapestry of borrowed moves, mediated images, clichés. Parodying Hoss's musical education, Crow mocks, "So ya' wanna be a rocker. Study the moves. Jerry Lee Lewis. Buy some blue suede shoes. Move her head like Rod Stewart. Put yer ass in a grind. Talkin' sock it to it, get the image in line." Hoss insists that he's an "original" and can't be sucked into Crow's "jive rhythms"—but Crow has struck a painful chord. "Collectin' the South. Collectin' the blues. . . . Tries trainin' his voice to sound like a frog. Sound like a Dylan, sound like a Jagger. . . . Wearin' a shag now, looks like a fag now" (61–62). Crow's accusation that Hoss is a composite of the cultural forces that formed him—Dylan, Jagger, the same "big ones" Hoss had previously invoked as cats who "broke codes"—is difficult to negate, since the difference between influence and imitation is open to insinuation. Hoss's weakness is his need to be part of a past and a tradition—a need that allows for Crow's attack. Crow's strength is his freedom from the burden of memory or a past. He is indifferent to "depth" mythology; in true postmodernist fashion, he celebrates image over essence—"I believe in my mask—The man I made up is me," as the refrain to "Crow's Song" goes (49–50). Where memory is not valued, its loss can not be missed.

This distinction between a modernist and a postmodernist stance—between a memoried consciousness and one free of the past—is the crux of Hoss's failed reconstruction after he loses the match, and the source of his suicide. Crow agrees, for a price, to "help" Hoss into the winning style, and begins Hoss's reeducation by "re-program[ming] the tapes." He teaches Hoss a new body language, a new emotional language—"get mean. There's too much pity, man. Too much empathy. . . . Just kill with the eyes" (66)— and how to imagine a new "me," without a past, without memory. "Empty your head. . . . Shake off the image," Crow insists (69). The new image Crow offers is of a "blank" screen, an empty surface that will be clothed in style, not textualized memory—"Put on his gestures," Crow says of his fantasy construction of the "new" Hoss, "Wear him like a suit a' clothes." Crow recreates Hoss's memories, describes a different young Hoss: "More dangerous. Takes bigger changes. No doubt. No fear." Hoss tries to adopt this new image of his own past, even speaks his new image in a long monologue of platitudes. But the experience of this "Pitiless. Indifferent" and unmemoried postmodern state of being breaks Hoss and leads to his shouts of "It ain't me! IT AIN'T ME! IT AIN'T ME!!" (71). Hoss chooses to prove his authenticity with "a true gesture that won't never cheat on itself 'cause it's the last of its kind. It can't be taught or copied or stolen or sold. It's mine. An original"—that is, his suicide (74).

Hoss's suicide is, of course, an irrelevant, no longer potent romantic gesture that changes nothing. His body is left to lie midstage as Becky, representing industry's invariable alliance with success and fashion, transfers the symbols of power from the dead "cowboy" to the new punk-rock king. But Hoss's suicide is an important move precisely because of its irrelevancy. It is a resistant gesture filled with the tradition and sources (authentic or not) to which Hoss insists on attaching himself, and thus continues and culminates his side of the battle lines. The importance Shepard attaches to this gesture—and his empathy for Hoss, who "went out in the old style"—are given in a final stage instruction: the suicide must not use "any jive theatrical gimmicks," Shepard writes, "other than the actor's own courage on stage" (74). As in his earlier *La Turista* and *Operation Sidewinder,* "authenticity" is defined by Shepard as antitheatrical, as outside the theater frame, the frame of representation. The ending of *The Tooth of Crime* predicts—or confirms—the victory of surface and style, of the theatrical over the authentic. It is a victory that Shepard understands but cannot accept. In a sense, the defeat of a memoried consciousness by a postmodern discourse of cold surface leaves Shepard nowhere to go but into apocalyptic despair—as becomes apparent in *Action,* written shortly after *Tooth*—or to revert to a form of realism that allows myth and memory to reemerge through more centered conventions, as occurs in Shepard's subsequent work.

Action and the Apocalypse

"I'm getting fucking tired of apocalypses. All I ever hear anymore is apocalypse, apocalypse. What about something with some hope?"[51] These lines, spoken by rock singer Kosmo to his sidekick Yahoodi at the start of Shepard's broadest cultural pastiche, *Mad Dog Blues* (1971), mark Shepard's attempt to find an alternative to the cultural pessimism implicit in many of his earlier plays. Those plays—*Forensic and the Navigators* (1967) and *The Holy Ghostly* (1969), for example—end with predictions of chaos and ruin as smoke and flames spread from the stage to the audience, erasing both the world and its theatrical representation. The earlier *Icarus's Mother* (1965) ends with orgasmic visual and verbal fireworks and descriptions of cosmic conflagration. Overtly political apocalyptic motifs occur as well in *Shaved Splits* (1969), *The Unseen Hand* (1970), and *Operation Sidewinder* (1970). Michael Bloom claims that this preoccupation with apocalypse was not unusual in American literature of the 1960s. Faced with a society "that suppressed the awareness of danger, Shepard, like many other writers, turned to apocalypse as the only way to describe the turmoil of American life . . . the feeling of betrayal, the grief about America."[52] Perhaps tired of this trend and of his own misgivings, Shepard allows all of Yahoodi's playful "visions"—his waking dreams—to come to life: his invocations of Marlene Dietrich and Mae West, for example. But when Yahoodi draws from his cultural stock of visuals the image of "A giant American bald eagle flying through a smoke-filled sky with the world clutched in his talons. He flies higher and higher until he can't fly anymore and then he lets the world drop," Kosmo rebels and declares a yearning for hope. "It's up to you, boy," Yahoodi says.[53] Indeed, *Mad Dog Blues,* part rock musical, part fantasy adventure-tale, assembles a cast of bright, suggestive characters from America's film and folklore cultural heritage—Marlene Dietrich, Mae West, Captain Kidd, Jesse James, Paul Bunyan—and ends with them all singing the rallying song "Home." This foray into "hope" and cultural affirmation is, however, short-lived. *Mad Dog Blues* precedes by only three years Shepard's darkest play on the erasure of society, community, and memory and on the menacing link between the loss of a rooted past and the threat of a destroyed future: *Action*.

   Action is Shepard's most radical study of an unmemoried state of being. Written in London, directly after *The Tooth of Crime,* the play reverses the *jouissance* and performative energy found in that postmodern pastiche of contemporary America and replaces it with stasis and void. *Action* offers us a world in which memory no longer exists; it is a world born of Crow's victory, but devoid of his energizing emotional indifference. Not only has the past been erased in this play, the present too shifts from one depleted movement to the next, without carryover, without memoried accumulation. Unlike some of the earlier plays, which represent anxieties of erased or lost memory in images of cosmic destruction (in *Icarus's Mother,* or *Operation Sidewinder*), *Action* is set *after* the apocalypse, in a world of traces and psychic constriction. Whereas "world's end" was previously performed by Shepard in spectacular terms, as climactic disasters either approaching or already besetting a society, here the catastrophe has moved inward. *Action* differs from Shepard's earlier imagistic plays in being less dependent on American pop culture and pastiche. It also differs from his later "family" plays in that it is devoid of anything but the most fragmentary realism. "It's very special to me," Shepard wrote of *Action* in a letter to Joseph Chaikin. "In writing it I found a whole new area."[54] Indeed, *Action* is unusual in Shepard's oeuvre. It is his most "theoretical" play, Shepard in Peter Handke's clothing, an analytical Shepard with overtones of Beckett and Pinter and undertows of poststructuralist theory. Unlike *Tooth,* with its *High Noon* shoot-out structure and two strong protagonists, the ironically titled *Action* is a plotless, almost static, group play sapped of any real activity. Postapocalyptic and deeply alarming, it withholds any explanation for the existing crisis or for the central "event" of the play—some sort of commemoration. No one seems to remember what or why they are celebrating, and though a crucial book is obsessively circulated among the characters, no one manages to read aloud from it—since none can remember where they last "left off" reading, and thus none can "find their place." The unread book becomes an ever-present center of loss and displacement, parallel to the lost and forgotten past/present that is the play's implicit theme.

Visually, Shepard presents us with a dichotomized stage, split into dark and light halves. On the upper, dark half, a Christmas tree with tiny blinking lights, set on a small table, accompanies the entire play, recalling the foundation story of Christ's birth. In the darkness of the remote upstage area, these lights resemble random stars flickering in an empty black cosmos, an image that gathers strength as the play develops. On the lower, lit half of the stage, we find the reduced remains of a realistic salon with simple table and chairs, coffee cups and plates. Running above the middle of the stage, dividing the darkness from the light, is a clothesline. The room has no doors or windows; characters enter and exit through the upstage darkness, dissolved and reformulated by a pale yellow-and-white light "which pulses brighter and dimmer every ten minutes or so, as though the power were very weak" (125). Weakly powered, stringently dichotomized, this strange stage is both hallucinatory and a semiotic puzzle.

The four characters, two women and two identically dressed men, almost constantly present on stage, are described in the same dichotomized fashion as the stage itself, eluding any grounded locality or historical context. The two men, Shooter and Jeep, wear identical long dark overcoats and heavy boots; both have shaved heads. They reflect each other as do Reader and Listener in Beckett's *Ohio Impromptu,* mirror images with opposed functions. And (to continue the comparison with Beckett) like Didi and Gogo in *Waiting for Godot,* Jeep remembers—useless, odd pieces from a mostly forgotten past—while Shooter forgets almost everything. The two women, Liza and Lupe, have only background roles (as is usual in Shepard's plays until *Fool for Love*), but visually, they continue the stage dichotomy, dressed in summer clothes as opposed to the men's winter coats, dressed in city heels and sandals, as opposed to the men's lumberjack shirts and boots. Thus, the stage sets up ever-multiplying divisions and intersecting oppositions that undercut any "grounded" stable reality. At the same time, it arouses expectations: of celebration, of family (there seem, after all, to be two couples), of some decoding of the apocalyptic riddle, of some *action* that might pull the opposed elements together into relation to each other. Expectations that remain unfulfilled.

Apocalypse is *Action*'s underlying image. Never explicitly discussed, the occurrence of some cataclysm is signified through absences and disconnected hints. Food is scarce, water must be fetched from a well, there is no "outside" to this claustrophobic "inside" world, and memory has all but disappeared. Moreover, the five passages randomly quoted from the unread book hint at a cosmic catastrophe. "Were we past the part where the comet exploded?" Liza asks; "Wasn't it around where the space ship had collided with the neutron?" Lupe asks. Or had they perhaps last left off "near the place where the sky rained fire?" These unexplained references, which sound like quotes from a work of science fiction, are the only hints we get to the nature of some disaster that underlies the noncohering traces of civilization left on stage. The disaster itself is never experienced. The vision we imagine might be found in the unread book is perhaps like the one supplied at the end of *Icarus's Mother*—where orgasmic devastation is sensually reflected through the sounds and colors of exploding fireworks and airplanes. Parallel to that explosion, a frenzied monologue describes an inconceivable eruption in lush, theatrical terms:

> a recognized world tragedy of the greatest proportion and exhilaration to make the backs of the very bravest shudder . . . lighting up the air with a gold tint and a yellow tint and smacking the water so that waves go up to five hundred feet in silver white and blue. Exploding the water for a hundred miles in diameter around itself. Sending a wake to Japan. An eruption of froth and smoke and flame blowing itself up over and over again. Going on and on. (79)

Such embodied destruction is also theatricalized in *Forensic and the Navigators* and *The Holy Ghostly*. In all of these plays, devastation is passionate, depicted through excess and theatrical contagion. In *Action,* on the contrary, all excess is drained, all passion is gone. Smoke and flame give way to emptied signifiers that the play assembles but never decodes. The fullness of terror—crashing planes, tidal waves—is replaced by traces and remains, the unremembered and unread. The apocalypse has been turned into signs of lack and loss; and it has been inscribed in a text that can no longer be read or used or recovered as a narrative.

The sense of epigonism, of coming *after* (in this case) a catastrophic break that has split the sign from the signified, is central to this play. Both the stage and the characters of *Action* are stranded in permanent fragmentation, alienated from any source of meaning. From the start, the dramatic text disintegrates into a series of gestural "scenes" that neither move a "story" nor interrelate. Characters smash chairs, imitate bears, dance a softshoe. Jeep pours water over his hands and dissects a fish, Shooter locks himself into an armchair from which he can no longer move. The actions accumulate but never converge. We seem to be viewing a collection of false starts, of phenomenological units that never *refer* to anything. Lack of reference—the play ends with the line, "I had no references for this"—implicates a world without causal progressions or a memoried ground; we are always beginning over, without memory or past. The first line of the play

reads "I'm looking forward to my life," as though that life were only beginning now, without a past on which to draw. David Savran has written that
Action depicts "a space of separation and crisis" such "that it effaces its own
origin[,] introducing a breach between past and present."[55] We have here
an "after" world whose ground has been so thoroughly dislocated that no
way of discussing a precrisis time, or recalling the origin of the catastrophe,
remains.[56]

Despite the fragment and disintegration implicit in this description, the
play is filled with traces of a once-recognizable and centered world. It enacts
what might be described as the drained and deformed remains of a communal ritual celebration. There is a turkey—a hard thing to come by, we're
repeatedly told. There is the eating: three of the four characters eat. There
is the seemingly significant blinking tree (never referred to by the characters). And above all, there is the book. "Maybe we should read," is one of
the first lines of the play. The book passes from one character to the other
as each seeks the "place" where they last left off. This pattern of searching,
quoting a random passage, giving up and passing the book on to the next
character continues for most of the play. It is a constant background activity. The five cataclysmic passages quoted from the book and the dozen variations of the statement that they cannot "find their place" become the only
consistent text in the play. The juxtaposition of random acts of performance
and violence with the characters' incapacity to "find their place" suggests a
correlation between the loss or "displacement" of a text—the loss of a
shared "scripture"—and the incoherent "actions" of the play.

Although the cataclysm described in the book is never verified, the
position of that book at the feast table, around which all gather for communal eating and reading, in front of the ever-blinking Christmas tree, marks
the book as a form of scripture, as a type of "Bible"—a foundation text that
normally functions to transmit and thus sustain the memory of a culture.
The characters' lapses of memory echo their inability to remember where
they were in the book. Shooter goes out for a chair but returns having forgotten why he went. When Lupe asks if anyone remembers "the days of
mass entertainment" (138), no one does. Shooter does not remember eating. Jeep, the only one with any memory, speaks of a collective past that no
one but he can comprehend. Shepard's "forgotten" pasts here differ from
his earlier cowboys, Indians, or rock singers. Jeep recalls some of the central
figures, and the central national crisis, against which American identity was
formed and through which it cohered: Lincoln, Whitman, and the Civil
War. Of Walt Whitman he says, "he was a great man."

> *Lupe:* I don't know anything about him . . .
> *Jeep:* He expected something from America. He had this great expectation.
> *Lupe:* I don't know. I never heard about it.
> *Jeep:* He was like what Tolstoy was to Russia.
> *Liza:* I don't know much about it either.
> *Jeep:* A Father. A passionate father bleeding for his country.

None of the others can recall Whitman or Tolstoy or even Lincoln "all dark and somber . . . the face of war in his eyes." Jeep's uncontextualized memories of an essential American past alert us to the erasure of communal, and thus national, memory. The "reality" of Lincoln or Whitman, the fact that "Walt was a witness" to the wounded, wet soldiers lying in every doorway of Civil War America (135)—these moving pieces of historical information cannot reverberate in an unmemoried and thus unhistoried world, where the past no longer maintains a collective identity.

More explicitly than in any of his other plays, *Action* suggests a connection between the longing for coherence and the reality of its loss, between the fragments and their missing mold. In *Action* we find a "tragic" correlation between the loss of a shared foundation text, a rooted and memoried originary narrative, and the chaotic, incommensurate, and disconnected postmodern world of the play—a world of textual fragmentation, of montage, indeterminacy, and unbearable randomness. The instability of the self and the emphasis on performance over representation are, of course, typical of postmodern drama. But even more pertinent for *Action* is postmodernism's opposition to foundational philosophies. Ideologically, postmodernism differs from the modern in its relation to "metaconcepts," its "incredulity" toward what Jean-François Lyotard has famously called the "master narratives" of modernism—whether liberal or Marxist.[57] Such *grands récits* had provided universal guiding principles that validated the social bond and offered a common purpose for action. That is, within them, local actions appealed to broader implicit narratives (such as humanism or nationalism) as ways of connecting past formations to present actions, in the name of a credible (future) goal.

That connecting context, the thread that ties history and memory to a vision of the future, is precisely what is no longer available in a postmodern world; and for Shepard the breakdown of these organizing narratives is both a prod toward stylistic freedom and a constant source of anxiety. *Action* might be usefully discussed in terms of the liberal social "utopia" outlined by Richard Rorty, whose career as a philosopher parallels Shepard's as a dramatist; thus both certainly drew from a common discursive and experiential pool. Rorty is America's foremost representative of a philosophical antifoundationalist position. He champions contemporary philosophy as emancipatory, freeing societies from constricting nationalist and historical self-definitions. Liberal societies, he claims, should be seen as historical contingencies without essence or foundations, without transhistorical meaning. The individual too, for Rorty, is denied any universal human nature, or moral absolutes. Following Lyotard, Rorty advocates a world free of "first definitions" and coercive metanarratives. His image of this free society is a nonideological plurality of voices within a loose, unessentialized cultural "conversation." The citizens of his "liberal utopia," writes Rorty, "would be people who had a sense of the contingency of their language of moral deliberation, and thus of their consciences, and thus of their community."[58] Such a rationalist liberal community would proceed not upon epistemological criteria, but rather through specific "tasks," through limited, ad hoc practices—through a set of not necessarily connected "actions." In this view, no ideology or foundation text would restrict or define the community, or the individuals within it, who would seek nonexclusionary "solidarity" through pragmatic forms of negotiation and persuasion.

The optimistic side of such nonhierarchical social thought is paralleled by Shepard through the emphasis in most of his plays on diversity, on parallel activities, on the lack of determination, and on performance itself. But, clearly, the emotional correlative of such an "ideal" foundationless society is, for Shepard, postmodernist angst. "What is a community?" Jeep asks at one point in the play—a question none of the characters can really answer. "You know. It doesn't need words," Lupe finally suggests. "Just a kind of feeling" (138). But community—the very subject of Rorty's social inquiry—is very much missing in *Action*. The four characters have little in common. From dress to memory to activity, each seems to exist in random isolation; the only link is the Book—wherein they can no longer place themselves. Shepard's anxiety in face of Rorty's ungrounded world is extended to the depiction of his unbearably anxious characters. Without foundations it is not only difficult to define community, but to define a self. "We're not completely stranded like that," says Jeep, in reaction to Shooter's story about a guy he once knew who feared his own body, spied on it, kept watch over it until one day the body killed him and continued to "walk around." "[I]f we ran into this body," Jeep wants to know, "could we tell it was vacant?" What are the criteria by which we would *know*, in face of a world devoid of categorical and binding fundaments? "You'd know," Jeep concludes.

I'd know. I mean with us, we know. We know. We hear each other. We hear our voices. We know each other's voice. We can see. We recognize each other. We have a certain— We can tell who's who. We know our names. We respond. We call each other. We sort of— We— We're not completely stranded like that. . . . It's not like that. (139)

But Shepard is not convinced. Rorty's utopian vision of free and equal citizens of a liberal society devoid of grounding or primal text to which we might refer in order to "know"—to validate, to certify—the meaning of community, or how to recognize a "self," is, for Shepard, a vision of chaos and terror. In this light, the omnipresent "book"—with its hint of history and myth, and its placement at the center of the play—suggests the absence of a metanarrative that might "shore up the ruins" and provide some form of grounding to social and individual identity. Indeed, it is this absence that the play enacts and whose loss it laments. Deprived of a cohesive metanarrative, of a memoried continuum that allows for innate essence, the figures cannot "place" themselves or find points of reference for their actions. This loss is paralleled by the play itself, which refuses to cohere as a text, constantly fragmenting and shifting focus. In the end, what remains is indeed a plurality of separate voices and disconnected actions, like so many random atoms on a split, dimly lit, anxiety-filled stage.

This image of disconnectedness underlies the play's final monologue, spoken by an isolated Jeep on an unresponsive stage. Jeep's monologue differs from Shooter's earlier stories—the parable of the moth, or the story of the body that killed the man within it—in that it is autobiographical, the one time in the play that a character betrays a concrete past. For no apparent reason, Jeep begins to tell his fragmented memory of family—"Once I was in a family. . . . I lived in different houses. . . . I found myself in schools. In cars"—and how it all "changed" when he got arrested. That traumatic experience revealed to him his "true position" in the world. The subsequent story of his trial and imprisonment (we're never told for what) expresses Jeep's (and Shepard's?) ontological panic on finding himself objectified into a collection of scars, marks, the "lines in my fingers. Hair. Eyes." He fears being taken away by "something bigger," powerless in a world of disparate details, permanent fragmentation, missing references: "I was up for grabs. . . . My frame of reference changed" (144). The claustrophobic prison experience evokes panic: "the walls were moving in. It was like a sweeping kind of terror that struck me." As the memory expands, his body begins to shake; the recalled panic turns into a present panic, fear of those walls conflated with fear of the space he now inhabits. Shepard's stage instruction make this clear:

Jeep begins to move around the stage. The words animate him as though the space is the cell he's talking about but not as though he's recalling a past experience but rather that he's attempting his own escape from the space he's playing in. (145)

Even in the one memoried moment of the play, Shepard rejects the idea of grounded recall and insists that this past memory of lost freedom is a present, bodily experience. The terrifying knowledge of his impotence is both narrated, in the past tense, and experienced by Jeep in the present, in his shaking, frightened body. He looks at the theater walls, at the "walls" of the room he's in, into the walls of his memory, and they all collapse into "a sweeping kind of terror" of incomprehension and total loss.[59] Past and present cannot be separated, the text of theater and the text of life interpenetrate, no separation of realms remains. "Everything disappeared," he says in the last lines of the play. "I had no idea what the world was. I had no idea how I got there or why or who did it. *I had no references for this*" (145; emphasis added).

This enigmatic final scene, with its sense of unreferenced fragment and lost context, is reinscribed on a stage whose original reduced realism has now disintegrated into a visual field of dispersal and alienation. While Jeep speaks, Lupe, standing on a chair, strings up wet laundry that slowly makes its way above the stage, dividing it in half; Shooter, hidden beneath an upturned armchair, arms flapping from the sides, rocks "like a headless turtle" (143); while on the table are the remains of the fish Jeep previously scaled and carved. Each character is oblivious of the others, continuing "in their own rhythm" as though moving in parallel universes. Common objects—fish, laundry, armchair—transform into a world of stranded objects, stranded within the emptiness of contextless action, of forgotten reference. Thus the play ends with a set of unreferenced and unrelated objects and actions, denying any common source or foundation; and with the explicitly expressed pain of living in a world, and in a self, devoid of grounded meaning, of any stable, shared memory.

A Reemerging Buried Memory

Shepard's theatricalization of the tension between memory and forgetting undergoes a striking change with his stylistic move toward greater realism. Inversely, we might say that Shepard's greater realism reveals a need to revise his vision of a rootless, unmemoried world, through a form that would allow greater stability. I have claimed that an implicit erasure of historical memory and a sense of lost origins underlie Shepard's postmodern tactics. In the "family plays," beginning with *The Curse of the Starving Class* (1977) and especially with *Buried Child* (1978), Shepard does something about these losses: he goes out to recover them. Instead of marking the sites of memory's disappearance into commodification or amnesia, Shepard embarks on a search for its buried roots, testing the soil and knotted family bonds from which an American (and personal) memory have vanished. Instead of iconic and depthless figures, we find in these later plays characters with recognizable (if complex and unstable) relations to each other. Instead of the earlier sense of collective amnesia and atomized parallel existences, the individual is reinscribed into a bloodline, into an almost tribal identity from which there is no escape. "We've got a pact," Eddie says in *Fool for Love*. "You know we're connected, May. We'll always be connected. That was decided a long time ago."[60] These plays seek new routes toward an emotional recovery of the past—an uncovering of hidden secrets, a laying to rest of past guilt; and they seek these routes through more conventional dramatic strategies of integration.

Shepard's plays about the American family—especially *Buried Child, Fool for Love,* and *Lie of the Mind*—turn away from the floating icons and parallel universes of his earlier work, and turn *back* toward the root-themes of more traditional American realist drama: homecoming, heritage, dynastic curse, and the intertwined fate of the clan. They retain, however, Shepard's earlier fixation on memory. Memory is here both highlighted and *reformed* in terms that slip out of postmodern discourse; memory has a location, and it is recoverable. The past, as Freud had theorized, may be buried and hidden, but it is never lost, never irretrievable. "Homecoming"—with its localization of "home" in the homestead and the blood tie—promises a measure of fated restoration. Vince will inherit Dodge (*Buried Child*), May and Eddie will eternally repeat their ritual of connectedness (*Fool for Love*), Travis will escape his desert of forgetting and come "home" to (at least a part of) the family he had lost—in the screenplay Shepard wrote for Wim Wenders, *Paris, Texas.*

Buried Child is the clearest example of such recovery. Thematically grounded in forgetting, the play unfolds toward rejuvenation and the recall of a linear inheritance. In the falling-apart midwestern farmhouse of that play, everyone forgets. Neither Dodge nor Tilden can remember his grandson/son Vince. Dodge, the nearly decrepit patriarch, has forgotten everything. "What's to remember?" he asks. "A long line of corpses! There's not a living soul behind me. Not a one. Who's holding me in their memory? Who gives a damn about bones in the ground?" (112). The paradigmatic scene of ineluctable tribal memory occurs when Vince tries to escape from the repression and rejection of his memoryless family by driving off "clear to the Iowa border." During that attempted escape from memory (or forgetting) and identity (or its loss) he discovers the futility of flight. Having literally turned his back on his family and origins, he discovers in his reflection in the windshield a confirmation of genetic memory, proof that family is a tie written into the flesh.

> As though I was looking at another man. As though I could see his whole race behind him. . . . His face became his father's face. Same bones. Same eyes. Same nose. Same breath. And his father's face changed to his Grandfather's face. And it went on like that. Changing. Clear on back to faces I'd never seen before but still recognized. Still recognized the bones underneath. (130)

This is the "face inside his face" that Tilden had previously recognized in Vince (100); it is the "genetic memory" that wreaks such havoc in *Curse of the Starving Class* and that finally overcomes forgetting and allows reintegration in *Buried Child*. "In *Buried Child*," writes Una Chaudhuri, "the figures of home and family become the site for an exceptional homecoming—that of the dramatist."[61] Samuel Shepard Rogers VII, who bore the name of seven generations of ancestors, and who changed his name and persona at the beginning of his career, returns, with this play, to the rooted bloodline and representational literary terrain within which the past had traditionally been inscribed in American culture.

Fool for Love continues this image of blooded linkage by giving May and Eddie, lovers in a transient roadside motel, a common genetic root that will always keep them connected. Their common father, the Old Man, may—as Shepard writes in the stage instructions—exist only in their minds, but his physical appearance on stage creates a site of constant, unresolved tension between the mythic and the real. Memory is placed center stage in this play, and memory always has its versions. The three retellings of the past do not vie for our belief. In a *Rashomon* of subjective remembrance, all of the versions coexist, and all point to the inescapability of a shared past and to the fateful hold of such ties, no matter how difficult or even horrifying. *Lie of the Mind* too creates knotted blood ties "as immutable as a tribal code," to quote Frank Rich.[62] Amnesia here becomes a form of release from the lock of personality and upbringing. Mind-damaged, language-damaged, full of forgetting, Beth finds release from one form of connectedness through her contact with another—the brother of her battering husband, whose face is also inside the new lover's face. Even in leaving her past, Beth (with Shepard) maintains a remembering link.

Shepard has said that he was led to this new focus on family as a way out of "the instinctive stuff" he had spent ten years writing within "an experimental maze—poking around, fishing in the dark."[63] His "fishing" in the exploded forms of postmodernism is not abrogated in these more controlled plays, with their discipline of linear development, their historied characters and language that moves plot. These are indeed the elements of a grounded reality that have little in common with the parallel worlds, pastiche conflations, imagistic indirection, randomness, and incursions of floating icons that filled his earlier stages. With this turn toward a greater rootedness through more traditional dramatic conventions, Shepard does leave the landscape of postmodern indeterminacy to return to the living room and backyard where Willy Lowman played out his alienation from the dreams of America—but with a difference. Shepard's "homecoming" remains filled with unease, fearful of cliché, fully cognizant of the lessons of his postmodern portrayals of America. The historicity of the institution of the family in these later plays, writes Chaudhuri, is shown, paradoxically, to have "arisen out of the *decline* of the family—from immemorial myth to stereotype steeped in oblivion."[64] With this knowledge in hand, Shepard cannot sustain a simplistic return to the deterministic realist form that previously contained the theme of "family." Indeed, Shepard never merely appropriates realism's package-deal of form and worldview. He expands the one and, to an extent, undermines the other. In these plays of motels and decrepit farmhouses, with their versions of the past and their magical corn, we find a "mixed application of the realistic and the unrealistic," writes William Demastes, involving both "flesh and blood actions" and a mythic "movement beneath or beyond consistent characterization."[65] There is a hope in the unresolved tensions within these plays that the opening of boundaries found in postmodernism might imbue the "homecoming" with a new view of the self and of America. Michael Vanden Heuvel insists on Shepard's attempt to "ironize the realist framework, and thereby suggest that within even the status quo lies the potential for transformation and difference, the possibility of 'another kind of world.'"[66] As such, these family plays are, for Shepard, an optimistic departure from postmodernism's obsession with cultural commodification, historical amnesia, and political erasure, without being an about-face.[67] In them, Shepard rejects his own alienation and anxieties of unrootedness in favor of a mythical search—even if not always successful—for intimations of origins, and for a more situated personal and national memory.

Chapter 5

Suzan-Lori Parks and the Empty (W)hole of Memory

[B]ecause so much of African-American history has been unrecorded, dismembered, washed out, one of my tasks as playwright is to—through literature and the special strange relationship between theater and real-life—locate the ancestral burial ground, dig for bones, find bones, hear the bones sing, write it down.

—Suzan-Lori Parks, "Possession"

Sam Shepard's theater work began at the fringes and moved toward a more central position in terms of both style and popularity. There is, however, a sense in which Shepard has always spoken from a well "centered" posture: identified with a Midwest terrain, with a mid-1950s popular imagination, with a centered masculinity (some feminists have accused him of recruiting "women as handmaidens";[1] some gay activists call him homophobic).[2] Shepard was attacked as racist by African-American students at Yale who in 1968 protested his "stereotyped" black revolutionaries in *Operation Sidewinder* and prevented the play's production at the school.[3] While these ideological reactions to Shepard's work are peripheral and wrongheaded, they highlight the perception—especially among those who feel marginalized—that, for all his formal experimentation, Shepard speaks from an automatic and safe "center." There is no real reason to compare Sam Shepard and Suzan-Lori Parks. Intuition warns us, in fact, that they are quite unlike: of different generations and different genders, they were brought up in different landscapes (although Parks, like Shepard, grew up as a soldier's child, moving with her father's postings from base to base), to families of different colors. Both write a rich and idiomatic American language, but their idioms are differently inflected since their ears were trained by different voices, and their memories—even the memories *of* their memories—emerge from very different sources. What they do share, from the point of view of this book, is a grievous sense of rupture from a grounded past—albeit ruptures very differently inflicted. They also share a postmodern dramaturgy that summons the past(s) and seeks identity, through an appeal to memory and its erasure.

155

Suzan-Lori Parks is a young black American woman (born 1963)[4] whose historical and personal "memory" of America is very different from her white male compatriot, Shepard. Hers is the inherited memory of enslavement, marginalization, discrimination, and a systematically erased past. Parks, who has so far written eight (produced) plays, various essays, and a screenplay that became Spike Lee's film *Girl 6,* has often protested against being identified first as a black playwright, then as a woman playwright, and only last as a "theater person" and artist. "Why does everyone think that white artists make art and black artists make statements?" she has asked. "Why doesn't anyone ever ask me about *form?*"[5] Her poetic and highly original work certainly calls for aesthetic appraisal; but it would be disingenuous and diminishing to pretend that Parks does not represent an additional element of the American imagination: one spiced precisely by her position as a black urban woman who writes about black experience in a language and voice shaped by cultural forces that had little or no impact on Shepard.

Parks's dramatic terrain is transhistorical and intertextual. Her plays contain figures drawn from history and myth or appropriated from other texts. Sections of the farce *Our American Cousin* (1851), the play Lincoln was watching when he was assassinated, are, for example, inserted into *The America Play* (1993), and both this play and *Imperceptible Mutations in the Third Kingdom* (1989) contain footnotes that are either quoted within the spoken text or appended to the dialogue in the manner of an academic text. A theater of voice and image, her plays, like those of Heiner Müller and Thomas Bernhard, are devoid of scenic descriptions or explicit stage directions. These attributes, together with a fluid sense of time and place, a multidirectional structure of events, the abundant use of repetitions and revisions, all exhibit a well-integrated postmodern sensibility. Robert Brustein, who has called Parks, admiringly, "a writer with more on her mind than race," noted that "she is as much a product of Western postmodernism as of black consciousness"[6]—an assessment that tallies with Parks's own statements. Parks's writing combines a highly personal poetic voice, almost hermetic in its richness of imagery, together with what she terms "epic stakes"—that is, political potential. Her characters ("They are not *characters,*" Parks writes, "They are *figures, figments, ghosts, roles*")[7] "are *signs* of something and not people just like people we know," signs that are socially representative rather than narratively unique. "We're a people who are often honored or damned because of the actions of one of our group," Parks said in interview. "One of us stands for all of us. Those are epic stakes."[8] Unlike Adrienne Kennedy, whose intimate, spectral plays so strongly inspired her, Suzan-Lori Parks's dreamscape, writes Alisa Solomon, "is specifically situated in history and culture."[9] Hers is a collective voice speaking for a people and its experience in broad mythic tones and incantatory rhetoric, combining facts and visions on an ever transforming—mutating—stage. Parks's theatrical inventiveness and her language of loss and mourning (for a forgotten history, a stunted memory) have created new ways of experiencing memory in the theater. Parks has shaped a unique theatrical vocabulary out of a profound sense of absence, a vocabulary that, in stylistic terms, might be compared with the work of Heiner Müller—who, in contrast, works with a surfeit of memory from which he cannot liberate himself. Both draw from a variety of sources and idioms, fusing the epic and poetic, the historical and the fantastic in a typically postmodern rejection of generic integrity, and in a frenzied need to "represent" the present through the losses of the past.

Longing for a lost past is the underlying impetus of Parks's plays; forgetting and erasure are her overt themes. These are inscribed into her dramas through a powerful set of strategies, foremost among which is the attempt to induce the past to reappear through a structure of repetition. The same scenes recur, the same lines repeat, a nonnarrative accumulation of the same images—each time with slight variations—is the grillage upon which her plays are hung. This is a conscious and significant procedure. Parks has explained that her dramatic technique is based on principles of jazz construction, through which her "memory agenda" is shaped into a theater poetics. In jazz, as Parks puts it, "we are not moving from A-B but rather, for example, from A-A-A-B-A. Through such movement, we refigure A. And if we wish to call the movement FORWARD PROGRESSION, which I think it is, then we refigure the concept of forward progression."[10] This progression through repetition (the repeating of A) culminates in the *revision* of A after it passes through B. Parks's use of "rep & rev" (as she calls this strategy) is more than just a structural borrowing from a musical language; it is an ideological component of her writing. To "repeat and revise" is to reject linearity and causal rationality in favor of a spatially open view of time and process. It is to favor multidirectionality and re-visions of a "past" (the past of the early A, for example) as definitions of progress. This is the practice that Gilles Deleuze has termed "clothed repetition," a mode that mirrors mechanical repetition but challenges its pretence to some essential reality by adding variation, slight shifts, that deny sameness and proclaim the principle of difference.[11] When, for example, variants of the line "You should write that down and you should hide it under uh rock" recur in *The Death of the Last Black Man in the Whole Entire World* (1992)—and they recur often—each repetition contains the trace of the form and context of its previous use. Each repetition also rethinks the past utterance through its variation. The past is thus contained and transformed through its subsequent variation. Through this procedure, the line expands, becoming a "semiotic machine" of accumulating, even clashing, connotations—rather than being "emptied out" as a mere mechanical refrain. This type of "forward progression" is used by Parks, as we will see, in order to excavate a lacking, and irretrievable, past.

For Parks, the principle of "rep & rev" is a recuperative maneuver aimed at overcoming fixity, or stereotyping, through the returns of memory. To "recuperate" implies a recovery, a saving of the past—perhaps as Walter Benjamin meant to save the past by recalling it and returning it to the present "at a moment of danger."[12] Benjamin believed that the past *could* be repossessed in the aid of a present need. But what of a past that is severely, perhaps fatally lost, forgotten, interred? Its memory, Parks believes, must then be invented, or rather—*made* to happen. "I'm working theater like an incubator to create 'new' historical events," Parks writes. "I'm remembering and staging historical events which, *through their happening on stage,* are ripe for inclusion in the canon of history."[13] In a foundationless postmodern world, where time and experience do not accumulate progressively, theater can become a retroactive restorative procedure in the sense that it *creates* memories no longer available to their rightful owners. Parks compares her stage to an "incubator" where not quite fully born incarnations from the past are nurtured into existence and through their staging are "born" as part of a collective memory. This theatrical midwifery is a response to the challenge posed by the paucity of actual black American memory. In an interview with Steven Drukman, Parks elaborated on the role that absence plays in her creative process, the extent to which absence is a spur to her imagination. The passage is worth repeating:

> *Drukman:* Let's talk about history . . . Toni Morrison said in *Playing in the Dark* that what she calls American Africanism are the ways in which the Africanist presence or persona is constructed in the United States by literature, and the imaginative uses that this fabricated presence has served. Now it seems that when you make a stage figure or character, you start from that point, from the fabricated presence. In other words, you assume that the figure is a historical construction.
> *Parks:* From the fabricated . . .
> *Drukman:* From the fabricated presence.
> *Parks:* From the fabricated absence, actually. It's a fabricated absence . . . It's the story that you're told that goes, "once upon a time you weren't here." (*Laughter*) You weren't here and you didn't do shit! And it's that, that fabricated absence.[14]

Parks coins the phrase "fabricated absence" in an almost reflex reaction against the conventional formulation repeated by Drukman, against the automatism of jargoned language. But the term is also precise: for Parks, history has "constructed" not a black historical presence in America, but a hole; and from within that "hole," that negative presence—the Great Hole of History—Parks's writing gathers its strength and emerges.

Parks's plays evince a deep self-awareness of the language used. Her relation to language is closely connected to the "task" she has set herself: to restore, to re-create, to make "present" through performance an irretrievable black American memory. To "hear the bones sing" and "write it down." Parks is aware that the consciousness she "chronicles" is one that was drained of its "original" language, and thus of a means by which to remember the past. Her figures thus often seek to retrieve a time before their affliction by a "foreign" language, a language that was a deformation of the language of the oppressors. "[B]ack tuh that," says one of the choral figures in Last Black Man. "Yes . . . Skirtin back tuh that . . . Far uhway. Uhway tuh where they dont speak thuh language and where they don't want tuh. Huh. Go on back tuh that" (114). That is: back to "Columbus. Before," before the imposition of a syntax and a grammar that razed the past and put Parks's figures "in their place" of linguistic, and political, subservience. Linda Ben-Zvi has suggested that Parks's writing "stages the process of linguistic deformation itself, the imposition of language and culture."[15] The result of this reflexivity is a language that fights against its own sanction, that speaks its historical deformity while reaching back to a time before historical inscription. This doubleness gives shape to a unique form of spoken/written language in her plays. "Saint mines," says Black Man of the watermelon attached to him in Last Black Man. "Saint mines. Iduhnt it. Nope: iduhnt. Saint mines cause everythin I calls mines got uh print uh me someway on it" (105). Note the difficulty in reading this transcription of a form of black language. It comes alive, however, and becomes transparent when read aloud, when performed as an oral text. The obscure written form attests to a conscious rejection of standardized scripture as itself a form of control. The readers' difficulty in scanning Parks's texts is increased by her transcription not only of black speech, but also of black "voice": the visceral soundings of her figures. Nonsemiotic noises are often written onto her pages as musical moans that evoke an uninscribed—perhaps uninscribable—preliterate world. In a list of "foreign words & phrases" appended to her published collection of plays, Parks explains "words" such as *uuh! thup, ssnuch,* or *gaw.* Each is parsed in terms of the breathing or tongue movement

needed to create these emotive sounds. Their exact connotations are, however, more difficult to pin down since their meaning emerges through their
physical expression.[16] Parks speaks of language and words as carnal, "something which involves your entire body." Words perform on stage; they are
"spells which an actor consumes and digests—and through digesting creates
a performance on stage."[17] The audience is then drawn into the play
through the spell of the language with its combination of incantatory
regress, its musical appeal to nonverbal roots in a lost past, and its specific
connotations of, and resistance to, a deformed social world.

Parks's style is thus a route into the missing roots of an African-American past, that which Paul Gilroy has called the missing story of black
Atlantic "roots 'n' routes." Gilroy, seeking the tools for a restoration of
black memory within art, suggests that it involves "a deliberate and self-
conscious *move beyond language* in ways that are informed by the social memory of the earlier experiences of enforced separation from the world of written communication."[18] The memory of a time of pure orality, or forced
orality, and the desire to incorporate these unversed "pasts" into the ver-
nacular of her social/poetic figures can partially account for Parks's idiosyn-
cratic transcriptions. The result is a double language: both English and not,
both contemporary and not. The idea of a double movement of language
between (white) American English and a black memorial idiom has been
developed in the writings of Henry Louis Gates Jr., who is clearly a theoretical source for Parks's magical but precise use of language. Gates describes
African-American dialect as a language that spans and conflates two verbal
shores—the one, English, the other, a language lost in some mythical, irretrievable linguistic kingdom. Dialect, he claims, is "our only key to that
unknown tongue,"[19] a tongue Parks "reconstitutes" through her memoried
"ear" for suppressed expression.

In addition to this view, Parks's language, as Robert Brustein has
pointed out, is also a form of verbal deconstruction. "Like other verbal
adventurers," Brustein writes, "especially Joyce and Stein, Parks is preoccupied with deconstructing language"; this is "partly an effort to exalt
black English into a kind of poetic code. It is also an effort to adapt English
words to the black experience."[20] Parks's self-conscious deconstruction of
language is both formally innovative and a political tool. Her language is
often keenly punning and incisive, recalling and exposing the ideologies
imprinted within words. In *The America Play,* for example, she plays with
the standard coins and historical clichés of America's self-image, erecting a
vocabulary that mutates into its opposite when applied to her black protagonists. Thus, for example, the nationalistic reverberations of "our Forefa-

thers" become, in a changed context, the dissipated ruin of our "faux-fathers." The verbal pun actualizes the historical disinheritance that under-writes her language, a disinheritance that has deprived black America of a memoried past. For Parks, as for Shepard, there is no memory without a history. Being written "out of history" (Parks's absent black history) creates, as Shepard put it, a "kind of chaos, a kind of terror."[21] But in Parks this "terror" is rerouted through language into mourning, outrage, and resistance against a vocabulary from which she has been forcibly excluded.

In the following discussion, I will focus on *The Death of the Last Black Man in the Whole Entire World* (1992), as well as the celebrated *America Play* (1993). I will also address aspects of Parks's first play, *Imperceptible Mutabilities in the Third Kingdom* (1989), which won her an Obie for the best off-Broadway play in 1990.

Waving across Time: *Imperceptible Mutabilities*

Suzan-Lori Parks's first two plays, *Imperceptible Mutabilities in the Third Kingdom* and *The Death of the Last Black Man in the Whole Entire World,* span the entire history of black American consciousness: from the imagined roots in pharaonic Egypt to the search for roots in contemporary America; from the dreams of paradise in pre-Columbian Africa "before uh demarcation made it mapped" (*Last Black Man,* 114), to the metaphoric execution of the last black man that "sparked controlled displays of jubilation in all corners of the world" (*Last Black Man,* 110); from enslavement and persecution to emancipation and persecution; from daily segregation in the southern states to urban struggles in the north. Both plays are imagistic, poetic embodiments of longing and anguish that try to piece together an identity and "history" out of the usurped memory of black America. *Imperceptible Mutabilities* is actually a composite of four separate, thematically connected playlets "so abstract in form and language as to make any attempts at interpretation provisional at best," wrote one of Parks's earliest critics, Alisa Solomon. "[I]t is, at the same time," Solomon continues, "clearly and firmly rooted in a forth-right political sensibility, one absolutely concerned with African-American experience under the weight of a hostile world."[22] Each of these playlets is subdivided into additional units, and each could be performed separately, though all, at least obliquely, refer to each other. The first and last playlets take place in contemporary and 1950s America, framing the more mythical middle sections within the perspective of present and semiautobiographical history. Section 3, "Open House," takes place on the eve of Emancipation. These three sections all make theatrical use of photography. Parks has called

Imperceptible Mutabilities an "African-American history in the shadow of the photographic image," in the shadow of the "official version" of history. Slide shows accompany various scenes, functioning as a form of (fraudulent) documentation. "You have these fixed pictures projected up there" on the back stage screen, Parks explains, "and down below there's a little person mutating like hell on the stage. I'm obsessed with the gap between these two things." The dynamic between the fixed and the mutating, the static and the evolving is paralleled by Parks to the relationship between "preconceived images of African-Americans and real people."[23]

The dichotomy between the (projected) document and (performed) experience is conflated in the two choral sections of *Imperceptible Mutabilities*—part 2, and an appendage to part 3 titled, respectively, "Third Kingdom" and "Third Kingdom (Reprise)." In these deeply poetic, hallucinatory segments, a group of strangely named figures—Kin-Seer, Us-Seer, Shark-Seer, Soul-Seer, and finally, ironically, Over-Seer—function as the play's collective subconscious voice. They seem static, almost disembodied, and perform the double task of reliving the trauma of "a people lost in middle passage, floating in the hyphenated space between Africa and America,"[24] and, at the same time, of describing this crossing as though they were witnessing its occurrence from an epic, alienated distance. This compounding of contradictory dramatic stances—reliving and reporting—is caught in the (often revised) repeated lines:

> *Kin-Seer:* Should I jump? Shouldijumporwhut?
> *Shark-Seer:* But we are not in uh boat!
> *Us-Seer:* But we iz. Iz iz iz uh huhn.
>
> (40)

Are these figures in the boat they're describing? Or are they remembering the collective passage from the distance of another world? Both choral sections circle around an attempt to remember and return to "where I comed from." The crucial line, spoken by Kin-Seer and often revised and repeated, reads: "Last night I dreamed of where I comed from. But where I comed from diduhnt look like nowhere like I been." The figures try to situate the unknown, unremembered dream-place "where I comed from" on a map. It is located, they learn, between a shore and a sea of sharks, between two cliffs "where thuh world had cleaved intuh 2" (37): a cosmology of pain that split the world in half. "Half the world had fallen away making 2 worlds and a sea between. Those 2 worlds inscribe the Third Kingdom" (39). The splitting of the world through the enforced bondage of Africa is imaged too as a splitting of subjectivity. Standing on the shore, Kin-Seer "was wavin. Wavin. Wavin at my uther me who I could barely see," and the me on the boat "waved back. . . . But my uther me whuduhnt wavin at me." Out of these two unseeing, waving "me"s appears a "third Self made by thuh space in between" (38–39). This poetic description of an identity split and lost, of a language cleaved between Gates's two verbal shores, of a search for origins that uncovers only a past drowned and unrecoverable—this description is repeated and crucially *revised* to stress grammatical forms of "being" in the choral "Reprise."

> *Kin-Seer:* Tonight I dream of where I be-camin from. And where I
> be-camin from duhduhnt look like nowhere like I been.
> *Soul-Seer:* The tale of how we *were* when we *were*–
> *Over-Seer:* You woke up screaming.
> *Shark-Seer:* How we *will* be when we *will* be–
> *Over-Seer:* You woke up screaming.
> *Us-Seer:* And how we be, now that we iz. . . .
> *Kin-Seer:* Should I jump? Should I jump?? Should I jump
> shouldijumporwhat? . . .
> *Soul-Seer:* But we are not in uh boat!
> *Us-Seer:* But we iz. Iz uh–huhn–uh–huhn–iz.
>
> (54–55)

The absence of origins is translated here into a dream in which all tenses collide ("tonight I dream"), turning the essence of a black identity into one outside of chronology, and thus outside of grammar. The linear search for "where I be-camin from" cannot be conjugated. Deprived of a rooted history, identity eludes the order of language and remains the same nightmare of bereavement ("You woke up screaming") in all tenses, past, future, and present. Thus the splitting of the world through slavery is also a splitting of the *word,* of language itself. This tragic pun—world/word—is overtly developed in a reprise of the geography of origins (quoted above). Now, instead of "2 cliffs where thuh world had cleaved intuh 2" we have "2 cliffs where the Word had cleaved. Half the Word has fallen away making 2 Words and a space between. Those 2 Words inscribe the third Kingdom" (56). Language, including the language of temporality and self-representation, takes on a traumatized structure in Parks's plays, a structure of displacement, repetition, intrusive dreams. Cathy Caruth, developing Freud's discussion of trauma, explains that traumatic events cannot be assimilated at the time of occurrence. Trauma is only felt belatedly, "in its repeated *possession*" of the one (or collective) who were harmed. To be traumatized "is precisely to be possessed by an image or an event" that overtakes the victim(s)[25]—such as the image of the boat that black America has never left ("But we iz. Iz iz iz uh huhn"), and the waving of selves across a mythical divide that language can no longer bridge. If, as I discussed in an earlier chapter, trauma does not remember its source, but rather replays the moment of cognitive disruption,[26] then the point of this ungrammatical dream of origins is that there *is* no "place" at which the real identity of these figures any longer resides, and no originary memory that can be recovered.

The center playlet of *Imperceptible Mutabilities,* "Open House," zooms into the trauma itself and further reflects on the complex relations between the fixity of recorded history and the chaos of a bereaved memory. It begins with the projection of a double-frame slide-show presenting Aretha Saxon, a black slave about to be freed, hugging two white children who have been in her care. With each slide, the smiles on the three faces grow wider; the frame moves ever closer in, finally focusing on the teeth. Meanwhile, on the semidark stage, we find the figures of Aretha and the two children, discussing teeth and smiles—"Smile," she tells the children, "Smile for show" (41). They also discuss Aretha's "last day" of enslavement and employment with the family. The projected photos fix the memory of the three as a memory of intimacy and joy. This is contrasted to the central subscene of the playlet that portrays the ex-slave, Aretha, sick and dying, having her teeth extracted on Emancipation day in 1865. The teeth are being pulled with a large pair of pliers in order that they may be photographed and "entered into the book . . . Think of it as getting yourself chronicled, Mrs. Saxon," she is told; "You are becoming a full part of the great chronicle!" (46). These extractions are experienced by Aretha as a series of discontinuous moments from her life, plucked out of her through her teeth. The tension between chronicle and loss, between the facts recorded in this section and the experiences barely related, creates a composite "third Self" (as Shark-Seer tells us): a self no longer enslaved yet far from free, a hybrid, unlanguaged (toothless, speechless) creation of history. "You dont want to be forgotten do you?" Miss Faith, the tooth-puller says to the dying Aretha: "AAAh! Open. Hmmmm. Canine next, I think. Find solace in the book. Find order in the book. Find find find the book. Where is the book. Go find it. Find it. Go on. Get up" (46). The rhetoric of the book invoked by Miss Faith rhymes with the language of the Good Book, from which Aretha, in her agony, quotes. But Miss Faith is actually referring to an unidentified history, or rather chronology, of the buying, selling, births, and deaths of black slaves. This "book" is clearly the white history of black America, a chattel listing.

> *Miss Faith:* The power of the book lies in its contents. Its contents are facts. Through examination of the facts therein we may see what is to come. Through the examination of what comes we may turn to our book and see from whence it came. Example: The book has let us know for quite some time that you expire 19-5-65, do you not Mrs. Saxon. You expire. (Footnote #5: "Juneteenth," June 19th in 1865, was when, a good many months after the Emancipation Proclamation, the slaves in Texas heard they were free.) You expire. Along with your lease. Expiration 19-6-65 with no option to renew. (47)

The perceived factuality of "the book," with the scientific footnote inserted into the spoken text—a notation that, horribly, conflates Aretha's death ("you expire") with the expiration of her lease as a slave—offers a depressing level of positivistic historicity that hides the death it records. Miss Faith, dentist and historian, speaks almost entirely in terms of chronicle and footnote. In section B of "Open House," Aretha acts as a witness to the origins of slavery. She is interviewed by Miss Faith and "remembers" the ships in midocean, picking up lines that had previously been spoken by the choral figures of "Third Kingdom." These imprecisions are translated by Miss Faith into footnotes for her "book." "You give me the facts," she tells Aretha. "I draw from them in accordance with the book" (44)—a book whose rules and rhetoric have little to do with Aretha's experiences. The dialogue between the two women, between recall and record, is a poignant clash between two incompatible languages, as different as the fluidity of dreams and the fixity of scientific register.

In later sections of "Open House"—sections that takes place, we're told, in "Dreamtime"—Charles appears. Charles is an unclear figure. Possibly Aretha's husband, he is also the father of the two white children she cares for. Thus he speaks as both master and kin, in the authoritative voice of white superiority, as well as in the voice of conscience. In one of his appearances he admonishes Aretha for having naively surrendered her teeth in the belief that her "mouth" will be recorded in a way that actually captures the truth of her experience:

> Charles: You let them take out the teeth you're giving up the last of the verifying evidence. All'll be obliterated. All's left will be conjecture. We won't be able to tell you apart from the others. We won't even know

thus historicizing the lyrical recollections and bringing them up to "now." These names are not merely a literary device meant for the reading audience, they are part of the memoried fabric of the play as a whole. While rehearsing the play, director Liz Diamond prepared an audio track of the figures whispering their names. "Those whispers helped create the feeling of *Last Black Man* as a visitation," Parks has said, a visitation of the voices of memory returned to haunt the living.[29] In order that the theater audience too might hear the strange, sometimes embarrassing names, the play begins with an overture in which the characters introduce themselves directly to the spectators, requiring the audience to "place" the names within their own memories—and preconceptions.

Although *Last Black Man* is a play full of mutations, its structure is stringent. There are five scenes, called panels—"partly from the Stations of the Cross, the tableau of Christ which hangs in churches," Parks explains.[30] Scenes 1, 3, and 5 are intimate dialogues between Black Man and Black Woman; all of the other scenes—scenes 2 and 4, the opening overture and the final chorus—are choral and include the entire cast of weirdly named roles. This structure recalls Greek tragedy with its narrative "episodes" separated by choral *stasima,* with its opening *parados* and closing *exodos.* But Parks imitates a classical structure in order to subvert it from within. As his generic name implies, Black Man does not stand for an individual; nor does his death. As he says early in the play: "Make me uh space 6 feet by 6 feet by 6. Make it big and mark it . . . uh mass grave-site. Theres company comin soonish" (109). The many deaths discussed in the play implicate a long history of black suffering in America. They are recited ahistorically, nonsequentially, in interlaced stories and transforming images that, rather than unfold, circulate and expand poetically, finally implicating every object on the stage and in nature—chair, food, lake, tree and sky—until the entire world is mythically transmuted into a memorial space inscribed with Black Man's deaths. In panel 1, Black Man, sitting on the porch with his wife, a watermelon at his feet, tells of how they put leather straps across his forearms and chest and "juiced me some" in the very chair he has now returned to. The melons, which he doesn't recognize as his own, are symbols of his deaths, and they accumulate during the play—one for every death he's endured. They grow "from one tuh 3 tuh many" (125), and as they encircle him and bring him closer to the play's final death, he comes to say "Melon. Melon. Melon: mines. I remember" (126)—thus embracing those collective deaths as his own. In panel 3, Black Man appears with a rope choking him and a tree branch still attached to the rope. He tells about his lynching: "When I dieded they cut me down. Didnt have no need for me no more. They let me go" (119). But where did he go to once he'd "been dismissed"? "Must be somewhere else tuh go aside from just go gone. Huh," says Black Woman (120). This is one of the central questions posed by the play, repeated throughout: "Where you gonna go now, now that you done dieded?" It is seriously addressed in panel 5, which, together with the final chorus, is the culmination of Black Man's dying. Together, these scenes confirm that there is nowhere for him to "go" but into history ("You should write that down"), into the memory of the audience ("Remember me")—or back into oblivion.

Parks notes the time of the play as "The Present," presumably referring to the time of performance (the past is created as history through its "happening on stage").[31] But time is entirely hallucinatory in *Last Black Man,* purposely conflated. We are told that the last black man was executed "Yesterday today next summer tomorrow just uh moment uhgoh in 1317." We are taken "Back. Back. Back tuh that" (102), to a time "before Columbus," confronted with the immediacy of a television newscast, with the beginnings of racial memory, with the future, thus canceling all temporality and forcing the pasts to reappear as *presented* in the present. This collapsing of time, as in *Imperceptible Mutabilities,* is consciously imparted to the grammatical structure of Parks's sentences as well—"In the future when they came along I meeting them" (104). The connection between the way time is *spoken,* and the way it is experienced and remembered, is, once again, central to Parks's dramaturgy. This is strongly captured, for example, in the one "realistic" image that threads through the play—the image of Black Man and Black Woman sitting together on their porch. Without ever moving, their entire past is interjected onto that nearly parodic porch, so common (together with front and back yards) to realistic American drama. "Today you sit in your chair where you sat yesterday and thuh day afore yesterday afore they comed and tooked you," Black Woman says in panel 1. "Things today is just as they are yesterday cept nothin is familiar cause it was such uh long time uhgoh." To which Black Man answers: "Later oughta be now by now huh?" (107). In panel 5, the dislocation and simultaneity of times is captured by Black Man in a long monologue in which he remembers this porch as the one they have sat on throughout time—compounding all the memories into a single intuition of being: "There is uh Now and there is uh Then. Ssall there is," Black Man says:

> I bein in uh Now: uh Now being in uh Then: I bein, in Now in Then, in I will be. I was be too but thats uh Then thats past. That me that was-be is uh me-has-been. Thuh Then that was-be is uh has-been Then too. Thuh me-

exclusionary historical method. More to the point, it exposes the ways the trauma of slavery (SOLD) and deprivation of identity (the crazed forms of address) have been hidden by the obscure mechanism of scientific notation, and thus lost as a memoried narrative. Language, as often in Parks, is used to reveal and subvert it's own cruel consequences.

Last Black Man is an elusive and allusive play. Part of its difficulty is due to its very richness—it is "too densely written for one mind to absorb at a single sitting," wrote Robert Brustein after seeing Liz Diamond's direction of the play at Yale's Winterfest Theater in New Haven.[34] Reading the play is in many ways even more difficult. The text is disembodied and narratively opaque, lacking stage directions or character description. Its metaphors are tangled and not meant to be easily unknotted and analyzed. In her 1992 production of the play, Liz Diamond framed the elusive text within a ceremonial setting, "a sort of surreal cathedral/burial ground," and directed the play as though enacting Black Man's remembrances and his final, literal burial in a black sarcophagus—not mentioned in the play itself.[35] This literalization of the play's obsession with death is an interpretation not necessarily supported by the text. Unlike *The America Play,* where the Foundling Father returns to be buried in the "hole" he had dug and his son had explored, within the coffin Parks writes is brought on stage, *Last Black Man*'s ending is less clear. Despite repeated references to "uh space 6 feet by 6 feet by 6," and to images of death and erasure, concrete indications of actual interment are highly ambivalent in the text, and their literalization is perhaps detrimental to an activist reading of the play. In a metaphoric sense, *Last Black Man* is clearly a play of mourning, approximating Freud's description of actively "working through" the trauma of loss by remembering, repeating, and "re-experiencing" that loss.[36] Alice Rayner and Harry Elam Jr. describe the play, in fact, as a eulogy "of repeated litanies by which the dead are laid to rest," thereby bringing an end to "the haunting" of the living by the dead.[37] I would take issue with this cathartic reading that sees a restoration of order and peace as the outcome of a nearly literal burying of the past. Despite the mourning and "re-experiencing," I find the play far too chaotic, and its memory agenda far more political, than such a reading would allow.

The rejection of linearity and closure is overtly addressed in the last panel and final chorus of the play. There, Parks fuses a ritual call to remember with an activist call to inscribe and hold onto the past, rather than to let it go through burial. At the end of panel 5, after Black Man's monologic erasure of time and self on his porch (discussed above), we find a new set of repetitions: the words "Miss me. Remember me." These are picked up in the final chorus by the other figures, and added to Parks's leitmotif sentence, a sentence recurring a dozen times from the first pages of the play to the last: variations of the line, "You should write that down and you should hide it under a rock." This choral refrain is structured into the play as a response to the oral memories being woven by the characters, underlining their ephemerality, and stressing as well that only that which is written and recorded will be remembered and transformed into power and "history." As one of the line's early revisions reads: "You should write it down because if you dont write it down then they will come along and tell the future that we did not exist" (104). This Benjaminian admonition that the past belongs to the "victors," to those who write the narrative of the past, is strengthened through subsequent revisions of the sentence until, in the final chorus, it turns into an insistent exhortation, almost biblical in tone, commanding, "You will write down thuh past and you will write down thuh present and in what in thuh future. You will write it down" (131). These seemingly programmatic lines in favor of giving memory textual form do not build toward any coherent line of thought, nor do they imply that the time has come to add the final *d* to black experience and to make it "round." Rather, Parks allows these repetitions to seep through the text and grow like the gathering voice of a collective subconscious wish for a place in history, a place that must be hewn out of the gathered memories of a black past—and in the voice and language *of* those memories as they exist in the present. It is only through the language that, for Parks, the past can be retrieved and turned into "history"—and this is the voice she "invents" through her "memoried" ear, the voice she hears in the singing "bones."

The connection between voice, inscription, and memory is beautifully, musically climaxed in the closing repetitions of the play. In addition to "Miss me. Remember me" and "You will write that down," a new sequence appears for the first time in the final chorus, adding serious weight to Parks's entreaty to remember and record. The final chorus begins with the words, "Somethins turnin. Thuh page," and adds, "Somethins burnin. Thuh tongue."

> *Old Man River Jordan:* Uh blank page turnin with thuh sound of it.
> Thuh sound of movin hands . . .
> *Black Woman With Fried Drumstick:* Where he gonna go now now now
> now now that he done diedihuh? . . .
> *Prunes and Prisms:* Somethins turnin. Thuh page.
> *And Bigger And Bigger And Bigger:* Somethins burnin. Thuh tongue.
> *Black Man With Watermelon:* Thuh tongue itself burns.
> *Old Man River Jordan:* He jumps in thuh river. These words for partin.

customer who, for a penny, is allowed to participate in the ritual reassas-
sination. The pattern is constant: the visitor chooses a pistol, stands in
position, waits for the Foundling Father, as Abraham Lincoln, to laugh
Lincoln's guffaw—"Haw Haw Haw Haw"—and with this cue, shoots
him. The Foundling Father then "slumps in his chair," and the customer
jumps from his box as Booth and proclaims, "Thus to the tyrants!" (the
line purportedly spoken in Latin by Booth "as he slew Lincoln and leapt
from the presidential box to the stage of Ford's Theater in Washington
DC on 14 April 1865" [165, footnote 8]), or "The South is avenged" (also
Booth's alleged words), or "Now he belongs to the ages" (Secretary of
War Edwin Stanton's epitaph), or "Theyve killed the president" (Mary
Todd's words). The detailed replayings of Lincoln's death, in all its lore—
repeated, with variations, seven times—marks it as a moment that surfaces
in the collective memory as a still potent trauma. Parks has thus chosen a
still painful historical scar, "burnt" into the communal memory, as the site
within which she will seek a black trace.

When we think of Lincoln's death, we imagine him sitting in an all-
white theater in the nation's capitol, watching an all-white cast perform *My
American Cousin,* and being shot by a white assassin. Parks replays this
famous, perhaps defining scene of American history—the shooting of "O
Captain my Captain"—with a twist: this time the revered leader, his assas-
sin(s), and even the players on stage (in the second-act replay of sections of
My American Cousin), are all black. Through this carnavalization of the past
as a penny-theatrical in "blackface," Parks underscores the absence of blacks
within the American historical imagination, exposing, as well, the dependence of African-American identity on images propagated by a history from
which they have, for the most part, been represented as absent. *The America
Play* is an attempt to "implant" a different memory of America's past, restoring a black presence. During his monologue, we experience the Lesser
Known as both an actor who dons false beards and discusses the mechanics
of impersonation ("fakin"), and an aspirant to become a *real* Lincoln, no less
revered or acknowledged. At the end of the play, the Foundling Father will
die like Lincoln, dressed like Lincoln, with a "great black hole" in his look-
alike head: but he will remain black, Lesser Known, and unmourned—
except perhaps by the audience of the play. The point of successful impersonation, Parks has said, is that it inserts "fakin" "into real life and sort of
makes history."[42] Through this play, Parks enters the skin of American history through a black door—and tries to revision it, to remake "history."
"Every time the Foundling Father sits in 'Lincoln's Chair' at 'Ford's theater'
and 'dies,'" writes Marc Robinson in a variation of Parks's thought, "he is

doing more than merely returning to a legendary moment. He is also forcing the past back into the present, and thus enabling himself to revise history."[43] Memory is remade retroactively, through its performance in the
present.

As the Lesser Known tells us in his opening autobiographical monologue, two factors fueled his obsession with Lincoln: the first was his
uncanny resemblance to the Great Man, "Being told from birth practically
that he and the Great Man were dead ringers, more or less" (161). They
shared the same gait and manner, the same long legs and short torso; the two
were virtually twins, "taking into account of course [the Lesser Known's]
natural God-given limitations" (163). The second factor was a direct
encounter the Lesser Known had had with American history. On their hon-
eymoon, Lucy and the Lesser Known visited a huge theme park "with historical parades," a sort of nationalistic Disneyland of "Reconstructed His-
toricities" displayed with such order and beauty that it consumed his entire
being. The Foundling Father remembers the thrill of discovering what
might be considered the "official story" of American history: the "Greats on
parade," the cannons lit, the rockets' blare, the slain enemy "stretched out
and smoldering"—images that continued to "march before him in his
minds eye," possessing him "like an echo in his head." The Lesser Known
experienced this encounter with history as a "summoning" ("Memories
sometimes stuck like that") (162–63)—summoned from his ordinary life
into the defining magic of history. He subsequently left his wife and child
to undertake the perilous, "monumentous" journey westward, where he
would re-create the wonders of history—with himself inserted as a major
player. "In making the mythical journey West," writes Una Chaudhuri,
picking up on the historical deconstruction implicit in this description,

> the Lesser Known was reenacting the core principle of American History. But
> a feature of his identity—that he was a digger (and nigger)—puts him in
> absolute conflict with the expected benefits of following that principle. Irrev-
> ocably separated . . . from the enabling narratives of the (white) past, the Lesser
> Known's efforts to connect his identity to the Great Man's prove futile.[44]

It is the futility of his efforts to become imprinted in history, and thus celebrated and remembered, that is overtly mourned in the second act of the
play. Act 2 extricates memory from monologic musings and places it physically on stage. Parks concretizes the hidden space of memory, of the past,
through a stage image so simple and so dominant that it immediately
becomes the very replica of memory and memory processes: the actual
excavation of the "Great Hole." Lucy and Brazil have come out West in

search of the remnants of their disappeared husband and father. For much of the second act, Lucy, whose prophetic gift is the ability to hear and hold the secrets of the dead, roams the circumference of the Hole with an ear trumpet, listening, in vain, for echoes, or "whispers," of her husband and their lost past, while Brazil digs for clues. In this act, Parks extends her metaphoric displacement of Lincoln by a Lesser Known black man, by turning the impersonator himself into a piece of lost history in need of reconstruction. Brazil, a digger like his father, seeks for relics and for his roots in his father's heritage—"This Hole is our inheritance of sorts," he explains (185). But as he digs ever deeper into the Hole—"Cant stop diggin till you dig up somethin," Lucy tells him—all he comes up with are mean and meaningless trifles where a past should be, "faux historical nick-knacks" buried by the black "faux-father." He finds the box where the Foundling Father had kept his fake beards, the bust of Lincoln that stood by his chair, a pair of wooden teeth ("uh top and bottom pair of nibblers"), a glass bead, whale's blubber, some documents, and medals

> for bravery and honesty; for trustworthiness and for standing straight; for standing tall; for standing still. For advancing and retreating. For makin do . . . For cookin and for cleanin. For bowin and scrapin. Uh medal for fakin? Huh. This could uh been his. Zsis his? This is his! This is his!!! (186).

Having found the one object that identifies the father for what he was—an impersonator, a pretender, an actor, a fake and forgotten imitation—Brazil bursts into lengthy weeping and mourning.

Mourning is in fact Brazil's special talent. In addition to being a digger, Brazil was brought up to be a professional mourner, "a weeper" who performs gestures of bereavement at funerals. As Brazil tells us, "On thuh day he claimed to be the 100th anniversary of the founding of our country," his father taught him the first gesture of grief: the Wail. Each year after that, presumably on that same memorial day of the country's birth, the son was taught another mourning technique: "the Weep," "the Sob," "the Moan," and finally, reserved for special occasions, "the Gnash" (182). Thus, Parks connects the act of mourning, rather explicitly, with the commemoration of the country that had enslaved and then excluded her characters from its history. Through Brazil, Parks objectifies and makes discursive that which had comprised the haunting fabric of her previous plays: mourning for a missing past. By the end of the play, Brazil will have actual occasion to use the techniques taught to him by his father, to mourn the unmourned passing of that father.

Parks's play on the erasure of a black presence in American history is also a replay of the audience's conventionalized memory of their own history. Among the few artifacts left by the Foundling Father to his son are his words and wisdoms, familiar to us from act 1. Lucy teaches her son those wisdoms: if the father could see him now, she tells Brazil, "He'd say: 'Uh house divided cannot stand!' He'd say: '4score and 7 years uhgoh.' Say: 'Of thuh people by thuh people and for thuh people.' Say: 'Malice toward none and charity toward all.' Say: 'Cheat some of thuh people some of thuh time'" (192). This collage of stock quotes from Lincoln's most famous speeches—appropriated by the Foundling Father as his own—ring hollow, almost grotesque in their stitched-together form. When repeated by Lucy, as remembered from the Lesser Known, these overfamiliar citations become the displacement of a displacement, in the same way that the Foundling Father as Lincoln problematizes our memory of Lincoln as a Founding Father. One of the many ironies in this play full of ironies is precisely the idea that Lincoln *was* a "Founding Father." After all, by Lincoln's time, the nation had long been "founded" by "greats" such as Washington, Jefferson, Adams, Franklin. The incorporation of Lincoln into the "historical pantheon of the Founding Fathers" was, writes historian Eyal Naveh, a conscious historical process resulting from the trauma of Lincoln's assassination, a process that served "to embed it forever in the collective memory and thus to render it meaningful 'to the ages.'"[45] Parks's punning invention of the term "Foundling Father" reflects back on the questionable epitaph "Founding Father" that has attached itself to Lincoln's name. Through their overlap, both labels are revealed as historical constructions saturated with ideological agendas that the audience is free to decipher. At the same time, the differences between the two men, and between the success of their constructions *as* historical forefathers, remains clear. It was Lincoln's death—endlessly repeated by the Lesser Known—that raised him to the "pantheon" of Founders. The Foundling Father, on the other hand, dies orphaned and barely remembered, leaving behind as his inheritance nothing but a spade and borrowed quotations.

The games of impersonation and reflection are incorporated into the structure of act 2. This act "remembers" and revises act one, "quoting" whole sections from the earlier act, developing speeches hinted at earlier, and allowing the dead Foundling Father to return as a "ghost." Unlike act 1 (titled "The Hall of Wonders"), act 2 is subdivided into short scenes. Scenes between Lucy and Brazil alternate with snatches of scenes from *My American Cousin,* introduced, and even acted, by the Foundling Father himself. In scene D, the Foundling Father appears as a female character in *My American*

Cousin, stretching his "fakin" and stretching too the humiliation of always playing someone "other" than himself. The protagonist as pretender without a "self" is further underscored through a TV set on which the Lesser Known is transmitted as a simulation of himself. In the last scene, the play's first act, "The Lincoln Act," is broadcast on TV in images devoid of sound. Brazil comments on the video replay: "They just gunned him down uhgain . . . He's dead but not really . . . Only fakin. Only fakin. See? Hesupuhgain," thus summarizing the repeated shootings, slumpings, sitting ups, we the audience had watched seven times in act 1, and encouraging us to "remember" the past we experienced. This is the type of textual repetition Parks has called "a literal incorporation of the past" within the present of the play,[46] a form of textual "remembering" that recurs throughout the second act. These insistent repetitions suggest a hope that, if often enough "rehearsed" and replayed, the death of the Lesser Known—this "memory" created by Parks through its performance—might too become a collective trauma remembered, mourned, and included in the "canon of history."

The depressing futility of this attempted recuperation comes to the fore in the final scene. Here we have the "return" of the Lesser Known, first as a TV image, and then as a "dead" version of himself. Lucy and Brazil plan the funeral, to which they have invited "hundreds upon thousands who knew of your Daddy, glorified his reputation, and would like to pay their respects" (196). They prepare the father's coffin and allow the Lesser Known to deliver his own eulogy—a variation of the quilt of Lincoln quotes Lucy had previously taught their son. A mock memorial ceremony ensues on the empty stage—a stage devoid of mourners aside from the son, who now prepares to "gnash" for his forgotten father. The Lesser Known again "slumps" in his chair, for the final time, and gunshot echoes recall the Lincoln assassinations of act 1. With this, Brazil turns to the audience and encourages it, the only "guests" at this memorial ceremony, to see the dead figure as worthy of collective mourning. Gesturing to the dead Foundling Father as Abraham Lincoln, Brazil points out, in the last lines of the play, "the top hat and frock coat, just like the greats. Note the death wound: thuh great black hole—thuh great black hole in thuh great head.—And how this great head is bleedin.—Note: thuh last words.—And thuh last breaths.—And how thuh nation mourns" (199). Thus everything about the Lesser Known's death is twinned with the death of the legend: everything except its impact and its memory.

The America Play is about memory and erasure, but it is not "memoried" in the same way as were Parks's earlier plays. With its witty language and historical deconstructions, Parks generates polemical images of a black absence, images inscribed into the play through stage and discussion, but especially through the play's self-reflective double verbal code. Language plays a very different role in this play than it did in *Last Black Man,* or in the choral sections of *Imperceptible Mutabilities.* Rather than cast an incantatory "spell," language tills a communal soil and unearths the ideology hidden in even the most common historical coins. Deliberately punning on national-istic idioms, Parks injects slight shifts that highlight how these idioms "sound" to those they exclude. In Todd London's summation, Parks

> broaches a new national narrative by means of puns, all self-contradictory. The Hole is the Whole; the forefather is the "faux-father," which means false and sounds like enemy; the digging is—even a generation after emancipation—"spadework" done by a family of "diggers," both of which echo racial epi-thets; and the black man who imitates and resembles the president is not the progenitor of the nation but its orphan or "Foundling Father." By trying to excavate a history for himself where there is none, Brazil digs his own grave—as his father had—out of which he must eventually climb.[47]

Once deciphered, the wit and painful irony of the play become clear and accusatory. This is a political play, a play of ideas that evinces the need to find some form of clarity, to test the evidence of a black imprint in Amer-ica. "Itssalways been important in my line to distinguish," Lucy tells her son. "Tuh know thuh difference. Not like your Fathuh. Your Fathuh became confused. His lonely death and lack of proper burial is our embarrassment . . . I need tuh know thuh real thing from thuh echo. Thuh truth from thuh hearsay" (175). This need for an understanding of the real place of black America within the scheme of American historical memory is crucially reflected in the register of the play's language—a language strikingly differ-ent from that of the earlier plays. The Lesser Known speaks a grammatical and correctly spelled English, as though he had been incorporated into the "official history" he impersonates. Lucy and Brazil speak a modified, far more transparent version of the black language found in *Last Black Man.* Through this, Parks loses the lyrical edge that nourished her "requiem mass in the jazz aesthetic," *Last Black Man,*[48] and gave us the vibrant chorus of memoried voices in *Imperceptible Mutabilities.* Consequently, we are not drawn into the play through the language in the same way. Memory is no longer "burnt" on the tongue, voice no longer carries traces of an unknow-able world, and the language no longer affords us an intuition of the "roots" of a lost past. The reason for this changed strategy is perhaps that the roots buried in *The America Play* are buried in America. Black history and mem-ory are not "lost" in some irretrievable kingdom, not cleaved on some mythic shore, not drowned and waving in Middle Passage. They are covered rather than missing: buried by a historical narrative whose representations (icons, theme parks) have excluded the black presence. In this play, Parks's memory agenda is more specifically corrective. By superimposing a black historical absence onto the overexposed white presence of Lincoln, Foundling Father onto Founding Father, the eminently remembered beneath the totally forgotten, she conflates and compares the two types of historical memories. The last line of *The America Play*, "And how thuh nation mourns," ironically intoned, spoken on a stage empty of mourners, is a call to rethink the representations, and the agendas, of national memory.

Chapter 6

Thomas Bernhard's Resentment and the Politics of Memory

Thomas Bernhard is renowned for his implacable memory, a memory permanently enraged against the collective amnesia of his *Heimat,* Austria. As famous in Austria for the scandals he created—even drawing personal attacks from the arch-amnesiac Kurt Waldheim himself—as for his thirty prose works, twenty plays, and numerous books of poetry, Bernhard's fight with Austria, with amnesia, with the euphemisms and hypocrisies of a German language inherited from a poisoned past, was long-standing and deep. It was not alleviated when, in 1986, the minister of defense officially welcomed home a war criminal released from an Italian prison. Nor was it helped by the scandal surrounding the exposure of two-time secretary general of the United Nations Kurt Waldheim's Nazi past and, worst, his subsequent election as president of Austria. It is these realities that underlie the ferocity of his attacks on "Austria / Österreich / L'Autriche / . . . a cesspool / in the pus-filled boil of Europe," as he puts it in his play *Histrionics (Der Theatermacher,* 1984).[1] And it was the collective denial of the memory of these realities that spurred him to write provocative, and, in the cases of *Heldenplatz (Hero's Square,* 1988) and *Eve of Retirement (Vor dem Ruhestand,* 1979), overtly political memory-plays.

Bernhard (1931–1989) had a talent for provocation and outspokenness—especially about the Austrian/German peoples and their history. He mocked them in play after play by unmasking their language, mentality, and especially their hypocrisy, in dense dramatic parables. Bernhard's reputation in his native Austria is that of their most respected writer and playwright, whose fame, together with that of Peter Handke and Elfriede Jelinek, extends well beyond Austria's borders. It is also that of Austria's most notorious *Nestbeschmutzer*—one who defiles his "nest," his homeland. "In Austria you have to be either Catholic / or a National Socialist," he wrote; "nothing else is tolerated / everything else is destroyed."[2] Bernhard's

enmity toward his country was rooted in Austria's problematic postwar situation: a country that was treated by the Allies as a "victim" nation, and that
gladly accepted this assumption—going so far as to label itself "Hitler's first
victim."[3] This self-serving historical distortion required that Austria repress
its own memory of ready collaboration and participation on all fronts of
Germany's war effort. The joyous welcome received by Hitler in March
1938, when hundreds of thousands of supporters gathered in Vienna's central square, Heldenplatz, to cheer Hitler's declaration of the *Anschluß*—the
annexation of Austria into the German *Reich*—was officially forgotten and
rarely referred to. In an interview, Bernhard recalled how, as a youth in the
early forties, he had attended the NS-Schülerheim (the National-Socialist
Boarding School) in Salzburg. After 1945 the school's name was changed to
the Johanneum, and "Instead of Hitler's picture, they hung a cross on the
wall," he explained, "exactly on the same nail."[4] "[T]hey're socialists / they
claim / and are only national socialists," Bernhard asserted bitterly in *Histrionics;* "they're Catholic / they claim / and are only national socialists" (218).
Repressed history was replaced by a vacuous and sentimental self-image
reflecting the "good old" prewar Austria of waltzes and bonhomie; unlike
Germany, no "mastering" of the past was required. The gap between this
constructed image and the awareness of its mendacity produced in many
writers and intellectuals "a perception of the world as parody and grotesque
and at the same time as suffocatingly banal and stereotypic."[5] In this analysis we find both the object of Bernhard's unbending contempt and the
style—parody and grotesque—through which, at least in part, he portrayed
that object.

The past is the stuff of which Bernhard's characters are made. His is a
theater of voice, of long, unpunctuated monologues delivered on
metaphoric stages presenting highly concentrated images of the world—a
stage not unlike Beckett's. But unlike Beckett's, Bernhard's language, alternately cynical and sentimental, mirrors the idioms and inflections of a concrete national past, still common to the present. His idiomatic voices might
belong to that other great Austrian ventriloquist, Ödön von Horváth,
except that Bernhard's voices are derealized through the extended monologue form, the obsessive repetitions and contradictions, and the minimal
narrative to which they are attached. While Heiner Müller called his stages
"landscapes beyond death,"[6] Bernhard's plays have been described as consisting of "a language after death, a language of relics (i.e., quotes) reconsti-
tuting a culture," and a society, as artifice.[7] Initially comfortingly familiar,
with its so particular cadence of Viennese German, Bernhard's language
finally evokes the mendacity and posturing that have colonized the language

and mentality of his people. His figures too are drawn from a familiar world: the *Schmaltz* and *Schlag* of Austrian self-identity—the opera singer, the musician, the matron, the circus director, actor, and politician. These self-performing characters rummage endlessly through memory, coming up with spite and contradictions, exposing different versions of their relations to each other, their parents, their past. Speech in Bernhard's plays is all-consuming and fluid; it moves in associative loops from one rumination to the next, circling and repeating private obsessions, aggressions, memories. Everything sounds overly familiar in his plays, as though all this had been said before, and the sense of unnatural repetition is underscored through repeated quotes: "Poverty is no longer necessary," Vera tells us in *Eve of Retirement,* "Poverty is caused / by the poor themselves / Don't ever help the poor / father used to say."[8] The characters are forever comparing themselves to their parents, seeing their parents in themselves, quoting and becoming the people they quote. "You took completely after father / if he could see / what you've achieved" (165)—Vera says to her Nazi brother. The appeal to "father"—that is, to Germany's past—as the authority and model, loved and despised but ultimately imitated, quoted, and repeated by his children, makes clear the memorial structure of historical repetition.

The past is always present in a Bernhardian play or novel. It is frozen as an indelible trace into the landscape, language, situations, and behavior of his characters. These traces make specific and provocative what would otherwise be parabolic and abstract in Bernhard's work. We might compare Bernhard's characters to, for example, Peter Handke's Kaspar, a character based on the historical figure of Kaspar Hauser. Handke's Kaspar is a blank character formed and created by Prompters—abstract voices that teach him language, thought, and behavior simultaneously. Kaspar learns well and finally comes to resemble his teachers fully. But when he first appears on stage, and before it is driven out of him, Kaspar carries within him a "trace" from the past: his one "original" sentence—"I want to be a person like somebody else was once."[9] Handke abstracted this sentence from the more specific one spoken by the historical Kaspar Hauser when he appeared in Nuremberg in 1828: "I want to be a horseman like my father was before me."[10] Handke's abstraction purposely displaces the influence of the biological—and historical—father onto the determinism of a discourse, a structure of language and ideas that become the mechanism for Kaspar's reconfiguration in the form of that discourse.[11] Kaspar finally performs the language forced upon him by the Prompters, but he is lost as a historical subject. Bernhard's stage characters begin, we might say, where Kaspar ends. They are already complete as "discourse" when we meet them, in no need of

Prompters; but this discourse is consciously steeped in, and reflexively evokes, the concrete remains of historical memory.

Through these remains, Bernhard portrays "mindscapes" that have been prewritten and overwritten by a collective past. The image of "inscripted" minds is ubiquitous in Bernhard's writings, but it is most overtly developed in his 1974 play *The Hunting Party* (*Die Jagdgesellschaft*), where the general says of the writer:

> You see he scribbles
> all over the walls of his mind
> all over
> a mind covered with writing
> a completely covered
> and therefore completely blackened mind
> scribbled on with such speed
> that already one line is scribbled right over the other
> like a madman.[12]

Consciousness is imaged by Bernhard as a Derridean primacy of writing over orality; the past is imprinted *as language* within memory. This image of memory as mental inscription recalls Freud's discussion of memory and the "trace" in his short article, "A Note upon the Mystic Writing-Pad." There, Freud compares the structure of memory to a writing pad consisting of a celluloid sheet covering a soft wax slab. As long as the cover sheet is pressed against the wax, we can read the imprint. Once it is lifted, however, the imprint disappears and the page is ready for a fresh inscription. The upper sheet is always reusable and retains nothing of what was previously written. Traces of the former inscriptions do, however, cohere to the soft wax below; and even as these are overwritten, their trace is never wholly extinguished. Thus this mystic writing-pad, like "our mental apparatus," retains permanent traces of what has been seemingly effaced on the surface[13]— traces that surface as a past buried and deeply inscribed, barely legible, conflicted, one line stumbling "right over the other" as in Bernhard's plays.

Bernhard's dramatic output was large, but not particularly varied. All of his plays show a group of static, talkative characters rehearsing their obsessions and misanthropy within an unchanging, theatrical setting—a circus, a hunting lodge, a party for paraplegics, a provincial stage, an opera singer's dressing room, a birthday party for Himmler. In all of Bernhard's novels and plays, the "family" is the central unit; and always, family "echoes the idea of nation."[14] Plot is minimal and most of the development is contained within the opening stage image, and within the endlessly moving language. Like

Beckett, to whom Bernhard is often compared,[15] the repetition of these central devices—circular voice and static image, remembrance and contradiction, a carefully honed language and an open, unfinalized structure—reflect a pessimistic worldview and a preoccupation with death. But death in Bernhard is less existential than in Beckett. I agree with Steve Dowden that "Bernhard's pessimism is at bottom anchored in historical experience," and especially in Austria's "morally blighted history."[16] Sharing many of Beckett's dramatic tactics, Bernhard grounds them in detailed historical and local references, in the concrete geography and specific idioms of Austria and Germany. His pessimism, and his unbending animosity, are less ontological than historical, less concerned with "human nature" than with the nature of the past.

The audience is always central in Bernhard's theater. Even his least realistic plays are "locally" inscribed, reflecting (and often parodying) the context of their performance, as well as their status as theater. Bernhard's plays fit easily into Linda Hutcheon's description of postmodern literature as manifesting the paradox "of complicity and critique, of reflexivity and historicity, that at once inscribes and subverts the conventions and ideologies of the dominant cultural and social forces."[17] A prime example of this is Bernhard's infamous ridicule of the Salzburg Festival—and its "cultured" Austrian audience—in many of the plays commissioned by and written *for* that festival. Each of the resulting scandals provoked divisive (and profitable) media coverage that certainly reflected Bernhard's "complicit and critical" relationship with the foremost venue of "official culture" in Austria.[18] But this doubleness of reflexivity and historicity goes further. As I will show in the discussion of the plays, Bernhard's theater is aggressively self-reflexive and openly aware of the specific audience that is always its subject. In *Eve of Retirement* and *Heldenplatz,* Bernhard refers directly to the audience, to current political scandals, to precise historical memories, thus requiring the "mediating" or oppositional function of an always complicit and implicated viewer. Bernhard's plays may begin on the stage, but they always end in the audience. This paradoxical double awareness, of remembered past and performed present, is translated into structures of temporal conflation within the plays and comprises one of Bernhard's most striking memory tactics.

I begin with a discussion of Bernhard's dramatic devices through his 1984 play *Histrionics,* a typical Bernhardian "comedy." Through it, I wish to explore a dramaturgy rooted in forms of repetition, in regressive rhetorics, in reflexivity and embeddedness, in the contradictions—recall and retraction—through which memory constantly revises itself, and through which a postmodern aesthetic of fragment, pastiche, and contrariness takes shape.

But I will concentrate predominantly on Bernhard's two overtly political memory-plays, *Eve of Retirement* and *Heldenplatz,* which contain Bernhard's usual dramatic tactics, but applied more concretely than usual to a collectively repressed past and its present manifestation in Bernhard's specific audience. What will especially interest me is the relation between the plays and the memory produced and "performed" in the scandals surrounding these plays: that is, the interrelations between performance and reception. Both plays were written with a particular audience in mind, and at a particular historical moment. Both provoked "memory scandals"—*Eve of Retirement* in Germany, *Heldenplatz* in Austria. And both were directed by the controversial German director Claus Peymann (who directed the premieres of almost all of Bernhard plays), the first in Stuttgart, the latter in Vienna. The circumstances of these performances turned both productions into dialogues with the knowledge and memory of the audience and with the consequences of repression.

Histrionics: Staging Postmodern History

Histrionics was written for, and premiered at, the Salzburg Festival of 1985. It is a play about the performance of a play. The characters represent a small troupe of actors—a family, as usual; and the setting is a provincial stage in Austria. As such, the play is automatically self-reflexive and audience-inclusive. The central figure is the "nationally recognized actor" Bruscon— "who played Faust in Berlin / and Mephisto in Zurich" (191)—now on tour of the provincial theaters with a play he himself has written, *The Wheel of History:* a play we will never get to see. The village at which he and his family have now arrived is Utzbach—"Utzbach like Butzbach," runs the refrain—a town of 280 people that, like the surrounding villages, has little to offer "but pig breeding institutes / and churches / and Nazis" (191). A bully and a tyrant whose treatment of his ever-coughing wife and docile children—his only actors—is outrageous, Bruscon is a parody of the self-important man of histrionics and a familiar Bernhardian tyrant-hero. Bernhard's use of theater is as a metaphor for the seedy provincialism of Austria as a whole. His play within a play—Bruscon's *humana comedia,* his "sort of *theatrum mundi*" (198) starring "Nero Metternich Hitler / historic constellation / Churchill the link" (270)—then becomes a parody of both postmodern "history" and a derailed Austrian historical consciousness. A faithful Bernhard audience, which the Salzburg audience was, would easily have recognized Bernhard's signature themes—artistic despair, national disgust, provincialism, dilettantism, tyranny, and a general misanthropy that finds its particular target in Austrians and their history. *Histrionics'* many local and geographic references assume the audience's knowledge on various levels, including a knowledge of Bernhard's own experiences at the festival within which this play was being shown, and to which it refers.

"Theater plays" draw much of their humor from the conflation of a fictive and a real audience, as Bernhard was well aware. Standing on the stage, looking over his "audience" of "Remarkably short people / remarkably short / and fat" (273), Bruscon speaks with disgust of the unworthiness of his spectators, and of the stage on which he is forced to appear—"This architectural helplessness / the horror of these walls / . . . this monument to bad taste" (208)—ridicule that reflected Bernhard's opinion of the Salzburg theater venues. Bernhard sets this "theater" within ever widening geographic circles through the comic device of naming real towns and cities, mapping a real world within his fictive play. He begins with the provinces around "Utzbach like Butzbach"—Gaspoltshofen, Frankenmarkt, Reid im Innbreis, Mattighofen, Zwicklett, Gallspach, St. Radegund, allowing Bruscon an anecdote about each, imbuing the repeated names with a certain absurd musicality. But provincial Austria is extended outward through self-centered stories that draw a map from Le Havre to Haag, from Berlin to Zurich, Cologne, Bochum, "the Rhineland or the Ruhr," from "Bergamo across the Alps / to Kiel / on the Baltic," from Hamburg to Copenhagen, Ostend, Palermo, Madrid, France, Italy, and finally always "Austria / Österreich / L'Autriche / . . . a cesspool / in the pus-filled boil of Europe" (218). This geography rhetorically collapses all of Europe onto Bruscon's shabby stage at the center of which are always the mendacious recesses of "Austria / Degenerate / . . . Austria / grotesque" (205).

The mapping of Europe is paralleled by Bruscon's reorganization of European history. Two temporalities intersect in the play. The minimal forward-moving action shows the rehearsal and preparation for that night's performance. Curtains are hung, soup is eaten, lines are practiced, costumes donned. "Time" in Utzbach is nothing if not banal—Tuesday is blood sausage day, pigs are fed at five, soup is served at three. On the other hand, temporal progression is totally lifted in Bruscon's *Wheel of History,* his "comedy of creation" (192) and the centerpiece of Bernhard's play. Metternich plays "a decisive role," as do Lady Churchill, Einstein, and Madame Curie. There is an encounter "between Metternich and Napoleon / on Zanzibar" (244). Hitler

encounters Napoleon and
has drinks with Roosevelt on the Obersalzberg

> . . . Goethe gets an attack of coughing
> and is carried out of the salon by Kierkegaard.
> (217–18)

It soon becomes clear that this historical clutter, this comedy "which in fact / is a tragedy" (190), is parodying the type of postmodern history play that Heiner Müller perfected in the seventies with *Germania Death in Berlin, The Battle,* or *Gundling's Life Frederick of Prussia Lessing's Sleep Dream Scream*—plays that put into practice Müller's dramaturgy of "flooding" the audience with collages of conflated pasts.[19] But such a collage structure is opposed to Bernhard's own concentrated form of drama. Unlike Müller, who investigates the consequences of historical memory upon his audience, Bernhard parodies the *in*consequence of historical memory within an audience adept at rewriting and repressing history. Within the fantasies of Buscon's historical imagination and the historical moments he evokes—all of which his audience would have known and understood—only one memory of the past is presented as factual and "traumatic." This is Bruscon's account of how he was nearly killed during the war in 1944: he was knocked down in St. Radegund, a mere ten kilometers from Utzbach, by a butcher's assistant "who mistook me for a candlemaker / alleged to have hailed from Mattighofen" (194). This was forty years ago, but Bruscon has never forgotten the incident that "might well have been the end of me." On the other hand, a picture of Hitler, found hanging on the stage wall, where it has "always hung," triggers no memories at all. "No one's taken umbrage about that / so far" (217) the landlord says. Bruscon contemplates whether to remove the picture from the stage, but looking out onto his Salzburg audience, he concludes that Hitler's picture would after all be necessary: "we've got to have Hitler here" (213), he says. History and memory, in this comedy of historical ungroundedness, are not invoked as coexistent or simultaneous in the audience's imagination—as they are, for example, in Müller's plays. Bernhard is not concerned here (as he *is* in the plays I discuss below) with the instability of memory and the psychosis of collective repression; rather, he admonishes Austria's willful distortion of the past, wagging an accusatory and parodic finger at an audience who, he has no doubt, remembers the past all too well.

Bernhard's mockery of his Salzburg audience, and of its memory, is structured into one of the central leitmotifs of the play: Bruscon's obsessive demand that the play must end in absolute darkness. "The climax of my comedy / is perfect darkness," he insists; "that is the sine qua non for the whole thing / if it isn't to be perverted into its opposite" (196). Hence, he

insists that the fire chief permit all lights—including the emergency exit
lights—be extinguished for the apocalyptic finale, which includes the lines

> Behold mankind annihilated
> The crucial sentence
> before it is totally dark
> Lady Churchill leaves her husband Winston
> and Stalin retracts his signature.
> (256)

This "fire light" subject is not just another piece of absurdity. It would have
brought much amusement to a Bernhard audience, who would have recognized in it the play's embeddedness not only in a specific national history
and geography, but also in Bernhard's own production history at the
Salzburg Festival. In 1972, Bernhard's play *Der Ignorant und der Wahnsinnige*
(*The Ignoramus and the Madman*) premiered at the festival and turned into his
first Salzburg scandal. In order to achieve a symbolic effect, Bernhard
demanded that all lights be turned off at the end of the play—fire exit signs
included. The fire marshal refused, as did the festival authorities. Bernhard
refused to relent, and the heated arguments soon attracted newspaper coverage, media interest, and a very histrionic public row. In Bruscon, Bernhard parodies himself and the entire incident—while also assuming an audience sufficiently versed in his theater history to recall this twelve-year-old
scandal.

Histrionics, like *Eve of Retirement,* ends in a theatrical reversal that parodies and explodes the play's two opposed temporal schemes. Scene 4 begins
with the distant sound of thunder. The actors are dressed as the historical
figures they are to portray—Madame Bruscon as Madame Curie, daughter
Sarah as Lady Churchill, the son as Metternich, Bruscon as Napoleon. As
they await the audience, who will soon see Bruscon's "high art / no arcane
nonsense / in a certain way I am / a fanatic for the truth" (275),[20] Bruscon
complains and redoes his wife's makeup. She is playing Madame Curie,
who, Bruscon tells us, is an "absolutely magnificent historic figure" he has
always loved. She does, however, require much black eye-shadow. Bruscon
applies the black shadow, circling and recircling the eye, extending it outward until her entire face "is finally completely black," scribbled over and
blackened like the writer's mind in the passage previously quoted. Meanwhile, he admits, looking at his wife's "rearranged" face, that Madame
Curie was "an eccentric Polish woman," uninspired and "boring in the
extreme / as history shows" (275–77). Such retractions and reversals are typical of Bernhard's postmodern refusal to allow absolutes or any uncontested

reality into his writings. This approach is now applied to the play's anecdotal ending. As the four historically dressed actors nervously prepare to perform their chaotic version of *The Wheel of History,* and thus also bring the play's "plot" to closure, the thunder and storm grow noisier until "dreadful rolls of thunder which refuse to stop" pour rain through the ceiling onto the stage. Shouts of "The parsonage is on fire" are heard in the audience—further mocking the "fire light" demand for darkness—who rush out of the theater leaving the four famous figures with no history to perform. Bruscon, who brawled and bullied throughout the play, is defeated by a thundering voice even louder than his own. Thus, postmodern history will not take place; and Bruscon's planned "apocalypse" is precluded by the *Götterdämmerung* taking shape outside of his little stage.

Performing Nazism: *Eve of Retirement*

Eve of Retirement (*Vor dem Ruhestand,* 1979) is one of Bernhard's most historically specific plays; it is also one of his most repetitive, ritualized, and memoried. A play of "doubleness" and unsynthesizable tensions, it is both realistic and metaphoric, structured both causally and cyclically, enacting a consciousness of historical specificity and ritualized changelessness. Steeped in public history, it simultaneously ritualizes history through private memory. This doubleness, the coexistence of historical and ahistorical consciousness, of development and stasis, time and timelessness, is contained within a self-reflexive theatrical mold that places the audience at the center of the performance. The multiple temporal codings, echoed in every gesture and object of the play and epitomized in its third-act ritual celebration, reflects—and implicates—the history and memory of its audience. A "ritual of remembrance," this play was intended as a political intervention into a memory-scandal at that time raging in Germany. As in *Heldenplatz,* there is no separation between past and present; memory, and its repression, are viewed as constituting the present.

With *Eve of Retirement,* Bernhard seemed to have written a realistic and narratively structured play, depicting contemporary German characters and their Nazi past in concrete, chronological detail, thus implying a political/historical drama. Simultaneously, however, this play is a metaphoric ritual in which action and language are circular repetitions of past repetitions and which, in Mircea Eliade's sense, takes place *in illo tempore,* in the "Great Time" of origins. In this sense, history is not portrayed but repeated, through archetypes that "restore" the past. Moreover, the apparent subject of the play, Nazism and its continuation in today's Germany, is aimed at an audience both implicated and affected by the subject, and within which (Bernhard seems to imply) both time-schemes and worldviews (progression and repetition) coexist and are conflated. Through the use of theater self-reflexivity—a third, critical time-scheme—Bernhard consciously turns the play into an ironic dialogue with, and serious attack on, his audience.

Eve of Retirement presents us with characters whose ages, activities, objects, and memories are calibrated to serve as markers for a specific, historically recognizable reality. Judge Rudolf Höller and his sisters Clara and Vera are situated in contemporary Germany (the late 1970s, when the play was written), possibly in Stuttgart, where the scandalous premiere performance took place and whose ranking politician was pointedly referred to in the text. Höller, in his late sixties and about to retire from the bench, is the matured version of the "youngest judge on the entire Eastern front" (196) and substitute commander of a Nazi concentration camp who, for decades, has secretly practiced the rituals of his loyalty to National Socialism. The play takes place on "October seventh. . . . everything in him is geared toward the seventh" (125)—the birthday of SS head Heinrich Himmler, and a date Rudolf has been commemorating for over thirty years. The play's minimal plot enacts this yearly ritual in a clear progression: there are Vera's preparations (ironing, cooking); Rudolf's second-act arrival and the annual act of incest between him and Vera; the third-act celebration meal and rituals of remembering; and a final ironic reversal.

The stage Bernhard describes represents a large, old-fashioned, deceptively ordinary living room unchanged since the days of their childhood. Clara, a paraplegic crippled during an American bomb raid, is first seen reading her leftist newspapers, while Vera chills the Fürst Von Metternich *sekt,* "the brand Rudolf likes so much" (118). This well-known champagne, recalling the ultraconservative Hapsburgian foreign minister who shaped Europe in the nineteenth century, was, we learn from Rudolf, what

> we drank at the camp
> That's something I always paid the greatest attention to
> that there was always enough Von Metternich at the camp
> otherwise we'd have never been able to take it.
>
> (194)

The details of Rudolf's past, his membership in the Hitlerjugend, volunteering for the army in 1939, the names of the cities where he served during the war, his description of Himmler, of the fate of the Hungarian and Polish Jews, of Auschwitz ("Two and a half million / that's what Eichmann said. . . . That's what Eichmann said to Gluecks" [202]), the false papers provided by Himmler in 1945 that allowed Rudolf to go underground, his ten years in hiding and subsequent emergence and integration into the legal system, where he has now achieved the position of chief justice, all these details are historically credible and doubly potent for being both accurate and taboo.

In the best naturalist tradition, not only is the play locally marked and realistically detailed, but the audience is also specific and marked. *Eve of Retirement* is doubly inscribed: reflecting both a general German/European audience thirty years "after" and the audience of the premiere performance in 1979. This audience would understand the nuanced political, historical, and local references and could react to the spare but vital stage icons. The play premiered in Stuttgart, the capital of Baden-Württemberg, some months after the divisive political scandal involving its powerful conservative minister president, Hans Karl Filbinger, a potential future CDU candidate for president of West Germany. Filbinger, like Höller, and like Kurt Waldheim in the 1980s, had long concealed his past as a (naval) "hanging" judge who, during World War II, zealously inflicted death sentences for trivial offenses. As would Waldheim a few years later, Filbinger first protested his innocence, then contested the importance of his activities, and only finally, and under severe pressure, resigned his post.[21] This political scandal is only the most obvious level of historical signification that runs throughout the play, but it is potent since, as many have noted, "Filbinger served as a symbol for the pernicious continuity between past and present in Germany."[22] The Stuttgart audience certainly understood the implications of this *Comedy of the German Soul* (*Eine Komödie von deutscher Seele*), as the play is subtitled, and reacted with boos.[23]

For all the localized realism of the setting, and historical markers notwithstanding, the texture of the play pulls in a quite different direction, that of an ahistorical parable, a grotesque and free-floating metaphor structured through monologues and repetitions. These circulate private aggressions and memories in typically obsessive Bernhardian language. As Vera says to her crippled sister:

> Say what you like
> It's all right
> I love you and protect you
> but it's hard with a person
> who despises me unnecessarily. . . .
> Rudolf often wonders
> if you wouldn't be better off
> in a sanitarium

Don't worry
we wouldn't dare
The three of us are a conspiracy
(124)

The characters are constructed of contradictory memories and open resentments. Rudolf, the symbol of continuing Nazism, is portrayed with Bernhard's usual irony: "Rudolf is a good good man," Vera insists,

You are proof of it
What's past doesn't matter
And who's to know how it really was
Now they are digging up the dirt again. . . .
Kindness creates enemies
father used to say
During the war there are no laws
father used to say. . . .
We know
and love our brother
He still is the child
he once was

(152–53)

Clara, the crippled leftist, the anti-Nazi enemy, is defamed, insulted, and
threatened with institutionalization. She rarely reacts, barely speaks, and it
soon becomes clear that the threats—and her silence—are built into the
relationship, part of its verbal stock, spoken almost by rote—as are the
repeated quotes from "father" and the childhood memories that have surely
been remembered before and never manage to sound spontaneous.

What we see is not so much enacted as reenacted. As in Strindberg's
Dance of Death, all this has been done before, said before. Already in act 1
Vera can tell us what will happen at the celebration in act 3, how Rudolf
"will sit here and suddenly not say a word," indicating that she is to bring
him the photo album. "I have to turn the pages / and I have to look at it
with him," she continues, "picture after picture / the same every year"
(141). This intuition of "sameness" is elaborated upon. "Father wouldn't
tolerate the slightest change," we are told. The furniture, the curtains, are
exactly as their grandparents had left them. Even the grime and gray of "this
ghastly house / this morgue" (143) is as it was: "nothing has changed . . .
nothing has changed" (144). This heavy sense of ahistorical stasis is countered, problematically, by narrative progression and the play's historical realism. Together they produce what Charles Russell, discussing postmodern

art, has described as "an art of shifting perspective, of double self-conscious-
ness, of local and extended meaning."[24] This shifting and simultaneity of
incommensurable perspectives achieves a typically postmodern political
effect. The play's historical grounding is subverted through stasis and return;
while the ritual celebration is deeply ironized through its historical grounding. Progression and return, narrative realism and ritual repetition, entropy
and stasis: these oppositions defeat a coherent reading of either the narrative
of German history or its ritualization through memory. Past and present
cease to function as discrete entities. Rudolf Höller will be read as much
through Hans Karl Filbinger as vice versa.

The plot develops causally in a nearly classical three-act structure: the
absent "hero" is anticipated; he arrives and complications develop among
the characters; the "hero" reveals himself in his true colors, threatens and
endangers the others, and is finally "overcome." Aside from the ending, this
could be a structural description of Molière's *Tartuffe* with the "hero's"
famous third-act entrance, his near destruction of the Orgon family, and the
ultimate deus ex machina that leads to a happy reversal. *Eve of Retirement* too
ends with an unexpected event, the sudden collapse of the "hero," reversing the plot and bringing an ironic "ending," though certainly no real closure, to the narrative structure.

At the same time, the play is structured as one complete and pre-
planned action, the preparation for and celebration of an annual ritual that
remains unchanged from year to year. The narrative development, which
seemingly traces a progress, is thus in fact a repetition, inevitable, without
spontaneity or unique action, aside from the ultimate *coup de théâtre*. These
two temporal schemes parallel Mircea Eliade's description of the differences
between "historical and archaic man" in *Cosmos and History*. In Eliade's thesis, historical consciousness is narrative and developmental and assumes "a
succession of events that are irreversible, unforeseeable, possessed of
autonomous value."[25] Archaic man, in Eliade's terminology, sets himself in
opposition to historical consciousness, and history, through an ideology that
is cyclical, based on repetition and return, and that refutes change. This ideology is expressed through the faithful reproduction of myths that transmit
"paradigmatic models revealed to men in mythical times."[26] Through "the
paradox of rite" (hallowed gestures performed *in* time in order to annul time
itself), human beings are projected "into the mythical epoch in which the
archetypes were first revealed." This enacts "an implicit abolition of profane
time, of duration, of 'history.'"[27]

Thus, what appears to take place over an evening *in* time is simultaneously a rejection *of* time. The celebration of the Höller's sacred archetype, Himmler, accomplishes a "revolt against concrete, historical time" and effects a "return to the mythical time of the beginning of things, to the 'Great Time'"[28]—which, for the Höllers, is the originary creation of the Nazi universe, rehearsed yearly through memorial practice. For the audience, however, the concrete and detailed references to a common past encourage a simultaneous *historical* evocation of Himmler and the *narrative* of German history. The play thus moves in two different directions simultaneously: the ritual repetitions of sanctified acts and memories deny change and appeal to the memories assumed still active in the audience, while the narrative structure and historical markers evoke a recognizable past whose plot progression implies change and history. These two contrary movements are not synthesized; we are in neither the realm of (historical) narrative realism nor of (ahistorical) ritual repetition. Eliade claims that mythical ideology "makes it impossible that what we today call a 'historical consciousness' should develop."[29] The two systems are, he argues, mutually exclusive. Yet in *Eve of Retirement* both are proposed and offered to the audience. Moreover, Bernhard implicitly suggests that both—ritualized memory and historical consciousness—already coexist *in* the audience.

Benjamin Heinrichs, in a review of *Eve of Retirement,* wrote with admiration of Bernhard's capacity to create a text on fascism written simultaneously from within and without, reflecting both "scornful remoteness and despairing proximity"[30]—both a shared memory structure and a critical historical consciousness. This doubleness does not remain binary but is itself problematized by Bernhard through abundant self-reflexive theater metaphors that remove the characters from both narrative time and ritual timelessness and place them in the suspended time of theater. As in many Bernhard plays, the characters here are also *players,* acting a role on the double stage of fictive reality and the real theater. "We've been acting our parts for so many years / we can't get out anymore," Vera says; "we keep acting our parts / to perfection / sometimes we don't understand it ourselves" (139). These "parts" are both the deadly habit that controls their repetitive day-to-day and the "parts" written for them by history. "We have rehearsed our play / the parts were cast thirty years ago / each of us got his role" (140). The parts are also, of course, the theater roles rehearsed and being played on stage. "Sometimes I actually see myself / on a stage / and I am not ashamed in front of the audience" (141), Vera continues, indicating that there is no need for shame in front of complicit supporters. The "loaded" moment of the play's first presentation in Stuttgart, at the peak of the Filbinger scandal, heightened the relevance and implications of this reflexivity. The co-optation of the audience into the play further emphasizes the present "time" (and context) of performance, asserts links between stage and outside reality, and accentuates the complicit and knowing "role" into which the spectator has been cast.

Eve of Retirement is situated, as are many of Bernhard's plays, in a bourgeois salon evoking the atmosphere of "old" Europe, the Europe of "then." As in *Heldenplatz,* tall windows dominate the stage, looking out on the old trees of Germany. Old-fashioned furnishings and the absence of modern appliances turn this into a timeless theatrical space. As the play opens, Vera stands, ironing Rudolf's judge's robes, the sign of his present rank and profession, while Clara sits, reading her newspapers. Soon, however, Vera begins to bring objects onto the stage that are not "natural" parts of the milieu. In a self-reflexive gesture, Bernhard sends Vera into the wings to bring out, one by one, objects marked as sites of taboo memory: a framed photograph of Himmler, an SS officer's uniform, the striped jacket of a concentration camp prisoner, SS boots. One by one, Vera irons, brushes, cleans, and polishes these objects. For two pages' worth of dialogue, Vera meticulously polishes the photograph by the light of the window, breathes on it, polishes, breathes, polishes. She sets in on the window sill, looks it over, and finally takes it backstage. The SS uniform receives much longer care: the jacket is hung on the window where it can be easily seen by the audience while the trousers are slowly ironed, held up against the light and inspected, ironed, held up and inspected, ironed, until they are finally hung with the SS jacket (onto which Vera pins the Iron Cross of the First Order). The entire process is slowly repeated for the striped prisoner's jacket—which, we're told, Clara is sometimes forced to wear during the ceremony—and then the SS officer's boots. The stage fills up with the specific historical symbols of Nazi power, aestheticized and sanctified through Vera's care. The exaggerated attention given these items and the repetition of purifying gestures, transforms them into fetishized and potent objects.

The stretch of these items is expanded in act 2 to include the body of Rudolf himself. Over the entire act he is slowly undressed by Vera, "objectified," turned into a locus of transgression through incestuous desire. Vera massages his neck, his back, removes his shirt, unzips his pants, kneels to massage his feet as the audience watches (participates in?) this taboo eroticism. As with the boots and jacket, the body is sanctified, fetishized. Simultaneously, the real historic body of a murderous Nazi becomes ever more evident through his speeches: "in our time we simply put the likes of you / under gas," he tells Clara (180):

whatever I did I was forced to do
and I did nothing
I couldn't justify
on the contrary. . . .
I have no bad conscience.

(175)

Finally, the very room they're in, indeed, the entire house, becomes
the object of this double coding, historical and ritual, past and present. We
learn that Rudolf had a great civic victory today, a victory worthy of October 7 since it parallels an act by Himmler himself forty years ago:

On this day the seventh of October a day of reckoning . . .
If it weren't for Himmler
this house wouldn't be here
you know what would be here instead
a poison plant
isn't it strange Vera that today
I too could prevent
the construction of a toxic gas plant
right in front of our windows
forty years ago Himmler prevented it
today I prevented it
There's no such thing as coincidence.

(161)

Thus, the house saved today by the judge, the house that belonged to his
parents and grandparents, is also Himmler's house, and "wouldn't be here"
but for him. The view from the window "where nature is still untouched"
would have been unbearable had Rudolf, or Himmler, allowed the "profit
mongers" to destroy the environment and cut down trees, "those beautiful
old trees / for the sake of a chemical plant / which produces nothing but
poison" (158). In the end, the house, or rather, the *stage,* with its timeless
German room and windows looking out on the "beautiful old trees" of
Germany, becomes a replica and metaphor for "Germany" of then and
now, and a conflation of the two.

   The choice of a gas factory, a "poison plant," as the objects of Rudolf's
and Himmler's humane objection is of course more than mere (crass) irony;
it is blatantly insulting, a refusal by Bernhard to be sensitive toward his audience. The word *gas* is one of the more loaded words for the contemporary
German consciousness, responsible perhaps for the fervent German fear of
nuclear attack (and retribution?).[31] Another "loaded" subject for the German audience is the Jews. Rudolf, in typical Bernhardian ventriloquism,

gives idiomatic voice to the most basic and mythical hatred, using "taboo" words taken from the Nazi vocabulary—"The Jews destroy annihilate the surface of the earth / and some day they will have achieved its final destruction" (163). At this point, Bernhard directly includes the audience and Germany's entire population "ninety-eight percent" of whom, Rudolf affirms, "hate the Jews / even as they claim just the opposite / that's the German nature." Not satisfied with these statements, Bernhard has Rudolf add "in a thousand years the Jews will still be hated in Germany / in a million years" (138). Bernhard's "abuse" of the audience led the German critic N. J. Meyerhofer to wonder if Bernhard hadn't devised *Eve of Retirement* as a *Rachestück,* a "revenge play" against the German audience in light of the Filbinger affair and the attempt of certain politicians to suppress the past.[32] The assumption of suppression—or rather *re*pression—underlies Bernhard's baiting of the audience, forcing a confrontation with collective historical memories that have become taboo topics best forgotten.

The birthday celebration (act 3) enacts the converging point of public history and repressed memory, of narrative progression and mythical (memory) return. The body we saw "objectified" in act 2 is now fully dressed in the clothes ironed and sanctified in act 1. As if enacting a role in a play within a play, Rudolf, fully costumed in the uniform, boots, and gun of an SS *Obersturmbannführer*—looking "like the very first day you wore it / absolutely perfect" (185)—sits across from Vera, the classic Nazi bride in braids and long brocade gown. Clara, dressed as before, silent throughout, sits between them. This tableau from the past transports us into the "eternal moment" the ritual is meant to recuperate; its "perfect" reproduction directs the audience's response. It also evoked the current context of the Nazi "memory debate": the Filbinger affair. Thus, the objects on stage had the multiple task of reflecting their "original" meaning, as well as all the meanings with which memory and subsequent use had imbued them. As Pierre Nora wrote about collective "sites" of memory, *lieux de mémoire* "are objects *mises en abîme*"—both preserving and transfiguring their original intention.[33] Visually, this scene reproduces the past and its continuation in the present (the "subject" of the play). Verbally, memory is ironized and politicized via the mawkish device of a family photo album.

Act 3 is intentionally provocative, pushing the act of anamnesis over the edge until it finally collapses. While the characters are statically viewing photographs and reminiscing about the past, memory becomes the play's overt subject. "Remembering / once a year / Nothing like memories" (186). The pictures they discuss follow Rudolf, among other places, from a "secret" mission to the Russian front, to the camp where he acted as substitute commander and met Himmler, to Cracow and Litzmannstadt, where Rudolf became the "youngest judge on the entire Eastern front," from the Ukraine, where Rudolf shot his first prisoners, to the outskirts of Leningrad in 1942, to Schitomir, "when I had bronchitis," to Warsaw and to Auschwitz, where Rudolf did not serve ("It wasn't meant to be"), from Berlin "after the first attack," to Verdun. Paradoxically, these memories, arranged by Rudolf—"that orderly man"—are chronological, in "perfect order" (141), beginning in "Christmas of thirty-nine" when Rudolf volunteered for the army, and tracing Rudolf—and German history—up to the American bombings of Freiburg in Breisgau and Würzburg. Thus, what at first appears as a random catalog of personal memories is in fact a thumbnail synopsis of the "plot" and "narrative" of German history from 1939 to 1945. Dates are given, cities and rivers named, and a career as varied and complex as the war it parallels, almost incarnates, is evoked in a mélange of trivial or horrific fragments—a cold caught here, a circus seen there, "happy" Poles in Cracow, the decayed faces of Jews from Hungary, the Führer on an inspection tour in Kattowitz, a beautiful Polish woman in Warsaw who "was gassed right away," Rudolf and Höss at Auschwitz. It is left to the audience to fill in the gaps, to produce their own versions of Rudolf's pictures. Memory and historical consciousness are *assumed* by Bernhard. His satiric portrayal of nostalgia requires an audience who can "remember" what else happened in Russia, the Ukraine, Schitomir, or Auschwitz.

As Vera had predicted in act 1, for every picture he has a story, "a horror story / as if his memory / consisted of nothing but piled-up corpses" (141). We get a composite of images, of verbal idioms and historical facts, drawing the audience into the act of memory and implicating them through their own understanding. Bernhard, insensitive as ever, plays on Nazi vocabulary. A high point of "comedy" and Nazi ventriloquism is reached in Rudolf's accusation that Roesch, commander of the concentration camp where he had been substitute commander, was "unscrupulous":

it didn't bother him
to send thousands and hundreds of thousands into the gas
it didn't bother him at all
for *me* it was an effort.[34]

Rudolf's use of escalating numbers—"thousands and hundreds of thousands"—and his "sensitivity" while murdering obviously recall (for a "knowing" audience) a number of Himmler's more famous speeches in which, for example, he describes the "effort" required of the "decent" German soldier "when we had to carry off thousands and tens of thousands and hundreds of thousands"; or Himmler's much-quoted speech to the SS group leaders in Posen on October 4, 1943, in which he said, in connection with "the extermination of the Jewish people": "Most of you know what it means to see a hundred corpses lying together, five hundred, or a thousand. To have gone through this and yet . . . to have remained decent, this has made us hard. This is a glorious page in our history that has never been written and never shall be written."[35] It is a page that Bernhard evokes, the knowledge of which Bernhard *assumes*. And it is the mixture of kitsch idealism and horrific image that Bernhard—critically, ironically—duplicates here.

While viewing these pictures of the concentration camp with its "lovely countryside / And there you swam in the Weichsel river," and discussing Himmler—"basically a very sensitive human being" (188), Vera switches on a recording of Beethoven's Fifth. Act 3 in fact begins with Vera's cliché about life having no meaning without music (Rudolf: "A civilized nation can make its own music" [192]). This becomes a double cliché within the visual context, recalling Heydrich and his violin, the chilling combination of culture and barbarism so well known a topos of Nazism and so overused as to evoke uncomfortable, Pavlovian laughter in the Stuttgart audience.[36] It is soon apparent that the semiotic overload—Nazi uniform, picture of Himmler, the photos, the champagne, the specific Nazi vocabulary, together with the heroic strains of Beethoven's Fifth—does not support realism but rather evokes a self-reflexive kitsch, pointedly parodic both of German pathos and of the kitsch elements in Nazism itself.[37] This, when combined with images of war and death-camps, of shootings and gassings, produces a stage reality simultaneously aestheticized and critical. Bernhard's kitsch, his trenchant parody of bourgeois sentimentality and nostalgia, is transparent, insulting, writ large. It does not, as some have claimed, "reproduce" fascist ideology—it is far too ironic and self-conscious for that; though it does, perhaps, force the audience to deconstruct the connections between kitsch emotion and the submission to fascism.[38] The kitsch is further undercut through the double ploy of Clara's silent, critical gaze, her refusal to "play," and the calculated theatrical self-reflexivity.

In this crucial section of the play, self-reflexivity takes the form of metadramatic discussions *of* memory and history, the objects of that very kitsch. "There is no way to falsify history," Rudolf says, "one day it will come to light / shining in its truest colors" (190). "Nobody can take these memories away from us / our memories," Vera says, "We can't lose them / Father always said that too" (203). These memories and longings are not presented as personal, but are rather considered by Vera and Rudolf as representative of the entire German people. The scene thus climaxes in an overt incorporation of the audience into the memories and history just presented. " . . . the majority thinks just like us," we are told but must do so "secretly." Even if they insist on the contrary "they still are National Socialists all of them / it's written all over their faces." Insinuation now gives way to the play's subtext in the audience—the present political "memory" scandal surrounding Filbinger's past and its suppression: "we do have a President now," Rudolf affirms, "who was a National Socialist. . . . this is proof of how far we've already come" (204). Thus, the Höller's secret veneration of National Socialism is expanded to include all of Germany and especially the audience, which has just participated in the Höller's ritual of remembrance through its role as coproducers of memory and meaning, and which, in its roles as citizens of Baden-Württemberg, has also played a part in the public "controversy" over the Filbinger affair. Like Peter Handke's *Publikumsbeschimpfung* (1966, *Insulting the Audience*), this section turns the audience into "actors" and seems to challenge the spectator to react, to defend himself or herself, to reject the power positions implicit in the hold of the stage (in the theater or the political arena) over the passive viewer. Through the extension of the stage into the audience, Bernhard draws direct links between present and past politics, between repression and recurrence, between passivity and complicity.

As in many of his plays (*The Force of Habit* or *Histrionics,* for example) Bernhard has created two temporal processes, conflated them, and now ironizes the entire undertaking in a final self-conscious *coup de théâtre*. *Eve of Retirement* draws to an end in a rage of pathos. Rudolf, drunk, inflamed with mythic potency, waves his gun and spits threats, declaring a soon to be reborn National Socialism. Suddenly, without preamble, he falls over onto the table. The remainder of the play involves the double-speed deconstruction of the stage, the removal of all Nazi objects, the undressing and redressing of Rudolf in order that Vera may call their Jewish doctor, Doctor Fromm, for help. In short: the play reverts from pathos to farce.

Very little dialogue is spoken during this final section. While Clara sits unmoving, silent, Vera drags the unconscious Rudolf to the sofa and begins to undo his SS uniform: his jacket, his boots, finally his trousers. Rudolf is now an inert object whose lifeless opposition to Vera's struggle to rid him of his clothing recalls Henri Bergson's description of comedy as the mechanical or inanimate encrusted upon the living body. Moreover, each piece of clothing that Vera struggles to remove is, for the audience, filled with memory and dramatic weight; we watched Vera iron and polish those clothes, we watched her undress Rudolf with erotic slowness and care.

Memory-Theater and Postmodern Drama

Now, those same clothes are not only torn off his body, they are shorn of their symbolic value, as the fetishized objects become a collection of theatrical props.

This speeded-up undressing scene almost reenacts the play in reverse. Vera runs back and forth, carrying out the same objects she had slowly carried on in act 1: Himmler's picture, the uniform, the boots, the pistol, thus accomplishing a comic de-rigging of the Nazi world. The ironic effect of these final actions is again underlined by their self-reflexive theatricality. Even before Vera begins to undress Rudolf, Bernhard has her "turn Beethoven's Fifth back on exactly where it was interrupted before" (207). Blatantly, tastelessly, this most heroic and overly familiar piece of music accompanies and comments ironically on the transformation of the "heroic" Nazi body into the collapsed remains of a dying old man. The ending of *Eve of Retirement* removes the play from the mythical "timelessness" of ritualized memory and relocates it within narrative progression, a progression toward the simultaneous ending of the ritual, of Rudolf's life, and of Bernhard's play. But above all, the ending returns the play to "theater" and to the role of the audience. Throughout the last section, indeed, throughout act 3, Clara has sat stage center, looking on and listening without moving or speaking. She neither answers her siblings' questions nor reacts to their accusations—reflecting, perhaps, the silent gaze of the audience. "It's your fault," Vera says to her sister in the penultimate words of the play, "you and your silence / you and your endless silence" (207). This is not the first time that Clara's passivity and the audience's have been equated. Toward the end of act 2, following prolonged invective against "what's going on in this country," Rudolf turns to Clara: "Speechless as always . . . she watches us and waits." To which Vera answers, "It's just a game. . . . we play this comedy" in which Clara, or the silent, watching, and waiting audience,

> plays the hardest part
> We only give her the cues
> With her speechlessness
> she keeps the comedy in motion
> (173)

Thus the ending of the play, rather than bringing closure to "this comedy," opens out accusingly to the "endless silence" of the passive and implicated spectator.

The performance of *Eve of Retirement* in Stuttgart in 1979 split its audience. The play has also split the reviewers. Donna L. Hoffmeister, for example, has protested that Bernhard's postmodern "disruption of time and memory" acts in this play to reduce "all politics to secret caprice, repression and perversion." The memories given "cancel each other out," are weightless, and lack a counterperspective.[39] "No idea is proposed in earnest," she writes, "and no reality is maintained as a locus of judgment."[40] Joseph A. Federico, on the other hand, insists that the play is nearly didactic, posing "a challenge to contemporary society to find an alternative to the historical compulsions which continue to preoccupy it." He objects to those critics who try to depoliticize *Eve of Retirement* by making of it a play not about Nazis at all but merely one more misanthropic, postmodern parable, "one more variation woven from Bernhard's central themes: repetition, theatricality, cruelty, obsession, death."[41] For Hoffmeister, the theatrical, contradictory gestures in *Eve of Retirement* remain outside of history, floating playfully above the audience; for Federico, the politically grounded fabula provides a critique and corrective to the position of the audience.

These opposing postures approximate Steven Connor's analysis of the double nature of theories of postmodern cultural politics: theories that offer the "dual prospect, on the one hand of a transformation of history by a sheer act of imaginative will, and on the other, of an absolute weightlessness in which anything is imaginatively possible, because nothing really matters."[42] Both prospects are available in Bernhard's play; they coexist in the play's double time scheme, its simultaneous evocation and dissipation of history, its rambling and its rectitude, its complex inscription and parodying of the viewer, within the act of theater itself. Hoffmeister's complaint that no counterperspective or "locus of judgment" frames Bernhard's play fails to take the context and viewer of the play into account, reading the play in isolation from its reception in a specific audience. Bernhard, in typical postmodern fashion, shifts the onus of a "locus of judgment" from the text to the interaction between the spectator and the performance, between text and context. Nor does he assume (as does Hoffmeister) a unified audience with "unifying memories" that can be "silenced" through disruptive discourses.[43] On the contrary. It is a split and fractured viewer, within whom the contrary discourses of the play can resonate, that Bernhard targets, and a split and unresolved national history that he invokes. In the end, Bernhard's conflation of cyclical and narrative time, of progression and return, seems to reflect, and seems the *effect* of, the open-ended text of recent German history—as found, among many other places, in the Filbinger affair. His play emerges from the text of history and its repression and carries on a dialogue with the memories assumed still active, and still hidden, in Germany, and within its target audience.

Past Hearing: *Heldenplatz* and the "Scandal" of Memory

Eve of Retirement generated extensive discussion, especially about the connections between the Filbinger scandal and Bernhard's provocative theater of memory. But this reaction was as nothing compared to the genuine political uproar—leading to demonstrations and attacks, involving intellectuals, journalists, politicians, and regular citizens—created nine years later by Bernhard's play *Heldenplatz*. To a far greater extent than was the case in *Eve of Retirement,* the context of *Heldenplatz*'s performance, the concrete historical situation within which it appeared, was very much part of the theatrical event. 1988 marked the hundredth anniversary of Vienna's famous Burgtheater building, and it was within those centenary festivities that Bernhard's play had been commissioned by Claus Peymann—the politically controversial German director who was then beginning his directorship of Austria's National Burgtheater. But the officially titled "memorial year" of 1988 also commemorated other events: *Heldenplatz* premiered under tight police security on November 4, 1988, fifty years after the *Anschluß,* Hitler's March 1938 annexation of Austria into the Third Reich, and fifty years almost to the day after *Kristallnacht* (November 9, 1938), for which Vienna has a particularly despicable record. On that night virtually all of Vienna's synagogues were burned down, over four thousand Jewish shops were looted or destroyed, and numerous atrocities took place on the streets of Vienna. In its wake, thousands of Jewish apartments were expropriated and thousands of Jews were sent to Dachau.[44] Peymann had been expected to commemorate a century of Austrian culture at the Burgtheater. A play that evoked the fiftieth anniversary of the *Anschluß* and the memory of Austria's Jews and their destruction was not considered by most observers to be a fitting tribute.

Heldenplatz centers on a Jewish family in the Vienna of 1988. The main character, Professor Josef Schuster, commits suicide by jumping out of his apartment window onto the historic Heldenplatz before the play begins. The metaphoric center of the play, his wife Hedwig Schuster, falls dead into her bowl of soup at the end of the play. Both of these extravagant and unheroic deaths are related to what Bernhard shows to be Austria's willing acceptance of the *Anschluß* and its active role in the destruction of its Jews. Between these two framing and accusatory deaths, Bernhard managed to infuriate much of Austria, including its Jews. Unlike most other post-Holocaust plays written in Germany or Austria, Bernhard produced a play in which the Jews are neither especially nice nor especially Jewish; in fact, they are not much different from Bernhard's usual cast of complex, misanthropic, self-centered, and slightly mad characters. Nor is the anger and bile expressed in the play mitigated by forgiveness or reconciliation. *Heldenplatz* erupted in an Austria still bruised by the campaign surrounding the election of Nazi collaborator Kurt Waldheim to the presidency. Waldheim, in his victory, proved Austria's determination to ignore its past and continue to view itself as "Hitler's first victim"—an epithet long cherished in Bernhard's homeland. Bernhard's usual anti-Austrian rhetoric, a staple in Austrian theater for almost twenty years, hit a real nerve during that "memorial" year. With *Heldenplatz*, Bernhard created a memory-scandal within the deeply etched space of Austrian repression and denial. As in his other plays, Bernhard took aim against the hypocrisy of his people and refused to relent.

Heldenplatz is a square at the center of historic Vienna. It is positioned close to the lovely Volksgarten (the garden where scene 2 of Bernhard's play takes place), and near the famous Burgtheater (where the play was originally performed). Two large museums, the National Library, and the old Kaiser palace are situated around this central square. As many have noted, Heldenplatz embodies much of Austria's national identity.[45] Literally meaning "Hero's Square," Heldenplatz figures in Bernhard's play as geography, history, and fable. During Austria's First Republic, Heldenplatz was the place for military parades and troop call-ups. Already in 1932, the first Nazi demonstration with Goebbels and Röhm took place there. It was at Heldenplatz that the crowds gathered in 1934 to mourn the assassination of their right-wing chancellor, Engelbert Dollfuss. And in 1938—the important date for this play, and the most infamous event connected with that square—hundreds of thousands of cheering Austrians gathered at Heldenplatz to welcome Hitler and the *Anschluß* that ended the First Republic and made Austria part of the German Reich. Bernhard did not need to detail all this history within the play. As always, he wrote for a specific audience, at a specific place and time: he could thus assume the audience's knowledge of the history and centrality of Heldenplatz.

The play begins in the Schuster's apartment, three floors above Heldenplatz. Josef Schuster, a mathematics professor and a Jew, was driven from Vienna with his family by the *Anschluß;* he escaped to Oxford, where he lived and taught for many years. His brother Robert, a philosophy professor and the main speaker in the play, found work in Cambridge. Later, Schuster was invited back to teach at the University of Vienna, and he returned—so Robert tells us—because he missed the music of Vienna.

He wanted his music
he wanted his childhood

again
But the Viennese were no longer
the way he remembered them.

In fact "nothing was what he remembered / Memory always deceives / memory is always a totally wrong picture" (112). The Austria to which the Schusters returned was the Austria of denial and revisionism; everything about it seemed tainted, even the music. "The Austrians after the war / had become much more hateful and even more Jew hating / than before the war," Robert says, "no one could have foreseen that" (112). Schuster's daughter, Anna, goes even further, claiming that "the circumstances today are really / just as they were in thirty-eight" except that now there are even "more Nazis in Vienna" than then; "they're again coming up / out of all their holes" (62–63). These perceptions finally convinced the Schusters to leave Austria and return to Oxford. Before the play begins, all had been packed and made ready for the family's departure; a house had been bought in Oxford, the Heldenplatz apartment sold, when, on the eve of the fiftieth anniversary of the *Anschluß,* Josef jumped out of his third-floor window. The play consists of a series of discussions in Bernhard's usual monologic form. The life and reasons for Josef's suicide are interrogated by the Schusters' housekeepers, their two daughters, and brother Robert—who gives voice to most of the anti-Austrian invective. Characters evoke Austria's past, which drove the Schuster's into exile, and the unchanged present, which finally led to Schuster's suicide.

Another vital strand of the play concerns Schuster's wife Hedwig, who, since returning to Vienna, suffers auditory seizures in which she—and finally the audience too—relives the cheering of the masses as they applaud Hitler's triumphant 1938 speech on the square below. Hedwig has undergone various treatments for her "condition" at the Steinhof sanatorium, including shock therapy. But all to no avail. This is hardly surprising since disease (which is so often a subject in Bernhard's works) is not the point here: memory, in Bernhard, cannot be cured. Like resentment, it can only be overcome (if at all) through death. By the end of the play, the roaring repeating choruses of "Sieg Heil Sieg Heil" lead to Hedwig's final collapse. Through these two deaths, Bernhard performs the taboo evocation of Austria's destruction of its Jews, connecting it with Austrians' part in Nazism, with their willing acceptance of the *Anschluß,* and with their continued refusal to "hear" the voices of a still present past.

Enormous public outcry against Bernhard's play preceded its performance. Passages had been "leaked" to the press during rehearsals, especially provocative passages attacking the Austrians, their government, their mendacity and vulgarity.[46] "What they would really want / if they were honest," one of the Jewish characters says, "is to gas us again today / just as they did fifty years ago / it's in their nature" (115). These provocations encouraged the histrionic effects that followed. The media dedicated weeks of daily coverage to the reactions and debates surrounding the as yet unseen and unread play. Waldheim called the play an insult to all Austrians. He was joined by former chancellor Bruno Kreisky, among others, in calling for the play's removal from the National Theater. Bernhard was vilified and even attacked on the street by an angry citizen. "What writers write / is nothing compared with the reality," one of the characters in Bernhard's play says,

> yes yes they write that everything is terrible
> that everything is ruined and depraved
> that it's all a catastrophe
> that it's hopeless
> but all of this
> is nothing compared with the reality.
> (115)

Bernhard claimed that he had to keep revising and "sharpening" his text during rehearsals in order, as he put it, "not to be left behind by reality"[47]— that is, by the uproar raging in the press, the parliament, and on the streets. Egon Schwarz summarized it well: "One could say that the play was already being performed in the country, while it was still in rehearsal at the Burgtheater."[48] And indeed, on opening day, two groups of protesters—for and against Bernhard—chanted and marched in front of the theater, and the night before, a group of rightists dumped horse manure on the theater steps. This *furor austriacus,* as the critic Bernhard Sorg called these displays,[49] had as much to do with the public determination not to face their own history of Nazi collaboration, as with the determined provocations of Bernhard's play.

The play, and the production, were far more nuanced and complex—though no less fierce—than these hysterical anticipations. Bernhard's tactics in *Heldenplatz* go beyond the litany of savage verbal attacks expected by his audience. This verbal layer is contained within a complex and sophisticated recreation of the geographic and historic "space" within which Austria and the audience are defined. The audience is always implicit in Bernhard's plays, and here it is signified both through direct reference and, more interestingly, through the spatial reinscription of the Burgtheater (within which the audience was sitting) and the Heldenplatz (geographically so close to the actual Burgtheater) on stage. Through this, the audience is imaged as contained within, and complicit with, the stage reality they are viewing. Bernhard confounded the play's fabula with the geography of the theater and city where the performance was being held; moreover, he evoked the past through the geography it shares with the present. Visual reinscription is one of Bernhard's central strategies for tying audience, city, and history into what Mikhail Bakhtin has called a "chronotope": that is, the unique space-time relationship that characterizes and underwrites every genre. *Heldenplatz* stresses the simultaneity of fictive stage and social world, of past and present, of Heldenplatz as diachronic and synchronic site of memory and identity.

Scene 1 of the play takes place in Professor Schuster's large linen-room. It contains one high window from which Herta, the maid, stares down onto the square below, directing the audience's attention to the spot where she had found Professor Schuster's broken body.[50] Scene 2 moves to the fog-filled Volksgarten, which divides Heldenplatz from the Burgtheater. For this scene, Peymann had his set designer, Karl-Ernst Herrmann, place a replica of a side wall of the Burgtheater within the garden, that is, *on stage,* thus reflecting the outside of the building inside of which the audience watching this play was sitting.[51] The Volksgarten, so close to the Burg-theater, is one of Vienna's most famous and revered venues. As Bernhard's translator Gitta Honegger, originally from Vienna, wrote of this scene:

> The evocative setting touches at the core of every Viennese's most intimate experiences. . . . All of us, (including the playwright) have surrendered at one time or another to the exquisite melancholy that spreads over this historic part of the city, under the comforting cover of fog that shields its beauty and mutes its memories. It takes the full force of Bernhard's frustrated anger to clear the fog and expose our own contradictions.[52]

With the Burgtheater wall at one side, and Heldenplatz in the distance on the other, Josef's daughters and their Uncle Robert sit on a park bench facing what would, if the onstage geography were extended to the auditorium, be the parliament building. Like the French historian Pierre Nora, Bernhard and Peymann mapped out the central *lieux de mémoire* of Vienna (and thus of Austria): the central square, the acclaimed and tradition-filled theater, the garden at the heart of the capital city, the parliament to which Bernhard often refers—and placed the audience at the center of this reflexive geography. Looking into the audience, the daughters rehearse their grievances, their resentment of the Jew-hating Viennese: "the Jews are afraid in Vienna / they were always afraid in Vienna" (83); and their longing for Oxford: "in Oxford there is no Heldenplatz," we are told, "in Oxford Hitler never came

/ in Oxford there are no Viennese / in Oxford the masses never screamed"
(13).

Scene 3 returns to the Schuster apartment, this time to the living room.
Against the back wall of the stage Bernhard placed "Three large high windows which look out onto Heldenplatz" (117). In this scene, the audience
can actually *see* the square for which the play is named. The stage area is thus
centered between Heldenplatz, clearly viewed through the three windows
behind, and the audience sitting in front. This positioning becomes vital for
the final effect of the performance, with its convergence of past and present.
Throughout the play we have hear references to Mrs. Schuster's unusual
form of memory madness: her constant reliving of the screams of welcome
that greeted Hitler's arrival at Heldenplatz in 1938. These screams invade
her most trivial rituals. "Barely has she eaten a few spoons of soup," the
housekeeper tells us, "when her face turns white and she goes completely
stiff" (13). This has been going on for at least ten years, "all day continuously
/ continuously continuously" (27). At the end of scene 3, Mrs. Schuster
enters the stage for the first time. She has come to join the family for a last
supper before leaving the apartment for good. As she begins to eat her soup,
Mrs. Schuster's affliction suddenly becomes a reality: the audience—
together with her—hears the "slowly swelling cheers of the masses at
Hitler's arrival on Heldenplatz nineteen-thirty-eight" (159). These cheers,
as though struggling to break through the barrier of collective repression,
begin as barely audible background noise. Mrs. Schuster goes stiff and pale
in her chair. Meanwhile, as the chanting from Heldenplatz swells, Robert,
unaware, continues to discuss present Vienna: "In this most terrible of all
cities," he says,

> an unbearable stink spreads itself out
> from the Hofburg and the Ballhausplatz
> and from the Parliament
> over the entire wretched and despoiled land,

thus remapping a circle around the same Heldenplatz. "This little city is one
huge pile of garbage" (164), Robert concludes, as "the shouts of the masses
in Heldenplatz swell to the limits of the bearable"—and Mrs. Schuster falls
face forward into her soup bowl.[53] "All react with fear" (165).

The unbearable shouts of the masses welcoming Hitler fifty years ago,
at a spot close enough to the theater for the shouts to have indeed been
heard *inside* the theater—those same shouts filled the theater for the last long
stretch of the play. Peymann, however, did not turn off the horrible noise

with the play's end. Gitta Honegger, who was in the audience that night, describes how the first performance ended:

> The . . . four-hour long performance was followed by forty minutes of thundering applause, standing ovations, boos and whistles, with the Austrian flag and banners unfolding from the balcony both in support of and against Peymann, who bowed next to Bernhard. . . . To some, the two men, their hands clasped and held up high, appeared like a triumphant pair of conquerors as the "Sieg Heil" choruses on stage segued hauntingly into the warring choruses in the auditorium.[54]

Thus, the relentless shouts coming from the wings—from the stage's (and history's?) hidden recesses—merged with the cheers and boos coming from the front, from the audience that was simultaneously acclaiming and despising the performance of memory they had just participated in. Together, these concrete gestures, and the dead Mrs. Schuster on stage, made an iconic—and ironic—statement about Austria's willing part in Nazism, in the destruction of its Jews, and in the repression of its past. Bernhard's concrete positioning of Austrian history within the geography and memory of his concrete audience turned the performance into a platform, and an instrument, for political intervention. Vienna was his extended stage, just as his actual theater-stage reflected the geography of Vienna. The concreteness of this reflexivity had everything to do with the type of memory Bernhard was calling forth: of a specific past everywhere blurred and obfuscated in his country, for fifty years ignored or denied. It was this specific past that Bernhard insisted on calling forth for, and from, his audience.

The insistence with which Bernhard forced his audience to confront their past recalls another Austrian whose story and voice is unmistakably echoed in Bernhard's play. Josef Schuster was loosely based on the life and suicide of the Austrian writer, philosopher, and concentration camp survivor Hans Maier—better known under the anagram of Jean Améry. After the *Anschluß*, Maier, son of a Jewish father, escaped from Vienna to Belgium, where he changed his name. He was captured in 1943, tortured by the Gestapo, and spent the rest of the war in concentration camps, including Auschwitz. He never returned to live in Austria. Améry, who retained his anagram as a sign of his radically rearranged post-torture identity, did, however, continue to write and lecture in his native German language, becoming one of Germany's most flagrant *Ruhestörer* ("disturbers of the peace"), as was Bernhard in Austria. Améry's uncompromising memory, his strict sense of resentment and his precise, dispassionate repetitions of how he had lost his "name," strongly link him to the character of Schuster. Améry

wrote and spoke relentlessly about the torture and destruction he experienced, refusing to allow forgetfulness to cover up the past. Like Schuster
and Bernhard, he retained permanent offense—and a keen memory—of
what the Germans and Austrians had done. Améry's most famous book on
the memory of his torture by the Gestapo, and on the eternal torture of that
memory, bears the Nietzschean title *Jenseits von Schuld und Sühne* (1966,
Beyond Guilt and Repentance—translated in the English as *At the Mind's Limits*). In a chapter of that book, titled "Resentments," Améry wrote of the
"antimoral natural process of healing that time brings."[55] Only active memory, he believed, could prevent the industrial murder of millions by the
Germans from being

> lumped with the bloody expulsion of the Armenians by the Turks or with the
> shameful acts of violence by the colonial French: as regrettable, but in no way
> unique. Everything will be submerged in a general "Century of Barbarism."
> *We,* the victims, will appear as the truly incorrigible, irreconcilable ones, as the
> antihistorical reactionaries in the exact sense of the word, and in the end it will
> seem like a technical mishap that some of us still survived.[56]

This view precisely fits Bernhard's portrayal of the Schusters: "antihistorical
reactionaries" who, fifty years later, still insist on hearing the roars that
greeted the *Anschluß* fifty years before, and who throw themselves out of
windows as though rebuffing the flow of history that decrees the "natural
process of healing."

Améry, in his refusal to forget, represents the same type of morality as
found in Bernhard's theater: the morality of memory—and of "resentment."
Resentment, Améry wrote, is the "emotional source of every genuine
morality, which was always a morality for the losers."[57] Literally meaning to
re-sense—to feel again, and again, the humiliation and pain experienced in
the past—Améry's use of this word echoes, and subverts, the writings of
Nietzsche. *Ressentiment,* according to Nietzsche, is characteristic of "natures
that are denied the true reaction, that of deeds, and compensate themselves
with an imaginary revenge."[58] For Nietzsche, the impotence of resentment
characterizes the slave, the *Untermensch,* such as Dostoyevsky's Underground
Man. The Master is always a person of action and of the future, who refuses
to internalize his enemies and injuries and can thus, as Nietzsche writes in
The Genealogy of Morals, "shake off with one shrug" resentments from the
past.[59] Michael André Bernstein rephrases Nietzsche's *ressentiment* into three
components: the "inability to forget, to rise above, or to avenge an injury."[60]
But how, we might ask, does one "rise above" or "avenge" an "injury" like
the Holocaust? What remains of this list—is to forget: and it is this that

people like Josef Schuster, Thomas Bernhard, and Jean Améry absolutely refuse to do. Their resentment takes the form of a "daemonically obsessive total recall"—on principle; a form of recall that Bernstein terms "reminiscence-as-suffering"[61] and that prefers the self-abuse of memory to the "antimoral natural process of healing." Bernhard, like Améry, made of resentment a creed. This comes fully to the fore in the dramatic, theatrical, political event of *Heldenplatz*. Here, through concrete and unforgiving remembrance—through *resentful* remembrance of the *Anschluß* and of Austria's determined distortion of its memory, and by theatrically "placing" the audience at the center of their own blighted past, Bernhard affirmed the power of recall, and forced his audience and compatriots—the object and subject of all of his plays—to participate in the performance of their own denial and complicity, both in the public and in the theatrical realms.

For Améry, as for Bernhard's character Schuster, only death could quell memory and resentment. "We victims must finish with our retroactive rancor," Améry wrote. "Soon we must and will be finished. Until that time has come, we request of those whose peace is disturbed by our grudge that they be patient."[62] And indeed, Améry, like Schuster, finished off his "retroactive rancor" by finishing off his life. In 1978 he returned to Austria, to Bernhard's city of Salzburg, rented a room, and hanged himself. Like Schuster—or Paul Celan, or Primo Levi—he left no note of explanation: his life and writings would serve as witnesses to the reasons for his death.[63]

The connection between memory, resentment, and performance has one final link in this context. That link is Bernhard's own death, which came suddenly, three months after the premiere of *Heldenplatz*. He died, in fact, during its run, some say as a result of the enormous scandal caused by this most provocative of his plays. Bernhard's death created an additional scandal. Like Josef Schuster, Bernhard left a will that specified he was to be buried privately, and that his death was to remain unannounced until after the burial. But most stunningly, Bernhard's will demanded that nothing he had ever written, directed, edited or produced, neither book nor poem nor essay nor play, was to be published or performed "within the borders of the Austrian state, however that state describes itself . . . for all time to come"[64]—or at least for the duration of his copyright (seventy years). He also forbade his own commemoration by Austria in any form whatsoever, or by any country supported by Austrian money or institutions. Thus Bernhard, in a sense, outdid both Schuster and Améry. His rancor and resentment live on after him in an act that continues to express his will to remember and, in a typical Bernhardian paradox, his refusal to *be* remembered in a country whose betrayals he could not forget.

Conclusion

Re-viewing the Performance of Recall

If even memory has a history,[1] it follows that the agendas of memory—especially collective memory—are, at least partially, historically formed. The plays and playwrights I have discussed (and others could be added) are all conscious of the wounds and commands of history as inscribed within their particular national, ethnic, or personal milieu. Their memory-theaters reflect these wounds and respond to the commands—but from a variety of positions. The question is: are these positions *critical,* implying resistant or activist "agendas" vis-à-vis the way memory has come to function in a particular society? Or are they rather neutral transmissions of depoliticized memory images, what Patrice Pavis has described as postmodernism's implacable but short-term memory, creating "an ephemeral, amnesiac theatre" that *stores* cultural references—without invoking meaning or seeking response from its audience?[2] And if they are critical, perhaps even pained and political protestations against the way memory has been used or erased in history, can the postmodern aesthetic I have been portraying—an aesthetic of ungrounded, nonhierarchical fragmentation, of collage and conflation—logically support such a stance?

The question of postmodernism and agency is one that has long occupied critics. Throughout this book, I have supported the view (variously elaborated by Foster, Auslander, Huyssen, and others)[3] that postmodern art can be positioned in a way that activates its audience, even though the multiple codings and ungrounded structures of this form (and worldview) do not lend themselves to unambiguous polemics or to dogmatic galvanization. The assumption underlying postmodern form is that the audience addressed by it is attuned to the openness of its structures and the memoried reach of its themes and is thus able to respond from within. As I have stressed throughout, the effect—and particularly the *political* effect—of postmodern (memoried) art depends crucially on its interaction with the (memoried) audience for whom it is meant at a given time. The authors I considered are fully aware of this. I used the word *activist* in connection with Suzan-Lori Parks's positioning of memory in her plays, and the idea is implicit too in my readings of Thomas Bernhard's manipulation of his "history" plays. Heiner Müller was a famous provocateur for whom the past and memory are always positioned in the present and are always politically loaded subjects. Sam Shepard's plays are, by turns, critical of, or nostalgic for, the erased memory of "America," a memory erased in a very different way for Parks, who also seeks its "recovery" in the present in ways distinct from Shepard's. All of these dramatists (I exclude Beckett) take critical, questioning, provocative stands towards the "memories" of which they themselves are constituted, memories they than grapple to transmit and critique. But these stands are not all of a piece, not all the same types of critique, not all doing—as I write in the introduction—the same kinds of "memory work."

For Müller, memory is the "stuff" of which his landscape is made. He, like his target audience, is saturated in memory—historical, literary, ideological, as well as personal. It is the overabundance of history and its effects, the glut of traumatic memories, that becomes the ever-shifting material of Müller's plays, shaped in ways that attempt to reopen the contours of his audience's memory stock. This struggle for openness is ideological and is the result of another historical circumstance: Müller's conscious stand against the deterministic mechanism of the Marxist dialectical-materialist version of history, from whose dictates he stems and against which his open form reacts. Müller's collage strategies release the texts of memory from social regimentation and from personal forgetting, working against repression but also against ideological formations or exclusions. This task is in the spirit of Walter Benjamin's injunction to "blast open" the official narrative of history and refute the causal continuum that serves only the victors[4] and is itself a type of forgetting.

In contrast to this suffusion of historical memory, the postmodern "amnesia" of Shepard's plays is positioned within a commodified landscape that has moved away from history and replaced the fullness of collective memory with the simulacra of commodified images. Commodification allows history to be "controlled" through the manipulation of its icons and the erasure of its costs. Shepard's plays illuminate the mechanisms of post-industrial consumerism wherein everything is forgotten in order to be returned as a sellable product. At the same time, the replacement of a meaningful past by ahistorical imagism is experienced as a source of great anxiety. That which Müller has called the "innocence" of a memoryless America[5] becomes a psychosis of emptiness in Shepard's postmodern work. Shepard—white, male, "cowboy"—is the rightful inheritor of this America. He inherits the advantages of amnesia, the "innocence" of a people who have forgotten their own violent, exploitative, expansionist past and are thus relieved of confronting the "nightmare of history" in Müller's sense. But the costs of such forgetting are, for Shepard (and, implicitly, for America), anxiety, paranoia, and lack of depth. Shepard's memory agenda is burdened by the very "weightlessness" that is its heritage: that unbearable lightness in which, Steven Connor writes, "anything is imaginatively possible, because nothing really matters."[6] This produces a longing in his work for "a trans-formation of history by a sheer act of imaginative will,"[7] a longing expressed through collisions between past and future, through apocalyptic imaginings, and through occasional slips into nostalgia or spiritualism. Finally, this long-ing leads him to seek a more rooted past through the more rooted poetics of his later, quasi-realistic plays.

Shepard's option of "homecoming" by embracing the more traditional roots of American poetics, and hence reverting, to an extent, to the more conservative way the past is traditionally represented, is an option not shared by his compatriot, Parks. For Suzan-Lori Parks there is no dramatic "tradi-tion" dedicated to sustaining her racial and historical memory, and a great part of her work is given to the "creation" of such a tradition. Parks shares with Shepard the sense of memory loss; she does not, however, share the stakes of that loss. For Parks, the stakes of memory are enormous. Her memory malaise reaches beyond anxiety; it derives from an urgent sense of memory deprivation, of having been "written out" of history and left with a "hole" where a memory should be. It is her difficult task to invent a new theatrical language of memory, including a new way to transcribe an African-American diction of memory. Out of these poetic elements she conjures and divines a memory "lost" to black America. This performative memory is not nostalgic, nor does it harbor hopes of recovering that which can no longer be found. Parks does not "search" for origins as much as cre-ate hallucinatory pasts released from oblivion through their performance in the present. Parks mourns the deprivation of a memoried past through an activist awareness that only in representation can the past be *re*presented and, thus, made useful for the present. Her postmodern performative approach to memory functions, like Müller's theater, to open up the memory stock of her audience, and calls for an active rethinking of the way black America figures in the collective American memory.

Parks's fully developed sense of memory as politically formed, and thus as a form of political intervention, is shared by the Austrian Thomas Bern-hard. Like Parks, Bernhard takes an activist stand against memory "loss"— in his case, against the strategic repression and willful distortion of the past so widespread both in his native Austria and in Germany. More so than any of the other playwrights I discuss, Bernhard's politically situated memory-plays, *Eve of Retirement* and especially *Heldenplatz,* have an unbendingly concrete and localized memory agenda. The past is always frozen into Bernhard's monologic "mindscapes" through the language, stage images, and the behavior of his characters. But the indelible traces of the past is shaped as specifically historical, and positioned within a concrete memory discourse, in these more overtly political plays. Like Müller, Bernhard reacts to a historical/political reality. Müller's reality is governed by the double failures of Nazism and East German Socialism. Bernhard's reality is the hypocrisy and calculated misrepresentation of the memory of the past. The plays I discussed function, of course, most forcefully when performed within the context *of* those realities. A good example of this is Bernhard's *Eve of Retirement,* which becomes a different play when removed from the German audience for whom it was written, and from the political scandal (the Filbinger case) on which it is based. Its goal is "local" and immediate, although its appeal, and its performances, have been much more far-reaching.[8] The complexity of Bernhard's memory-plays stems from his paramount concern with language and form, and from his theatrical innovations, which, as with Parks, reinvent the terms through which a specific collective memory can be performed and thus *re*formed.

All of these dramatists write from within their specific world, in an idiom—a postmodern idiom—that rejects, and reacts against, the dogmatic or parochial. Their "agendas" are not programmatic; they are rather multi-coded, reactive, audience-dependent. The tendency of these playwrights is to open up the discourses of memory found within their audiences, to expose repressed or dogmatic stances, to return the stakes of memory to the general public. The memory-theaters I have studied derive, for the most part, from the text of history. In turn, they replay the traces of history as memoried inscriptions through a theater founded in language as well as in images, contained within both a performative and a literary tradition. It has been my intention in this book to focus on the double matrix of, on the one hand, a distinctive postmodern theater aesthetic, and, on the other, a memoried—*textually* based—dramaturgy. I was aware that such a choice would necessarily lead me to exclude other forms of memoried theater that might come to mind (some of which have been abundantly studied elsewhere).[9] In conclusion, I will briefly mention some of these theaters, and their differences from the postmodern memory-drama I have addressed.

The most obvious of these exclusions are the choreographies and memory-filled installations of that theater-magician of the postmodern age, Robert Wilson. Wilson, who has deployed memory abundantly in his work, worked with Müller on numerous projects (discussed in chapter 3), and his more recent installations continue to quote that relationship. His approach to memory, unlike Müller's, is almost totally imagistic and harbors few political stakes. Memory in his theater comes, perhaps, closer to Pavis's "storehouse" of cultural references than to the resistant or even activist applications found in the language-based theaters of Müller, Shepard, Parks, and Bernhard. Wilson, who has done much of his most interesting work in Germany, has created a highly visual theater often woven out of borrowed images, memory shards that struck a chord in his imagination without necessarily having any place in his own memory, shards that are more specific to Europe than to his native America.

His 1987 "environment" displayed at the municipal gallery in Stuttgart, titled "Memory of a Revolution," is an example of this. The title of Wilson's project is identical to the subtitle of Müller's 1979 play, *The Task* (*Der Auftrag*), and as with Müller's play, its images are set in the French Revolution. An immobile "still life" that Johann-Karl Schmidt, in the catalog to the exhibition, described as "animated stasis . . . a continuous play in suspended motion,"[10] Wilson's installation consisted of an eighty-two-year-old (live) actor sitting, motionless, between the toes of a huge (constructed) elephant's foot, dressed in Napoleonic costume, holding the model of an empty stage on his lap, with sculptured rats scurrying around him. The source for this image was not Müller, but rather Victor Hugo's 1862 novel *Les Misérables,* in which street urchins seek shelter within the huge plaster statue of an elephant slowly being devoured by rats. Hugo based *his* description on historical fact. From 1811 until the 1840s, a twelve-meter-high bronzed plaster statue of an elephant, a model for a fountain commissioned by Napoleon, stood on the Place de la Bastille in Paris.[11] These historical layerings are aestheticized in Wilson's beautiful "scene," distanced from the viewer/voyeur by bars through which she or he might peep, made indistinct through dim lighting, and accompanied by the sound of Maria Callas singing arias from Cherubini's *Medea*. Although the environment contains some of the elements through which the French Revolution is perhaps remembered, the context of their re-creation had little to do with any specifically political context. Wilson created this scene in conjunction with an additional exhibition being held at that same museum: an exhibition titled "Baden and Württemberg in the Age of Napoleon." No other memory agenda is discernible. The same is true of another memoried Wilson installation, his 1993 award-winning "Memory/Loss" (awarded the Grand

Prix de Sculpture), displayed at the Venice Biennale. This installation again recalls Heiner Müller—this time his *Letter to Robert Wilson* (discussed in chapter 3). That letter, referring to a Mongolian text on memory-erasure through torture, a text Wilson had originally asked Müller to turn into a scenic text, prominently contains the words "There is no revolution without memory."[12] Wilson took Müller's letter and T. S. Eliot's *The Waste Land* and created an apocalyptic environment signifying an end to memory, to revolution, and perhaps also to affective art. In a stone-walled room in a granary, with a narrow door, one window, and a parched, fracturing clay floor, the wax bust of a blindfolded man with Wilson's own features stood buried to the shoulders in the dying earth. This scene was accompanied by Wilson's recorded voice reading Eliot's *The Waste Land,* interrupted by noises and screams until the poem finally disintegrated. While the effect of this might certainly have been devastating, and was surely apocalyptic, its memory agenda was in no way an intervention into some public discourse or into a specific historical memory. Wilson's use of memory comes close to Beckett's postures of memory, creating a theater vocabulary for imaging memory rather than intervening or participating in a situated discourse on memory. In Wilson's case, the vocabulary is often nonverbal and drawn from a broad "store" of cultural memory. "I find what he does important," Müller said about Wilson, "but I would never do it that way. . . . If we want to make theatre here in Europe, we need a theatre with text, a theatre with history, and for Wilson that doesn't exist."[13]

Another memoried stage choreographer worth consideration is the German dancer, Pina Bausch. Like Wilson, she works with obsessively repeated images and gestures gleaned from a collective unconscious. Her work, like Wilson's, is temporally distorted, dreamlike, and impregnated with a sense of anxiety and loss—both personal and historical. It is also, however, repeatedly marked by images that return the viewer to Europe of the 1920s and 1930s, a period crucial to the collective German memory—of which Bausch is a part. Through visual, musical, and gestural inscriptions—choices of clothing, song, and bodily attitudes—her work evokes a sometimes nostalgic, sometimes parodic, but always visceral sense of the past, or of how the past is frozen and mediated through film and photography. Historical memory in Bausch is always part of subjective experience, and thus, of memoried identity. In her 1986 dance-play *Viktor,* for example, the entire twentieth century is traversed. Without narrative grid or chronological development, an epoch is remembered from within a grave the size of the stage, surrounded by huge mounds of earth and leaning ladders. Her troupe of dancer-actors return us through music and imagery to the early decades of this century, while they themselves seem already entombed within the grave of century's end. Both Wilson and Bausch display an unrootedness and sensual flooding of images consonant with a postmodern aesthetic. Although the way memory operates within their theaters is not identical, both draw upon cultural artifacts to create (for the most part) non-textual theaters of images.

Other names that must be mentioned in connection with contemporary memory-theater are Tadeusz Kantor and George Tabori. Both of these East Europeans—Kantor is Polish, Tabori originally from Hungary—are theatrical innovators as well as playwrights whose careers spanned much of the twentieth century, a century deeply embedded within their work. Both are of an older generation of theater auteurs (Kantor, 1915–1990; Tabori b. 1914) who have become especially prominent and influential since the 1980s. Kantor and Tabori both work with the stuff of memory, placing particular stress on the body as the site of memory—often detached from the verbally expressive dimension. Kantor's theater company, Cricot-2, cocreators of many of his theater works, drew from materials of apocalyptic remembrance, which seemed to suggest as well an impending apocalypse.[14] Kantor, who lived through World War II and returned to images of war and personal obliteration in many of his plays, was always present in his performances as an implicit witness, but also as the embodied stage-magician. In *The Dead Class* (1975), he watches as the dead return to the precinct of the living—not in the present, but in the memories of his childhood. The dead demand their life again, but more than this, they demand their embodied place within memory. Returning to the school benches of Kantor's childhood, they push aside the living, the doubles who have taken their place in memory—puppet figures, fleshless, incapable of carrying the past. In this work, Kantor tried to recover from oblivion his own life, which, as he wrote, was in danger of being appropriated by

official
History,
the history of
mass Movements,
mass ideologies,
passing terms of Governments,
terror by power,
mass wars,
mass crimes.[15]

Notes

Introduction

1. Quoted in Francis A. Yates, *The Art of Memory* (1966; reprint, Chicago: University of Chicago Press, 1993), 132.

2. Yates, *The Art of Memory,* 129–30. Another useful work on Camillo is Lu Beery Wenneker's dissertation "An Examination of *L'Idea del Theatro* of Giulio Camillo, Including an Annotated Translation, with Special Attention to His Influence on Emblem Literature and Iconography" (Ann Arbor: University Microfilms, 1970). Also of interest is Jonathan D. Spence, *The Memory Palace of Matteo Ricci* (New York: Viking, 1984), which traces the spread of this memory system to China.

3. Camillo, *L'Idea del Theatro,* quoted by Yates, *The Art of Memory,* 143.

4. Richard Terdiman, *Present Past: Modernity and the Memory Crisis* (Ithaca: Cornell University Press, 1993), 3; emphasis added.

5. Cicero, *De Oratore,* trans. E. W. Sutton and H. Rackham, Loeb Classical Library, revised, II, lxxxvii, 358.

6. *Ad Herennium,* trans. Harry Caplan, Loeb Classical Library, III, xxii, 36–37.

7. Cicero, *De Oratore,* II, lxxxvii, 357.

8. See Patrick H. Hutton, "The Art of Memory Reconceived: From Rhetoric to Psychoanalysis," *Journal of the History of Ideas* 48, no. 3 (1987): 371–92, for a detailed discussion of these developments.

9. Terdiman, *Present Past,* 5.

10. Pierre Nora, "Between Memory and History: *Les Lieux de Mémoire,*" trans. Marc Roudebush, *Representations* 26 (spring 1989): 15. I discuss Nora at length in chapter 1.

11. Marcel Proust, in *A l'ombre des jeunes filles en fleurs,* ed. Jean-Yves Tardié, 4 vols. (Paris: Gallimard-Pléiade, 1987–89), 2:4, cited in Terdiman, *Present Past,* 202.

12. Walter Benjamin, "The Image of Proust" (1929), in *Illuminations,* ed. Hannah Arendt, trans. Harry Zohn (New York: Schocken, 1968), 202; emphasis added.

13. Israel Shenker quotes Beckett as saying of his characters, "My people seem to be falling to bits." "An Interview with Beckett," *New York Times,* May 5, 1956, sec. 2, 1, 3, reprinted in *Samuel Beckett: The Critical Heritage,* ed. Lawrence Graver and Raymond Federman (London: Routledge and Kegan Paul, 1979), 148.

14. Sam Shepard, *The Tooth of Crime,* in *The Tooth of Crime and Geography of a Horse Dreamer* (New York: Grove Press, 1974), 37.

15. Heiner Müller, "Walls," interview by Sylvère Lotringer (1981), reprinted

in *Germania,* ed. Sylvère Lotringer, trans. and annotated by Bernard and Caroline Schütze (New York: Semiotext[e] Foreign Agents Series, 1990), 24.

16. John Lahr, "Spectacle of Disintegration: *Operation Sidewinder,*" in *American Dreams: The Imagination of Sam Shepard,* ed. Bonnie Marranca (New York: Performing Arts Journal Publications, 1981), 55.

17. Suzan-Lori Parks, "Possession," in *The America Play and Other Works* (New York: Theatre Communications Group, 1995), 5.

18. Andreas Huyssen, *Twilight Memories: Marking Time in a Culture of Amnesia* (New York: Routledge, 1995), 6.

19. Michel Foucault, "Questions on Geography," in *Power/Knowledge: Selected Interviews and Other Writings, 1972–1977,* ed. Colin Gordon (New York: Pantheon, 1980), 70.

20. Nora, "Between Memory and History," 7.

21. Nora, "Between Memory and History," 13.

22. James E. Young, "The Counter-Monument: Memory against Itself in Germany Today," *Critical Inquiry* 18, no. 2 (1992): 273.

23. My discussion of this monument is based on Young, "The Counter-Monument," 274–84. This material can also be found, in shortened form, in James E. Young, *The Texture of Memory: Holocaust Memorials and Meaning* (New Haven: Yale University Press, 1993), 27–37.

24. See Young, "The Counter-Monument," 281.

25. Joseph A. Federico, "Millenarianism, Legitimation, and the National Socialist Universe in Thomas Bernhard's *Vor dem Ruhestand,*" *Germanic Review* 59, no. 4 (1984): 147.

26. Donna L. Hoffmeister, "Post-Modern Theater: A Contradiction in Terms? Handke, Strauss, Bernhard, and the Contemporary Scene," *Monatshefte* 79, no. 4 (1987): 432–33.

27. See Frank Trommler, "Germany's Past as an Artifact," *Journal of Modern History* 61 (December 1989): 724–35.

28. Geoffrey H. Hartman, "Introduction: Darkness Visible," in *Holocaust Remembrance: The Shapes of Memory,* ed. Geoffrey H. Hartman (Oxford: Blackwell, 1994), 6.

Chapter 1

1. I discuss the hollowed-out subject of postmodernism at greater lengths in the introduction. A number of books on postmodern theater and drama have appeared in recent years, most notably (in English), Johannes Birringer, *Theatre, Theory, Postmodernism* (Bloomington: Indiana University Press, 1991); Michael Vanden Heuvel, *Performing Drama/Dramatizing Performance* (Ann Arbor: University of Michigan Press, 1991); and Deborah R. Geis, *Postmodern Theatric[k]s: Monologue in Contemporary American Drama* (Ann Arbor: University of Michigan Press, 1993). Other books, with a greater emphasis on performance, are Philip Auslander, *Presence and Resistance: Postmodernism and Cultural Politics in Contemporary American Performance* (Ann Arbor: University of Michigan Press, 1992); and Nick Kaye, *Postmodernism and Performance* (New York: St. Martin's, 1994). Each of these is differently

positioned within the discussion of postmodern theater, and the authors are occasionally divergent in views, but they offer overlapping theoretical constellations for the definition of postmodern theater. Rather than repeat these, I have chosen a more formalistic approach based on a less-often-cited theoretician. This definition of postmodern theater will be subsequently expanded.

2. Hal Foster, "Postmodernism: A Preface," in *The Anti-Aesthetic: Essays on Postmodern Culture,* ed. Hal Foster (Seattle: Bay Press, 1983), xv.

3. Erika Fischer-Lichte, "Avant-Garde and Postmodernism: Theatre between Cultural Crisis and Cultural Change," in *The Show and the Gaze of Theatre: A European Perspective,* trans. Jo Riley (Iowa City: University of Iowa Press, 1997), 269. This article originally appeared as "Postmodernism: Extension or End of Modernism? Theater between Cultural Crisis and Cultural Change," in *Zeitgeist in Babel: The Post-Modernist Controversy,* ed. Ingeborg Hoesterey (Bloomington: Indiana University Press, 1991), 216–28.

4. Fischer-Lichte, "Avant-Garde and Postmodernism," 273–74; emphasis added.

5. David Harvey, *The Condition of Postmodernity* (Oxford: Blackwell, 1989), 30.

6. See Arnold Aronson, "Postmodern Design," *Theatre Journal* 43 (1991): 1–13.

7. In *The Protean Self: Human Resilience in an Age of Fragmentation* (New York: Basic Books, 1993), the psychologist Robert Jay Lifton puts forth an argument similar to Fischer-Lichte's, although from the opposite perspective. He asserts that under pressure, such as changes in communication systems and basic ideological and epistemological frameworks, the "self," rather than collapsing, changes its (collective) psychological shape to fit the shapes demanded by the world. The self adapts, he writes, and becomes "fluid and many-sided. Without quite realizing it, we have been evolving a sense of self appropriate to the restlessness and flux of our time. This mode of being differs radically from that of the past, and enables us to engage in continuous exploration and personal experiment" (1). This new "self" is both the producer and the object of the forms of postmodern drama and theater.

8. Fischer-Lichte, "Avant-Garde and Postmodernism," 269.

9. See Jean-François Lyotard, *The Postmodern Condition: A Report on Knowledge,* trans. Geoffrey Bennington and Brian Massumi (Minneapolis: University of Minnesota Press, and Manchester: University of Manchester Press, 1984).

10. David Lyon, *Postmodernity* (Minneapolis: University of Minnesota Press, 1994), 75.

11. Steven Connor, *Postmodernist Culture: An Introduction to Theories of the Contemporary* (Oxford: Blackwell, 1989), 227.

12. Heiner Müller, "Literatur muß dem Theater Widerstand leisten," a conversation with Horst Laube (1975), reprinted in *Gesammelte Irrtümer: Interviews und Gespräche* (Frankfurt am Main: Verlag der Autoren, 1986), 20.

13. Linda Hutcheon, *The Politics of Postmodernism* (London: Routledge, 1989), 11. Hutcheon's almost mechanical application of this "doubleness" to a wide range of postmodern texts has been criticized as producing a closed and predictable model. See Brian McHale, "Postmodernism, or the Anxiety of Master Narratives," *Diacritics* 22, no. 1 (1992): 17–33.

14. Umberto Eco and Stefano Rosso, "A Correspondence on Postmodernism," in Hoesterey, *Zeitgeist in Babel,* 243.

15. The view of the past performed in many of these plays approximates Michel Foucault's concept of a resistant "counter-memory" that persists against the tyranny of gapless official accounts of historical development. Rather than use the past in order to reinscribe belief in a stable or continuous (national or historical) identity, Foucault's counter-memory functions through ruptures and *dis*continuities, eschewing the linear or the teleological, recalling the hidden and repressed. See Michel Foucault, *Language, Counter-Memory, Practice: Selected Essays and Interviews,* trans. Donald F. Bouchard and Sherry Simon (Ithaca: Cornell University Press, 1977), especially "Nietzsche, Genealogy, History," 139–64.

16. Tennessee Williams, *The Glass Menagerie* (1949; reprint, London: Heinemann Educational Books, 1988), xvii, xviii.

17. Williams, *The Glass Menagerie,* 2–3.

18. Peter Szondi, *Theory of the Modern Drama: A Critical Edition,* ed. and trans. Michael Hays (Minneapolis: University of Minnesota Press, 1987), 19–20.

19. Pierre Nora, *Les Lieux de mémoire,* 3 vols. (Paris: Editions Gallimard, 1984–92).

20. From the introduction by Natalie Zemon Davis and Randolph Starn to a special issue, "Memory and Counter-Memory," of *Representations* 26 (spring 1989): 3.

21. See Henri Bergson, *Matter and Memory,* 5th ed., trans. Nancy M. Paul and William S. Palmer (London: G. Allen and Unwin, 1991).

22. Mikhail Bakhtin, *The Dialogic Imagination: Four Essays,* ed. Michael Holquist, trans. Caryl Emerson and Michael Holquist (Austin: University of Texas Press, 1981), 293.

23. See Maurice Halbwachs, *On Collective Memory,* ed. and trans. Lewis A. Coser (Chicago: University of Chicago Press, 1992).

24. Pierre Nora, "Between Memory and History: *Les Lieux de Mémoire,*" trans. Marc Roudebush, *Representations* 26 (spring 1989): 8. This article is a translation of Nora's introductory essay to his collective work.

25. Nora, "Between Memory and History," 17.

26. Nora, "Between Memory and History," 7.

27. Walter Benjamin, thesis 9 of the "Theses on the Philosophy of History," in *Illuminations,* ed. Hannah Arendt, trans. Harry Zohn (New York: Schocken 1968), 257–58.

28. St. Augustine, *Confessions,* trans. R. S. Pine-Coffin (New York: Barnes and Noble, 1961), bk. 11, sec. 20.

29. Benjamin, "Theses on the Philosophy of History," 255.

30. Stéphane Mosès, "The Theological-Political Model of History in the Thought of Walter Benjamin," *History and Memory* 1, no. 2 (1989): 10. My discussion here draws from Mosès's reading of Benjamin (10–13).

31. Benjamin, "Theses on the Philosophy of History," 262; emphasis added.

32. Walter Benjamin, *Gesammelte Schriften* (Frankfurt am Main: Suhrkamp, 1980), vol. 1, pt. 3, 1243, 1244.

33. Richard Wolin, *Walter Benjamin: An Aesthetic of Redemption,* 2d ed. (Berkeley and Los Angeles: University of California Press, 1994), xl–xli.

34. Jean-François Lyotard, *The Differend: Phrases in Dispute,* trans. Georges Van Den Abbeele (Minneapolis: University of Minnesota Press, 1988), 56.

35. Heiner Müller: "There isn't a nation in Europe that didn't experience the Holocaust. This makes a difference in the subconscious." In Arthur Holmberg, "A Conversation with Robert Wilson and Heiner Müller," *Modern Drama* 31 (1988): 456.

36. Lyotard, *The Differend,* 56, 57.

37. Anton Kaes, "Holocaust and the End of History: Postmodern Historiography in Cinema," in *Probing the Limits of Representation: Nazism and the "Final Solution,"* ed. Saul Friedlander (Cambridge: Harvard University Press, 1992), 208; emphasis added. Writing on postmodernism in the cinema, and using the example of Hans-Jürgen Syberberg's highly controversial *Hitler: A Film from Germany,* Kaes focuses on what he defines as four concerns central for a postmodern historiography of film: the rejection of narrativity, the specularization of history, the proliferation of perspectives, and the affirmation of nostalgia. All of these are relevant for my memory-dramas, although I do not believe affirmation of nostalgia is a defining trait of postmodern visual arts.

38. Saul Friedlander, "Trauma, Memory, and Transference," in *Holocaust Remembrance: The Shapes of Memory,* ed. Geoffrey H. Hartman (Oxford: Blackwell, 1994), 260. Friedlander is referring to historians of the Holocaust and adds: "This evaluation applies also to my own work."

39. See, for example, Jonathan Shay, *Achilles in Vietnam: Combat Trauma and the Undoing of Character* (New York: Atheneum, 1994), 172.

40. Cathy Caruth, introduction to part 1 of *Trauma: Explorations in Memory,* ed. Cathy Caruth (Baltimore: Johns Hopkins University Press, 1995), 4–5.

41. Caruth, introduction to part 2 of *Trauma,* 153.

42. Caruth, introduction to part 1 of *Trauma,* 5; emphasis added.

43. Sigmund Freud, *Beyond the Pleasure Principle,* in *The Standard Edition of the Complete Psychological Works of Sigmund Freud,* ed. James Strachey, vol. 18 (London: Hogarth Press, 1953–1974), 29–30; emphasis added.

44. Caruth, introduction to part 2 of *Trauma,* 153, 154.

45. Müller, "Literatur muß dem Theater Widerstand leisten," 20.

46. Friedlander, "Trauma, Memory, and Transference," 254.

47. Charlotte Delbo, quoted in Lawrence Langer, *Holocaust Testimonies: The Ruins of Memory* (New Haven: Yale University Press, 1991), 7.

48. On the difference between superficial retellings of the past, and embodied recall, particularly in adults who carry the traumatic memory of child abuse, see Roberta Culbertson, "Embodied Memory, Transcendence, and Telling: Recounting Trauma, Re-establishing the Self," *New Literary History* 26 (1995): 170.

49. Friedlander, "Trauma, Memory, and Transference," 254. Friedlander is referring specifically to the trauma of the Holocaust, but the distinction between common and deep memory is valid for all serious collective traumas. See, for example, Shay, *Achilles in Vietnam.*

50. Eric L. Santner, "History beyond the Pleasure Principle: Some Thoughts on the Representation of Trauma," in Friedlander, *Probing the Limits,* 152.

51. See, for example, Andreas Huyssen, *Twilight Memories: Marking Time in a*

Culture of Amnesia, (New York: Routledge, 1995), esp. 1–9, for an extended discussion of these paradoxes.

52. Hillel Schwartz, *Century's End: A Cultural History of the Fin de Siècle from the 990s to the 1990s* (New York: Doubleday, 1990). Schwartz invents the term "janiform logic" (31) to describe the doubleness and paradoxes of the apocalyptic imagination.

53. Jean Baudrillard, "The Year 2000 Has Already Happened," in *Body Invaders: Panic Sex in America,* ed. Arthur Kroker and Marilouise Kroker (Montreal: New World Perspectives, 1988).

54. This is Jon R. Snyder's succinct summation of Vattimo's thought in his translator's introduction to Gianni Vattimo, *The End of Modernity: Nihilism and Hermeneutics in Postmodern Culture* (Baltimore: Johns Hopkins University Press, 1988), xlviii, xix.

55. Lutz Niethammer, *Posthistoire: Has History Come to an End?* trans. Patrick Camiller (London: Verso, 1992), 3.

56. Kaes, "Holocaust," 222.

57. Jean Baudrillard, *The Illusion of the End,* trans. Chris Turner (Stanford: Stanford University Press, 1994), 12. Already in *The Transparency of Evil: Essays on Extreme Phenomena,* trans. James Benedict (New York: Verso, 1990), Baudrillard discussed the phantomization of the past and the "new amnesia" that results from endless image-substitution, and thus the "re-writing" of reality.

58. Baudrillard, *Illusion of the End,* 9.

59. See Richard Terdiman, *Present Past: Modernity and the Memory Crisis,* (Ithaca: Cornell University Press, 1993), 247–56, for an excellent analysis.

60. See Nietzsche's *Of the Use and Misuse of History for Life,* as well as his attacks on archival historicism, in his foreword to the second of the four *Untimely Meditations.*

61. This is Ernest Gellner's elegant formulation in *Culture, Identity, and Politics* (Cambridge: Cambridge University Press, 1987), 6. Renan puts it more plainly: "the essence of a nation is that all individuals have many things in common, and also that they have forgotten many things." The diverse ethnic origins of the French, the devastating religious wars—such as the Saint Bartholomew's Day massacre—are some of the examples Renan brings of what must be forgotten in order for a nation to cohere. Ernest Renan, *Qu'est-ce qu'une nation?* (Paris, 1882) trans. Martin Thom as "What Is a Nation?" in *Nation and Narration,* ed. Homi K. Bhabha (London: Routledge, 1990), 11.

62. Jean Baudrillard, "Hunting Nazis and Losing Reality," *New Statesman,* February 19, 1988, 17.

63. Nora, "Between History and Memory," 19.

64. This is the wording of the resolution adopted by the Continental Congress in Philadelphia on June 14, 1777, and referring to the original thirteen colonies.

65. Nora, "Between History and Memory," 20.

66. The historical memory of Wilhelm Tell, for example, was forged on the stage through Schiller's play; and when this memory was subverted or travestied by, for example, Leopold Jessner's staging of the play in Berlin in the twenties, the audience went wild.

Chapter 2

1. Samuel Beckett, *Eh Joe,* in *The Collected Shorter Plays* (New York: Grove Press, 1984), 201.

2. H. Porter Abbott, *Beckett Writing Beckett: The Author in the Autograph* (Ithaca: Cornell University Press, 1996), 23. Numerous books and articles arguing for a modernist or postmodernist Beckett have been published since 1980. In recent years, as Abbott admits, "the postmodernist categorizers have steadily gained the high ground," 24. See chapter 2 of Abbott's book for a discussion of this "turf war."

3. See my discussion of postmodernism in chapter 1. Erika Fischer-Lichte's listing of the salient traits of postmodernism, in "Postmodernism: Extension or End of Modernism?" in *Zeitgeist in Babel: The Post-Modernist Controversy,* ed. Ingeborg Hoesterey (Bloomington: Indiana University Press, 1991), is almost a catalog of Beckett's late plays: "the redefinition of the relationship between time and space, the dissolution of the self and its boundaries . . . the shift of focus away from the work onto the reader . . . interaction between reader and text . . . the shift of the dominant as epistemological question to the dominant as ontological one . . . from monism to pluralism, from representation to performance, from referentiality to nonreferentiality . . . the self-reflexivity of a literary text" (217).

4. Enoch Brater, *Beyond Minimalism: Beckett's Late Style in the Theater* (New York: Oxford University Press, 1987), 176.

5. Israel Shenker, "An Interview with Beckett," *New York Times,* May 5, 1956, sec. 1, 2, 3, reprinted in *Samuel Beckett: The Critical Heritage,* ed. Lawrence Graver and Raymond Federman (London: Routledge and Kegan Paul, 1979), 148.

6. This is how Enoch Brater (*Beyond Minimalism,* 37) characterizes the "severed head" in *That Time,* but it holds true for all the central images in these late plays.

7. Cicero, *De Oratore,* trans. E. W. Sutton and H. Rackham, Loeb Classical Library, II, lxxxvii, 351–54.

8. Cicero, *De Oratore,* II, lxxxvii, 358.

9. Brater, *Beyond Minimalism,* 18.

10. Brater, *Beyond Minimalism,* 19; this is quoted by Brater from an interview with Tandy.

11. Cited by Enoch Brater in "Dada, Surrealism, and the Genesis of *Not I,*" *Modern Drama* 18 (1975): 53.

12. Michael Vanden Heuvel, *Performing Drama/Dramatizing Performance* (Ann Arbor: University of Michigan Press, 1991), 79.

13. S. E. Gontarski, *The Intent of Undoing in Samuel Beckett's Dramatic Texts* (Bloomington: Indiana University Press, 1985).

14. Samuel Beckett, *Proust* (New York: Grove Press, 1957), 71.

15. Charles R. Lyons, "Beckett's Fundamental Theater: The Plays from *Not I* to *What Where,*" in *Beckett's Later Fiction and Drama: Texts for Company,* ed. James Acheson and Kateryna Arthur (New York: St. Martin's, 1987), 90.

16. Natalie Crohn Schmitt, *Actors and Onlookers: Theater and Twentieth-Century Scientific Views of Nature* (Evanston, Ill.: Northwestern University Press, 1990), 9.

17. Herbert Blau, *The Audience* (Baltimore: Johns Hopkins Press, 1990), 124.

18. Crohn Schmitt, *Actors and Onlookers,* 9.

19. Samuel Beckett, *Not I,* in *The Collected Shorter Plays,* 222. Subsequent references are to this edition and will be cited parenthetically within the text.

20. St. Augustine, *Confessions,* trans. R. S. Pine-Coffin (New York: Barnes and Noble, 1961), 214 (section X.8).

21. Linda Ben-Zvi, *Samuel Beckett* (Boston: Twayne, 1986), 6.

22. St. Augustine, *Confessions,* 277 (section XI.28).

23. Beckett, *Proust,* 4–5.

24. James Olney, "Memory and the Narrative Imperative: St. Augustine and Samuel Beckett," *New Literary History* 24 (1993): 864.

25. Auditor's unclear function is attested by the fact that in a French version directed by Beckett in 1975, he omitted the figure altogether. Beckett also allowed the play to be filmed that same year by the BBC, again without the figure of Auditor. See Ben-Zvi, *Samuel Beckett,* 244, 245.

26. See Gilles Deleuze, *Difference and Repetition,* trans. Paul Patton (London: Athlone Press, 1994); and more specifically, Steven Connor's application of Deleuze to Beckett's use of repetition in *Samuel Beckett: Repetition, Theory, and Text* (Oxford: Blackwell, 1988), esp. chap. 1.

27. Brater, *Beyond Minimalism,* 23.

28. Paul Lawley, "Counterpoint, Absence, and the Medium in Beckett's *Not I,*" *Modern Drama* 26 (1983): 412.

29. St. Augustine, *Confessions,* 114 (section X.8).

30. This is how Gilles Deleuze defines Bergson's theory of memory in *Bergsonism,* trans. Hugh Tomlinson and Barbara Habberjam (New York: Zone Books, 1988), 58.

31. Henri Bergson, *Matter and Memory,* 5th ed., trans. Nancy M. Paul and William S. Palmer (London: G. Allen and Unwin, 1991).

32. Bergson, *Matter and Memory,* chap. 2, esp. 89–92.

33. Mary Warnock, *Memory* (London: Faber and Faber, 1987), 29–30.

34. Bergson, *Matter and Memory,* 95.

35. Deleuze, *Bergsonism,* 58–59.

36. Warnock, *Memory,* 30.

37. Samuel Beckett, "Dialogue Two," in *Proust and Three Dialogues with Georges Duthuit* (London: John Calder, 1965), 103.

38. See, for example, Charles R. Lyons, "Beckett, Shakespeare, and the Making of Theory," in *Around the Absurd: Essays on Modern and Postmodern Drama,* ed. Enoch Brater and Ruby Cohn (Ann Arbor: University of Michigan Press, 1990), 97–127; Keir Elam, "*Not I:* Beckett's Mouth and the Ars(e) Rhetorica," in *Beckett at 80/Beckett in Context,* ed. Enoch Brater (New York, Oxford: Oxford University Press, 1986), 124–48; Lawley, "Counterpoint."

39. See Billie Whitelaw, "Billie Whitelaw: Interviewed by Linda Ben-Zvi," in *Women in Beckett: Performance and Critical Perspectives,* ed. Linda Ben-Zvi (Urbana: University of Illinois Press, 1990), 3–10; and Toby Silverman Zinman, "Billie Whitelaw: What Beckett Said to Me," *American Theater* 11, no. 4 (1994): 24–25.

40. Whitelaw, "Billie Whitelaw: Interviewed by Linda Ben-Zvi," 4.

41. See chapter 1 for my discussion of the two parts of Proustian memory: unwilled recall and narrative reconstruction.

42. Connor, *Samuel Beckett,* 130.

43. Abbott, *Beckett Writing Beckett*, 28–29, emphasis added, and 40, respectively.

44. The actor Patrick Magee heard this from Beckett when he was playing Listener at the Royal Court Theater in 1976 (quoted by Brater, *Beyond Minimalism*, 37).

45. Cited in Brater, via the witness of S. E. Gontarski and James Knowlson (*Beyond Minimalism*, 37).

46. *That Time*, in *The Collected Shorter Plays*, 229. Subsequent references are to this edition and will be cited parenthetically within the text.

47. Brater, *Beyond Minimalism*, 45.

48. Kurt Vonnegut, *Slaughterhouse-Five or the Children's Crusade* (New York: Delta, 1969), 23.

49. Deleuze, *Bergsonism*, 58–59.

50. Walter D. Asmus, "Rehearsal Notes for the German Première of Beckett's *That Time* and *Footfalls* at the Schiller-Theater Werkstatt, Berlin," trans. Helen Watanabe, *Journal of Beckett Studies* 2 (1977): 94.

51. Cited by Beryl S. Fletcher and John Fletcher, in *A Student's Guide to the Plays of Samuel Beckett* (London: Faber and Faber, 1985), 220, from a letter written to them by Beckett on August 5, 1976.

52. Connor, *Samuel Beckett*, 138.

53. Seven years before Beckett wrote *That Time*, Peter Handke placed three loudspeakers, and three voices, above the figure of a clown/man, Kaspar (*Kaspar*, 1968). The voices, coming from three spaces above this figure, also recalled a world: a world of discourse, of idiomatic speech and grammatical correctness, of structures of thought and behavior that finally reform the figure on stage in their image. Handke's voices are clearly "outside" of Kaspar; but Kaspar will only become a part of the world once he has internalized them. These voices, Handke's "Prompters," are "memories" in the sense of being the memorialized structures of our discursive formation. In *That Time*, the inverse is taking place. The voices do not re-create Listener. Rather, they trace the mode of his existence as constituted by the coexistence of his and an intersubjective past.

54. Quoted in Jonathan Kalb, *Beckett in Performance* (Cambridge: Cambridge University Press, 1989), 202.

55. Bernard Beckerman, "Beckett and the Act of Listening," in Brater, *Beckett at 80*, 158.

56. Warnock, *Memory*, 30.

57. Samuel Beckett, *Footfalls*, in *The Collected Shorter Plays*, 240. Subsequent references are to this edition and will appear parenthetically within the text.

58. Samuel Beckett, *Rockaby*, in *The Collected Shorter Plays*, 280. Subsequent references are to this edition and will appear parenthetically within the text.

59. Quoted by Brater in *Beyond Minimalism*, 173–74, from a presentation by Daniel Labeille at the "Beckett Translating/Translating Beckett" conference, University of Texas, Austin, March 24, 1984.

60. Connor, *Samuel Beckett*, 3.

61. Jacques Derrida, *Writing and Difference*, trans. Alan Bass (London: Routledge and Kegan Paul, 1978), 297.

62. Samuel Beckett, *Ohio Impromptu,* in *The Collected Shorter Plays,* 287. Subsequent references are to this edition and will appear parenthetically within the text.

63. Sigmund Freud, "Mourning and Melancholia," in *Standard Edition,* vol. 14, 244–45; emphasis added.

64. Freud, "Mourning and Melancholia," 246.

65. Freud, "Mourning and Melancholia," 245.

66. "To be traumatized is precisely to be possessed by an image or event" (Cathy Caruth, introduction to part 1 of *Trauma: Explorations in Memory,* ed. Cathy Caruth [Baltimore: Johns Hopkins University Press, 1995], 4–5). See my discussion of trauma in chapter 1.

67. Fletcher and Fletcher, *Student's Guide,* 256.

68. Brater, *Beyond Minimalism,* 128.

Chapter 3

1. Ingo Schmidt and Florian Vaßen, foreword to *Bibliographie Heiner Müller: 1948–1992* (Bielefeld: Aisthesis Verlag, 1993), 4; my translation.

2. This is by now a common appellation for Müller's work. See especially Norbert Otto Eke, *Heiner Müller: Apokalypse und Utopie* (Paderborn: Ferdinand Schöningh, 1989), who emphasizes this aspect of Müller's very broad and varied oeuvre; and Andreas Keller, *Drama und Dramaturgie Heiner Müllers zwischen 1956 und 1988* (Frankfurt am Main: Peter Lang, 1992), esp. 90–95.

3. Heiner Müller, *A Letter to Robert Wilson* (1987), in *Explosion of a Memory: Writings by Heiner Müller,* ed. and trans. Carl Weber (New York: Performing Arts Journal Publications, 1989), 155.

4. Richard Wolin uses this phrase in his discussion of Benjamin in *Walter Benjamin: An Aesthetic of Redemption,* 2d ed. (Berkeley and Los Angeles: University of California Press, 1994), xl–xli.

5. See Keller, *Drama und Dramaturgie Heiner Müllers,* especially 67–90, for a good discussion of this division. Eke, *Heiner Müller,* rejects this division by period and prefers a division by style, arguing for "layers" of writing that often coexist.

6. See Keller, *Drama und Dramaturgie Heiner Müllers,* 71–73.

7. I discuss *posthistoire* in chapter 1. This subject is studied in depth in Lutz Niethammer's *Posthistoire.*

8. See my discussion of *The Foundling,* below.

9. A term used by the critic Hans-Thies Lehmann in "Theater der Blicke: Zu Heiner Müllers *Bildbeschreibung,*" in *Dramatik der DDR,* ed. Ulrich Profitlich (Frankfurt am Main: Suhrkamp Verlag, 1987), 201.

10. Schmidt and Vaßen, foreword, 7. Müller had a complex and varied career not only as a dramatist and director, but also as a dramaturg, poet, essayist, and translator.

11. Johannes Birringer, *Theater, Theory, Postmodernism* (Bloomington: Indiana University Press, 1991), 46.

12. Jonathan Kalb, "2 Stücke/2 Gegenstücke," *Theater* 21 (summer–fall 1990): 21.

13. Pierre Nora, "Between Memory and History: Lex Lieux de Mémoire,"

trans. Marc Roudebush, *Representations* 26 (spring 1989): 18. See my discussion of Nora and of *lieux de mémoire* in chapter 1.

14. Elinor Fuchs, *The Death of Character: Perspectives on Theater after Modernism* (Bloomington: Indiana University Press, 1996), 93.

15. In 1983, Müller wrote act 4 for Wilson's *CIVIL warS* by creating a collage from some of his own earlier plays and from his biography; he offered his *Medea* pieces for Wilson's operatic version of the Euripides tragedy; and his thirteen-page prose text, *Explosion of a Memory,* consisting of one endlessly transmuting sentence, became the prologue text for Wilson's 1986 American Repertory Theater production of *Alcestis.* That same year, Wilson also directed a stage version of an entire Müller play, *Hamletmachine.*

16. Müller, *Letter to Robert Wilson,* 153–55.

17. Müller, *Letter to Robert Wilson,* 153–55.

18. "'The Forest,' a Conversation with Christoph Rüter" (1988), reprinted in Heiner Müller, *Gesammelte Irrtümer 2: Interviews und Gespräche,* ed. G. Edelmann and R. Ziemer (Frankfurt am Main: Verlag der Autoren, 1990), 108; my translation.

19. Müller in Arthur Holmberg, "A Conversation with Robert Wilson and Heiner Müller," *Modern Drama* 31 (1988): 456.

20. Carl Weber, in *Explosion of a Memory,* 15.

21. Heiner Müller, "Reflections on Post-Modernism," trans. Jack Zipes, with Betty Nance Weber, in *New German Critique* 16 (winter 1979): 56.

22. From "Deutschland spielt noch immer die Nibelungen," Heiner Müller in conversation with Urs Jenny and Hellmuth Karasek, *Der Spiegel,* May 9, 1983, reprinted in *Spectaculum 39* (Frankfurt am Main: Suhrkamp Verlag, 1984), 258–59.

23. Walter Benjamin, thesis 16 of "Theses on the Philosophy of History," in *Illuminations,* ed. Hannah Arendt, trans. Harry Zohn (New York: Schocken, 1968), 262.

24. "19 Answers by Heiner Müller," to a questionnaire by Carl Weber, in *Hamletmachine and Other Texts for the Stage by Heiner Müller,* ed. and trans. Carl Weber (New York: Performing Arts Journal Publications, 1984), 139.

25. Carl Weber, from his introductory remarks to *Despoiled Shore Medeamaterial Landscape with Argonauts,* in *Hamletmachine and Other Texts,* 124.

26. Carl Weber, in "The PAJ Casebook: *Alcestis,*" *Performing Arts Journal* 28 (1986): 105.

27. Heiner Müller, "Ein Brief," in *Heiner Müller Theater-Arbeit: Texte 4* (Berlin: Rotbuch Verlag, 1975), 125.

28. *Ad Herennium,* trans. Harry Caplan, Loeb Classical Library, III, xxii, 37. I discuss this in chapter 1.

29. Pierre Bourdieu, *Outline of a Theory of Practice,* trans. Richard Nice (Cambridge: Cambridge University Press, 1977), 79.

30. Christopher Innes, *Avant Garde Theater: 1892–1992* (London: Routledge, 1993), 199.

31. Innes, *Avant Garde Theater,* 199.

32. Heiner Müller, *The Battle,* in *The Battle: Plays, Prose, Poems by Heiner Müller,* ed. and trans. Carl Weber (New York: Performing Arts Journal Publications, 1989), 145.

33. This story is translated as "The Iron Cross" in *Explosion of a Memory,* 18–19.

34. *The Battle,* 146. I added the hyphens to make the connections clearer. There is no ambivalence in the original German, in which each of the "sounds" described is fixed in one compound verb: "Reden Heil Saalschlacht Kristallnacht Krieg."

35. *The Battle,* 146–47.

36. *The Battle,* 148–49.

37. Helen Fehervary, "Enlightenment or Entanglement: History and Aesthetics in Bertolt Brecht and Heiner Müller," *New German Critique* 8 (spring 1976): 96.

38. "Literatur muß dem Theater Widerstand leisten," a conversation with Horst Laube (1975), reprinted in *Gesammelte Irrtümer: Interviews und Gespräche* (Frankfurt am Main: Verlag der Autoren, 1986), 20.

39. Heiner Müller, "Walls," interview by Sylvère Lotringer (1981), reprinted in *Germania,* ed. Sylvère Lotringer, trans. and annotated by Bernard and Caroline Schütze (New York: Semiotext[e] Foreign Agents Series, 1990), 24.

40. Sigmund Freud, *Beyond the Pleasure Principle,* in *The Standard Edition of Complete Psychological Works of Sigmund Freud,* ed. James Strachey, vol. 18 (London: Hogarth Press, 1953–1974), 29–30; discussed in chapter 1.

41. Judith Graves Miller on Mathias Langhoff's 1989 production of *The Task* in Avignon, "Theatricalizations of the French Revolution," *Theater* (winter–spring 1990): 13.

42. Carl Weber quoting Müller from a Deutschlandfunk radio interview; in his introductory notes to *The Task,* in *Hamletmachine and Other Texts,* 83.

43. Heiner Müller, *The Task,* in *Hamletmachine and Other Texts,* 85. Subsequent references are to this edition and will appear parenthetically within the text.

44. Müller, "Schreiben aus Lust an der Katastrophe: Gespräch mit Horst Laube," in *Rotwelsch* (Berlin: Merve, 1982), 181.

45. See Anne Ubersfeld, *Lire le théâtre* (Paris: Editions Sociales, 1977).

46. "Tribunal seiner Erinnerung," from Eke, *Heiner Müller,* 116.

47. Arlene Akiko Teraoka, in *The Silence of Entropy or Universal Discourse: The Postmodernist Poetics of Heiner Müller* (New York: Peter Lang, 1985), writes that "The 'Auftrag' will be accomplished within Antoine's memory, as a remembering and reliving of the revolutionary past . . . accomplished through the mediation of the 'angel of despair'" (132). She argues convincingly for the identity between the two "failed" intellectuals. See chapter 4.

48. See Joachim Fiebach, *Inseln der Unordnung: Fünf Versuche zu Heiner Müllers Theatertexten* (Berlin: Henschelverlag, 1990), 27.

49. *Übermalung* is the term used by Müller in a note appended to *Explosion of a Memory* to explain that that play "may be read as an overpainting of Euripides' *Alcestis.* . . .The text describes a landscape beyond death. The action is optional since its consequences are past, explosion of a memory in an extinct dramatic structure" (*Explosion of a Memory,* 102).

50. Heiner Müller, "The Luckless Angel" (1958), trans. Bernard and Caroline Schütze, in *Germania,* 99; the German original, "Der glücklose Engel," can be found in *Rotwelsch,* 87.

51. Benjamin, thesis 9 of "Theses on the Philosophy of History"; quotes are from 257–58.

52. Stéphane Mosès, "Theological-Political Model of History in the Thought of Walter Benjamin," *History and Memory* 1, no. 2 (1989): 6.

53. The marquis de Sade's (like Sasportas's) hatred of passionless industrial murder (doubled in Weiss as the French and Communist revolutions, and as Auschwitz) is countered through his own extreme excremental vision.

54. The reference is to the debate between the two revolutionaries in act 1, scene 6 of Georg Büchner's well-known play. Müller's savage imagery unlocks the irrational hinted at, but never made explicit, by Büchner.

55. See Keller, *Drama und Dramaturgie Heiner Müllers,* 94–95, on involuntary memory.

56. Reported by Henning Rischbieter, "Das Theaterwunder," *Theater Heute* 8 (1990): 23.

57. Gilles Deleuze and Félix Guattari, *Anti-Oedipus: Capitalism and Schizophrenia,* trans. Helen R. Lane and Robert Hurley (Minneapolis: University of Minnesota Press, 1983), 116.

58. "The Luckless Angel," 99.

59. Gilles Deleuze, "The Schizophrenic and Language: Surface and Depth in Lewis Carroll and Antonin Artaud," in *Textual Strategies: Perspectives in Post-Structuralist Criticism,* ed. Josué V. Harari (Ithaca: Cornell University Press, 1979), 287.

60. Quoted by Weber in his introduction to *The Task,* 83.

61. Marianne Streisand, " 'Experimenta 6—Heiner Müller' in Frankfurt/Main," in *Weimarer Beiträge* 36, no. 10 (1990): 1671–75. My description of the production is based largely on this report. Additional details were taken from Martin Linzer, "Müller und kein Ende? Nachbemerkungen zur EXPERIMENTA 6," *Theater der Zeit* 9 (1990): 58–59.

62. See Andrei S. Markovits and Philip S. Gorski, *The German Left: Red, Green, and Beyond* (New York: Oxford University Press, 1993), 67–70.

63. Streisand, " 'Experimenta 6," 1675.

64. Carl Weber, introduction to *Volokolamsk Highway,* in *Explosion of a Memory,* 112.

65. All translations from *Der Findling* are my own. My uses of capitalizations follow Müller's; capitalizations midline usually indicate the beginning of a sentence. Carl Weber has translated the entire play in *Explosion of a Memory,* 143–49. An additional English translation can be found in Heiner Müller, *Theatremachine,* trans. and ed. Marc von Henning (London: Faber and Faber, 1995), 170–76. Von Henning translates the title of the composite five texts as *The Road of Tanks.* I have chosen to do my own, often more literal, translations here. Page references, within the text, are to the German original published in *Die Schlacht. Wolokolamsker Chausee. Zwei Stücke* (Frankfurt am Main: Verlag der Autoren, 1988), 67–75; here 67.

66. Müller has explained that he sought to instill ambiguity into *The Task* "perhaps through a diffuse movement that cannot be fixed into a clear perspective or intention" ("Schreiben aus Lust an der Katastrophe," 181).

67. This opinion is expressed by Martin Linzer, in " . . . rückwärts in die Gegenwart," *Theater der Zeit* 11 (1991): 12. *Theater der Zeit* was the most important East German theater journal.

68. Müller's fellow playwright, Thomas Brasch, was in fact arrested and imprisoned for protesting the Soviet invasion and emigrated to the West in 1976.

69. From "The Father," trans. Carl Weber, in *Explosion of a Memory*, 27.

70. Müller, "Walls," 39.

71. Elaine Scarry, *The Body in Pain: The Making and Unmaking of the World* (New York: Oxford University Press, 1985), 4.

72. Scarry, *The Body in Pain*, 109–13ff.

73. Arthur Kleinman and Joan Kleinman, "How Bodies Remember: Social Memory and Bodily Experience of Criticism, Resistance, and Delegitimation Following China's Cultural Revolution," *New Literary History* 25, no. 3 (1994): 716–17.

74. In 1985, Müller wrote a prose piece called "I Want to Be a German" in which he speaks of the German people as "a people castrated of its civil courage by the bloody repression of a premature revolution and a resulting thirty-year war, whose spine was crushed by the beheading of its proletariat through the murder of two of its Jewish leaders forgotten by the majority, and a twelve-year reign of terror against the revolution. A nation with a broken spine that makes it its duty to break the spines of other nations" (*Germania*, 97). These are the exact images found in *The Foundling*, written some years later, underlining the role of the Father as "German History": castrated, crushed back, full of forgetting.

75. Heiner Müller, *Germania Death in Berlin*, in *Explosion of a Memory*, 84.

76. Susan Sontag, *Illness as Metaphor and Aids and Its Metaphors* (New York: Doubleday, reprint 1990), 23, quoting from *Reich Speaks of Freud*, ed. Mary Higgins and Chester M. Raphael, trans. Therese Pol (Harmondsworth, Middlesex: Penguin, 1975), 23.

77. Müller, *Letter to Robert Wilson*, 153.

78. As quoted above: "There isn't a nation in Europe that didn't experience the Holocaust. This makes a difference in the subconscious" (Müller, in Holmberg, "Conversation," 456).

79. "Jedem das Seine" and "Arbeit macht frei" (everyone gets what he deserves, and work brings freedom) were the signs hung over the entrances to several concentration camps, most notoriously, Auschwitz. Any German audience would recognize these infamous slogans.

80. Keller, *Drama und Dramaturgie Heiner Müllers*, 94–95.

81. This type of gender inversion is found, far more powerfully, in Müller's *Hamletmachine*, where Hamlet too rebels against his "role" as son to a loved/despised father (Hamlet and Stalin) by dressing as a woman. Gender inversion as a form of escape from historically assigned roles is paradigmatically found in *Quartet*.

82. John Rouse, "Heiner Müller and the Politics of Memory," *Theatre Journal* 45, no. 1 (1993): 65.

83. Müller had previously directed *Mauser/Quartet* with students at the Max Reinhardt Seminar in Vienna. See Eva Brenner, "Heiner Müller Directs Heiner Müller," *Drama Review* 36, no. 1 (1991): 161–66.

84. Linzer, in conversation with Müller, " . . . rückwärts in die Gegenwart," 10.

85. Müller, "Raising the Dead," in *Germania*, 225.

86. Heiner Müller and Reiner Geulen, interview with the *Tagesspiegel,* September 22, 1991, 23, cited by Rouse, "Politics of Memory," 65.

87. Brenner, "Heiner Müller Directs," 167.

88. Franz Wille, "Das Rad der Geschichte dreht durch," *Theater Heute* 10 (1991): 4. Information and descriptions of this production were taken from Wille, 2–6; as well as Rouse, "Politics of Memory," 68–73; Brenner, "Heiner Müller Directs," 166–68; and Linzer, " . . . rückwärts in die Gegenwart," 10–13.

89. This image is not uncommon in productions of Müller's bloody plays (often signifying the platitudinal "slaughterhouse of history"). It was famously used by the Frankfurt-based "Theater zwischen den Ufern" at the 1990 "Experimenta 6—Heiner Müller." There, the group performed Müller's prose text *Explosion of a Memory* at an actual slaughterhouse on the banks of the Main, to an audience who moved from room to room, viewing the clean, shining instruments of mechanical death, while actors recited the text. The text was spoken by two miked actors who led the audience from room to room of the slaughterhouse as they spoke, occasionally running into the chorus of six men, each dressed in a costume and hat from a different historical period (Streisand, " 'Experimenta 6,' " 1673–74). Nor is the smokestack image original. For Robert Wilson's 1986 production of *Alcestis* (at the American Repertory Theater in Cambridge), for which Müller supplied the prologue *Explosion of a Memory,* Wilson's designer Tom Kamm created three columns that transformed during the play from cypress trees into Corinthian columns, and finally into smokestacks. See Tom Kamm on *Alcestis* in Laurence Shyer, *Robert Wilson and His Collaborators* (New York: Theater Communications Group, 1989), 164–76.

90. Rouse, "Politics of Memory," 69.

91. The image of a "hole," of an underground trap in which history is stored (like Freud's unconscious from which nothing disappears, waiting merely to be recovered), was more recently used by Suzan-Lori Parks in her play about the absent black memory of an American past, *The America Play,* discussed in chapter 5.

92. Linzer, " . . . rückwärts in die Gegenwart," 11.

93. These, like other parts of the production, are obviously influenced by Müller's work with Robert Wilson: the static, statuary stagings, the repetition of identical bodies and gestures, the splitting and repeating of identities, the miking and echoing of voices, simultaneous actions, even the use of a wheelchair for one of the sons in *The Foundling*—all these had been used by Wilson in his staging of Müller's *Hamletmachine* (1986), and in previous productions on which Müller had worked.

94. Rouse, "Politics of Memory," 71.

95. Rouse, "Politics of Memory," 71.

96. For Santner, German history had bequeathed upon the present "a cultural inheritance fragmented and poisoned by an unspeakable horror," the horror of the Holocaust, which plays a lesser role in Müller's work. See Eric L. Santner, *Stranded Objects: Mourning, Memory, and Film in Postwar Germany* (Ithaca: Cornell University Press, 1990), xiii.

97. Sigmund Freud, "Mourning and Melancholia," in *Standard Edition,* vol. 14, 244–45; emphasis added.

98. Müller, "Walls," 24.

Chapter 4

1. C. W. E. Bigsby, *Modern American Drama: 1945–1990* (Cambridge: Cambridge University Press, 1992), 163.

2. Deborah R. Geis, *Postmodern Theatric[k]s: Monologue in Contemporary American Drama* (Ann Arbor: University of Michigan Press, 1993), 57–58. Shepard's work is commonly divided into an "early period" with plays from *Cowboys* and *Rock Garden* up to *La Turista* written in a style termed by David J. DeRose, *Sam Shepard* (New York: Twayne Publishers, 1992), the "theatrical expression of acute, and usually highly personal, states of psychic agitation" (4); a "middle period," where the plays attest the awakening of a greater social or cultural consciousness, beginning with *Forensic and the Navigators* (1967) according to DeRose (5), or with *Melodrama Play* (1967) according to Geis (57); and a "late period" with plays that turn to themes of family and roots in a quasi-realistic idiom, beginning with *Curse of the Starving Class* (1977).

3. Sam Shepard, "Language, Visualization, and the Inner Library," *Drama Review* 21, no. 4 (1977), reprinted in *American Dreams: The Imagination of Sam Shepard*, ed. Bonnie Marranca (New York: Performing Arts Journal Publications, 1981), 215.

4. Sam Shepard, *Geography of a Horse Dreamer*, in *The Tooth of Crime and Geography of a Horse Dreamer* (New York: Grove Press, 1974), 127. Subsequent references are to this edition and will appear parenthetically within the text.

5. DeRose, *Sam Shepard*, 6.

6. C. W. E. Bigsby, *A Critical Introduction to Twentieth-Century American Drama*, vol. 3, *Beyond Broadway* (Cambridge: Cambridge University Press, 1985), 249; emphasis added.

7. Fredric Jameson, *Postmodernism; or, The Cultural Logic of Late Capitalism* (London: Verso, and Durham, N.C.: Duke University Press, 1991), 18; emphasis added.

8. Sam Shepard, "Metaphors, Mad Dogs, and Old Time Cowboys," interview by Kenneth Chubb and the editors of *Theatre Quarterly*, in *Theatre Quarterly* 4, no. 15 (1974), reprinted in Marranca, *American Dreams*, 196.

9. Shepard, "Metaphors, Mad Dogs," 196.

10. *Icarus's Mother*, in Sam Shepard, *The Unseen Hand and Other Plays* (New York: Bantam Books, 1986), 77. Subsequent references are to this edition and will appear parenthetically within the text.

11. He changed his name from Samuel Shepard Rogers VII in 1963 when he came to New York.

12. Shepard, "Metaphors, Mad Dogs," 208.

13. Sam Shepard, *Action*, in *Angel City, Curse of the Starving Class, and Other Plays* (New York: Urizen Books, 1981), 137. Subsequent references are to this edition and will appear parenthetically within the text.

14. Sam Shepard, *Buried Child*, in *Seven Plays* (New York: Bantam Books, 1981), 111. This is a more realistic version of the rejection of past and memory. Subsequent references are to this edition and will appear parenthetically within the text.

15. Shepard, "Metaphors, Mad Dogs," 198.

16. See, for example, Leonard Wilcox, "Modernism vs. Postmodernism:

Shepard's *The Tooth of Crime* and the Discourses of Popular Culture," *Modern Drama* 30 (1987): 560–73. Wilcox sees Shepard ultimately as a postmodernist. Michael Vanden Heuvel, *Performing Drama/Dramatizing Performance* (Ann Arbor: University of Michigan Press, 1991), comes to the conclusion that "Shepard is essentially a modernist, as opposed to postmodernist, playwright" (199); DeRose, *Sam Shepard*, weighs in on the postmodern side, finding in Shepard the master of re-creating "the postmodern condition of media-fed consumer America" (47), and the creator of "a postmodern, intertextual pastiche of American popular culture" (41).

17. Sam Shepard, *The Unseen Hand*, in *The Unseen Hand and Other Plays*. This refrain is repeated a number of times during the play. Subsequent references are to this edition and will appear parenthetically within the text.

18. The release results from the *inversion* of the Kid's cliché-ridden text, its recitation backward as an "undone" text—a situation easily recognized in the text, but less so on the stage, where the text sounds theatrically indecipherable.

19. DeRose, *Sam Shepard*, 47.

20. Jean Baudrillard, "The Precession of Simulacra," in *Art after Modernism: Rethinking Representation*, ed. Brian Wallis (New York: New Museum of Contemporary Art, 1984), 253–81.

21. George Stambolian, "A Trip through Popular Culture: *Mad Dog Blues*," in Marranca, *American Dreams*, 87.

22. Vanden Heuvel, *Performing Drama*, 200.

23. Shepard, "Metaphors, Mad Dogs," 190.

24. DeRose, *Sam Shepard*, 3.

25. Kenneth Chubb, "Fruitful Difficulties of Directing Shepard," in *Theatre Quarterly* 4, no. 15 (1974): 19.

26. DeRose, *Sam Shepard*, 13–14.

27. Sam Shepard, interview by Amy Lippman, *Dialogue*, April 1985, 59.

28. Sam Shepard, "Hollywood," in *Motel Chronicles and Hawk Moon* (London: Faber and Faber, n.d.), 147. *Hawk Moon* was first copyrighted by Shepard in 1973.

29. Philip French, *Westerns* (London: Secker and Warburg, 1973), 24.

30. Cited by Carol Rosen in her "Interview with Shepard," *Modern Drama* 36, no. 1 (1993): 5.

31. Sam Shepard, *La Turista*, in *Seven Plays*, 270.

32. Rosen, "Interview with Shepard," 5.

33. Leonard Wilcox, "The Desert and the City: *Operation Sidewinder* and Shepard's Postmodern Allegory," in *Rereading Shepard: Contemporary Critical Essays on the Plays of Sam Shepard*, ed. Leonard Wilcox (New York: St. Martin's, 1993), 53.

34. Sam Shepard, *Operation Sidewinder*, in *The Unseen Hand and Other Plays*, 234. Subsequent references are to this edition and will appear parenthetically within the text.

35. John Lahr, "Spectacle of Disintegration: *Operation Sidewinder*," in Marranca, *American Dreams*, 53.

36. Leonard Wilcox, "The Desert and City: *Operation Sidewinder* and Shepard's Postmodern Allegory," in *Rereading Shepard: Contemporary Critical Essays on the Plays of Sam Shepard*, ed. Leonard Wilcox (New York: St. Martin's, 1993), 45.

37. Bigsby, *Modern American Drama*, 163.

38. Lahr, "Spectacle of Disintegration," 55.

39. Bigsby, *Modern American Drama,* 163.

40. Sam Shepard, *The Sad Lament of Pecos Bill on the Eve of Killing His Wife,* music by Sam Shepard and Catherine Stone, in Sam Shepard, *Fool for Love and The Sad Lament of Pecos Bill on the Eve of Killing His Wife* (San Francisco: City Lights Books, 1983). Since most of the lines repeat, I will not note page numbers for this short piece.

41. This is a recurring line in Beckett's mourning play *Ohio Impromptu,* discussed in chapter 2.

42. Carlos Fuentes, "La Mémoire du futur," trans. Céline Zins, *L'Écrit du Temps* 10 (autumn 1985): 95.

43. Wilcox, "Modernism vs. Postmodernism."

44. I discuss the language and discourses of *The Tooth of Crime* in Jeanette R. Malkin, *Verbal Violence in Contemporary Drama: From Handke to Shepard* (Cambridge: Cambridge University Press, 1992), 198–223.

45. Shepard, "Language, Visualization, and the Inner Library," in Marranca, *American Dreams,* 217.

46. Sam Shepard, *The Tooth of Crime,* 73. Subsequent references are to this edition and will appear parenthetically within the text.

47. From a letter by Shepard to Richard Schechner, quoted by Schechner in "The Writer and the Performance Group: Rehearsing *The Tooth of Crime,*" in Marranca, *American Dreams,* 166.

48. See Malkin, *Verbal Violence in Contemporary Drama,* 203.

49. Amos Funkenstein, "History, Counterhistory, and Narrative," in *Probing the Limits of Representation: Nazism and the "Final Solution,"* ed. Saul Friedlander (Cambridge: Harvard University Press, 1992), 69.

50. See Vanden Heuvel, *Performing Drama,* all of chapter 5, but especially 203–8.

51. Sam Shepard, *Mad Dog Blues,* in *The Unseen Hand and Other Plays,* 264.

52. Michael Bloom, "Visions of the End: The Early Plays," in Marranca, *American Dreams,* 77.

53. Shepard, *Mad Dog Blues,* 263–64.

54. Letter dated February 11, 1974, in *Joseph Chaikin and Sam Shepard: Letters and Texts, 1972–1984,* ed. Barry Daniels (New York: New American Library, 1989), 12.

55. David Savran, "Sam Shepard's Conceptual Prison: *Action* and the Unseen Hand," *Theatre Journal* 38 (1984): 59.

56. In chapter 1, I discuss Jean-François Lyotard's description of the destruction at Auschwitz of scientific reason and the desolation of the Enlightenment narrative of progress and rationality. His famous image of the seismic end of an era compounds the upheaval with the loss of those instruments used to measure, and thus rationally evaluate, the strength or meaning of that upheaval. In his words:

Suppose that an earthquake destroys not only lives, buildings, and objects but also the instruments used to measure earthquakes directly and indirectly. The impossibility of quantitatively measuring it does not prohibit, but rather inspires in the minds of the survivors the idea of a very great seismic force. The scholar claims to know nothing about it, but the common person has a complex feeling, the one aroused by the negative presentation of the indeterminate.

Such complete annihilation shatters not only the continuum of history, but also the shape of its representation, writes Lyotard. Similarly, although Shepard writes from within a totally different reality, the characters in *Action* are also filled with unease, split not only from the catastrophe that has occurred but from any way of discussing or "placing" that catastrophe within a recognizable context. See *The Differend: Phrases in Dispute,* trans. Georges Van Den Abbeele (Minneapolis: University of Minnesota Press, 1988), 56 and 57.

57. See Jean-François Lyotard, *The Postmodern Condition: A Report on Knowledge,* trans. Geoffrey Bennington and Brian Massumi (Minneapolis: University of Minnesota Press, and Manchester: University of Manchester Press, 1984).

58. Richard Rorty, *Contingency, Irony, and Solidarity* (Cambridge: Cambridge University Press, 1989), 61.

59. A prevalent reading of this play sees it as reflecting the anxiety of performance itself, exploring, as Gerry McCarthy puts it, "the actual problems encountered by the actor as he confronts his audience" without a consistent character to carry him through, and with only "the enduring presence of himself and the other actors on the stage, and the ever-present necessity of action to relieve the burden of existence." Gerry McCarthy, "'Acting It Out': Sam Shepard's *Action,*" *Modern Drama* 24 (1981): 2. David Savran goes even further, seeing the alienation and unease of the play as aligned with Shepard's view that the theater is "a prison for all those involved in its operation," an oppressive system of production "inscribed within an oppressive social network" ("Sam Shepard's Conceptual Prison," 58). Variations of this reading are also found in Vanden Heuvel, *Performing Drama,* and Geis, *Postmodern Theatric[k]s.* This reading works well for *Action,* which reflects on the need to both *act* and find motivations for action. The play's numerous performance metaphors overlie, of course, the broader anxieties and absences of the play. Jeep's attempt to escape "from the space he's playing in" invokes both the theater space and the space of an unscripted, unreferenced world.

60. Sam Shepard, *Fool for Love,* in *Fool for Love and Other Plays* (Toronto: Bantam Books, 1984), 31.

61. Una Chaudhuri, *Staging Place: The Geography of Modern Drama* (Ann Arbor: University of Michigan Press, 1995), 112.

62. Frank Rich, "Theater: *A Lie of the Mind,* by Sam Shepard," *New York Times,* December 6, 1985, C3.

63. Shepard, "The Man on the High Horse," interview by Jennifer Allen, *Esquire,* November 1988, 148.

64. Chaudhuri, *Staging Place,* 107.

65. William W. Demastes, "Understanding Sam Shepard's Realism," *Comparative Drama* 21, no. 3 (1987): 234–35.

66. Vanden Heuvel, *Performing Drama,* 214. In the absence of a suitable term for Shepard's expansion of realism, John Glore invented the term "nova-realism" to characterize Shepard's regenerative search for wholeness "beneath surfaces" and beyond causal constrictions. See John Glore, "The Canonization of Mojo Root-

force: Sam Shepard Live at the Pantheon," *Theater* 12 (summer–fall 1981): 57. DeRose came up with the term "suprareal"—not intending "any connection whatsoever to the 'hyper-realism' of postmodern criticism," he writes, but in the sense that certain images and moments "transcend the fictional 'realism' of the play" (*Sam Shepard,* 147 n. 6).

67. I find it difficult to agree with those, such as Deborah Geis, who, in *Postmodern Theatric[k]s,* sees Shepard's family plays as another idiom of postmodern drama. Geis writes, rightly, that the family plays continue "the rewriting and rereading of an American mythology," but she defines his reformation of realists tactics as "the postmodern grotesque, rooted in the corporeal (the visceral and sexual), that simultaneously shocks its audience and creates a Brechtian alienation effect in the comic way it is handled" (74). She argues that the plays are not "fully" realistic, are indeed "resist[ant] to coherence," and are thus "set against the seemingly traditional oedipal 'searches' and 'discoveries' that the narratives of these works play at enacting but do not genuinely fulfill" (76). In addition, she emphasizes that *narrativity,* the telling of stories, as opposed to authenticity, the telling of *true* stories (for example, in *Fool for Love*), is a postmodern characteristic. While her individual points are often convincing, they do not converge into a depiction of a postmodern dramaturgy. Since I have placed rootlessness, or the absence of foundations, at the center of my definition of the postmodern, I find it difficult to accept plays that crave homecoming, that are set in the kitchen or salon, and that cannot evade connections of blood and soil—as still belonging to a postmodern aesthetic, no matter how incomplete or "anti-Oedipal" the narrative may be.

Chapter 5

1. Florence Falk, "Men without Women: The Shepard Landscape," in *American Dreams: The Imagination of Sam Shepard,* ed. Bonnie Marranca (New York: Performing Arts Journal Publications, 1981), 95. Falk's article in fact defends Shepard against unbridled feminist attacks, claiming that "both his males and females are developed with unflinching irony. Nevertheless, men are the energy centers" (95).

2. See, for example, Alan Shepard, "The Ominous 'Bulgarian Threat' in Sam Shepard's Plays," *Theatre Journal* 44 (1992): 59–66.

3. See Robert Brustein, *Making Scenes: A Personal History of the Turbulent Years at Yale, 1966–1979* (New York: Limelight Editions, 1984), 73–79.

4. Parks was born in Fort Knox, Kentucky. As a child she lived in Kentucky, California, Texas, Vermont, and Maryland. She also spent four years in a German junior high school, where she was exposed to a different culture and learned the language.

5. Quoted by Alisa Solomon in "Signifying on the Signifyin': The Plays of Suzan-Lori Parks," *Theater* 21 (summer–fall 1990): 73; emphasis in the original.

6. Robert Brustein, review of *The Death of the Last Black Man in the Whole Entire World, New Republic,* April 13, 1992, 29.

7. Page references to Parks's plays and essays that appear parenthetically within the text refer to *The America Play and Other Works* (New York: Theater

Communications Group, 1995) unless otherwise noted. Suzan-Lori Parks, "Elements of Style," in *America Play and Other Works*, 121.

8. "Interview with Suzan-Lori Parks," interview by Lee A. Jacobus, in *Bedford Introduction to Drama*, ed. Lee A. Jacobus (Boston: Bedford Books of St. Martin's Press, 1993), 1372.

9. Solomon, "Signifying on the Signifyin'," 75.

10. Suzan-Lori Parks, quoted in Alisa Solomon, "Language in *The Last Black Man*," in *Bedford Introduction to Drama*, 1376.

11. See Gilles Deleuze, *Difference and Repetition*, trans. Paul Patton (London: Althone Press, 1994).

12. Walter Benjamin, "Theses on the Philosophy of History," in *Illuminations*, ed. Hannah Arendt, trans. Harry Zohn (New York: Schocken 1968). 255. See my discussion of Benjamin in chapter 1.

13. Parks, "Possession," in *America Play and Other Works*, 4–5; emphasis added.

14. Steven Drukman, "Suzan-Lori Parks and Liz Diamond: Doo-a-diddly-dit-dit," *Drama Review* 39, no. 3 (1995): 67.

15. Linda Ben-Zvi, "'Aroun the Worl': The Signifyin(g) Theater of Suzan-Lori Parks," in *The Theatrical Gamut: Notes for a Post-Beckettian Stage*, ed. Enoch Brater (Ann Arbor: University of Michigan Press, 1995), 191–92.

16. Parks, "Elements of Style," 17–18.

17. Parks, "Elements of Style," 11.

18. Paul Gilroy, *The Black Atlantic: Modernity and Double Consciousness* (Cambridge: Harvard University Press, 1993), 123; emphasis added.

19. Henry Louis Gates Jr., *Figures in Black: Words, Signs, and the "Racial" Self* (New York: Oxford University Press, 1987), 173.

20. Brustein, review, 29.

21. As I discuss in chapter 4, Shepard said of America that "you don't have any connection with the past, with what history means"; all that remains is "this emotional thing that goes a long way back, which creates a certain kind of chaos, a kind of terror" ("Metaphors, Mad Dogs," 196).

22. Solomon, "Signifying on the Signifyin'," 73.

23. Parks, quoted in Solomon, "Signifying on the Signifyin'," 75.

24. Liz Diamond, "Perceptible Mutability in the Word Kingdom," *Theater* 24, no. 3 (1993): 87.

25. Cathy Caruth, introduction to part 1 of *Trauma: Explorations in Memory*, ed. Cathy Caruth (Baltimore: Johns Hopkins University Press, 1995), 4–5.

26. See chapter 1 of this book, the section "'Trauma' of History: Flooding and Repression," for a more detailed discussion.

27. Mel Gussow, "Dangers of Becoming a Lost Culture," *New York Times*, September 25, 1990.

28. Frederick Douglass, from his speech "The Races," reprinted in the *Douglass Monthly*, August 1859, quoted by David W. Bright, "W. E. B. Du Bois and the Struggle for American Historical Memory," in *History and Memory in African-American Culture*, ed. Geneviève Fabre and Robert O'Meally (New York: Oxford University Press, 1994), 52.

29. Jacobus, "Interview with Suzan-Lori Parks," 1372.

30. Jacobus, "Interview with Suzan-Lori Parks," 1371.

31. Parks, "Possession," 5.

32. Gilles Deleuze, *Bergsonism,* trans. Hugh Tomlinson and Barbara Habberjam (New York: Zone Books, 1988), 58–59.

33. Walter Benjamin, *Gesammelte Schriften* (Franfurt am Main: Suhrkamp, 1980), vol. 1, pt. 3, 1243, 1244.

34. Brustein, review, 30.

35. Jacobus, "Interview with Suzan-Lori Parks," 1373.

36. Sigmund Freud, "Mourning and Melancholia," in The Standard Edition of the Complete Psychological Works of Sigmund Freud, ed. James Strachey, vol. 14 (London Hogarth Press, 1953–74), 244–45. I discuss this at greater length in chapter 2.

37. Alice Rayner and Harry J. Elam Jr., "Unfinished Business: Reconfiguring History in Suzan-Lori Parks's *The Death of the Last Black Man in the Whole Entire World," Theatre Journal* 46 (1994): 458.

38. Friedrich Nietzsche, *On the Genealogy of Morality,* ed. Keith Ansell-Pearson, trans. Carol Diethe (Cambridge: Cambridge University Press, 1994), 41.

39. Marc Robinson, *The Other American Drama* (Baltimore: Johns Hopkins University Press, 1994), 189.

40. Quoted by Ben-Zvi from her conversations with Parks, in "'Aroun the Worl'," 192.

41. Todd London, "Epic-Cure: History That Heals," *American Theater* 11, no. 6 (1994): 44.

42. "Making History," Suzan-Lori Parks interviewed by Tom Sellar, in *Theatre Forum* 9 (summer 1996): 38.

43. Robinson, *The Other American Drama,* 191.

44. Una Chaudhuri, *Staging Place: The Geography of Modern Drama* (Ann Arbor: University of Michigan Press, 1995), 263.

45. Eyal Naveh, "'He Belongs to the Ages': Lincoln's Image and the American Historical Consciousness," *Journal of American Culture* 16, no. 4 (1993): 49.

46. Parks, "Elements of Style," 10.

47. London, "Epic-Cure," 44.

48. Cited by Errol G. Hill, s.v. "Parks, Suzan-Lori," *Cambridge Guide to American Theatre,* ed. Don B. Wilmeth (Cambridge: Cambridge University Press, 1996), 300.

Chapter 6

1. Thomas Bernhard, *Histrionics,* in *Histrionics: Three Plays,* trans. Peter Jansen and Kenneth Northcott (Chicago: University of Chicago Press, 1990), 218. Subsequent references are to this edition and will appear parenthetically within the text.

2. Thomas Bernhard, *Heldenplatz* (Frankfurt am Main: Suhrkamp Verlag, 1988), 63. All translations from *Heldenplatz* are my own; the play has not yet been published in an English translation. Subsequent page references are to the German edition and will appear parenthetically within the text.

3. On Austria's *Lebenslüge* (survival lie)—that Austria was Hitler's victim—see Richard Mitten, *The Politics of Antisemitic Prejudice: The Waldheim Phenomenon in Austria* (Boulder, Colo.: Westview, 1992).

4. Thomas Bernhard, "Die Vergangenheit ist Unerforscht" (The past is unexamined), an interview with Viktor Suchy, March 5, 1967, reprinted in *Von einer Katastrophe in die andere: 13 Gespräche mit Thomas Bernhard,* ed. Sepp Dreissinger (Katsdorf: Bibliothek der Provinz, 1992), 21.

5. Gabrielle Robinson, "Slaughter and Language Slaughter in the Plays of Peter Turrini," *Theatre Journal* 43 (1991): 199.

6. Heiner Müller, "Raising the Dead," in *Germania,* ed. Sylvère Lotringer, trans. and annotated by Bernard and Caroline Schütze (New York: Semiotext[e] Foreign Agents Series, 1990), 225. For a discussion, see chapter 3.

7. Gitta Honegger, "The Theater of Thomas Bernhard," in Thomas Bernhard, *The President and Eve of Retirement,* trans. Gitta Honegger (New York: Performing Arts Journal Publications, 1982), 10.

8. Thomas Bernhard, *Eve of Retirement,* in *The President and Eve of Retirement,* 118. Subsequent references are to this edition and will appear parenthetically within the text.

9. Peter Handke, *Kaspar,* in *Kaspar and Other Plays,* trans. Michael Roloff (New York: Farrar, Straus and Giroux, 1969), 68–72 and passim.

10. "Ich möcht a sochener Reiter warn, wie mei Voter aner gween is." This is how his sentence was transcribed by A. Ritter von Feuerbach in *Kaspar Hauser, Beispiel eines Verbrechens am Seelenleben des Menschen* (Ansbach: J. M. Dollfuss, 1832).

11. I discuss this, and Handke's *Kaspar,* at some length in Jeanette R. Malkin, *Verbal Violence in Contemporary Drama: From Handke to Shepard* (Cambridge and New York: Cambridge University Press, 1992), chap. 1.

12. Thomas Bernhard, *The Hunting Party,* trans. Gitta Honegger, in *Performing Arts Journal* 13, no. 1 (1980): 127. Honegger discusses this section in "The Theater of Thomas Bernhard," 12.

13. Sigmund Freud, "A Note upon the Mystic Writing-Pad," in *The Penguin Freud Library,* vol. 11, *On Metapsychology* (London: Penguin Books, 1984), 428–34.

14. Stephen D. Dowden, *Understanding Thomas Bernhard* (Columbia: University of South Carolina Press, 1991), 75.

15. See, for example, Martin Esslin, "Beckett and Bernhard: A Comparison," *Modern Austrian Literature* 18, no. 2 (1985): 67–78; Franz Josef Görtz, "Hier spukt natürlich Beckett: Thomas Bernhard und die Kritik," in *Thomas Bernhard,* series editor Heinz Ludwig Arnold, 2d ed., *text + kritik* 43 (1982): 85–94; and Willi Huntemann, "Treue zum Scheitern: Bernhard, Beckett und die Postmoderne," *Thomas Bernhard,* series editor Heinz Ludwig Arnold, 3d ed., *text + kritik* 43 (1991): 42–74.

16. Steve Dowden, "Thomas Bernhard's Austria," *Partisan Review* 61, no. 4 (1994): 626.

17. Linda Hutcheon, *The Politics of Postmodernism* (London: Routledge, 1989), 11.

18. His 1975 play *Die Berühmten* (*The Famous*), for example, ridicules the "famous" names associated with the history of the festival itself. *Die Macht der Gewohnheit* (1974, *The Force of Habit*) accuses the festival and its audience of produc-

ing and viewing theater merely out of bloodless "habit." This reflexivity recurs in *Histrionics,* discussed below.

19. I discuss this in chapter 3.

20. Bernhard has been called a *Wahrheitsfanatiker*—a fanatic for the truth—by some of his supporters, as I discuss below in the *Heldenplatz* section. Here he again parodies himself and his audience, again assuming their shared knowledge of his reception in Austria.

21. For a concise description of the political background see Dowden, *Understanding Thomas Bernhard,* 77.

22. Dowden, *Understanding Thomas Bernhard,* 77.

23. This is reported by Nicholas J. Meyerhofer, *Thomas Bernhard* (Berlin: Colloquium Verlag, 1985), 77.

24. Charles Russell, "The Context of the Concept," in *Romanticism, Modernism, Postmodernism,* ed. Harry R. Garvin (Lewisburg, Pa.: Bucknell University Press, 1980), 192.

25. Mircea Eliade, *Cosmos and History: The Myth of the Eternal Return* (New York: Harper and Row, 1959), 95.

26. Eliade, *Cosmos and History,* viii.

27. Eliade, *Cosmos and History,* 35. Nazism, of course, claims roots in ancient Germanic myths and symbols; its ideology posits an inevitable return to prominence and power through the renewal of the ancient Reich.

28. Eliade, *Cosmos and History,* xi.

29. Eliade, *Cosmos and History,* viii.

30. *Die Zeit,* July 6, 1979, quoted in Helen Chambers, "Thomas Bernhard," in *After the "Death of Literature": West German Writing of the 1970s,* ed. Keith Bullivant (Oxford: Berg, 1989), 210; my translation.

31. For a discussion of this subject see Dan Diner, "Negative Symbiose: Germans and Jews after Auschwitz," in *Reworking the Past: Hitler, the Holocaust, and the Historians' Debate,* ed. Peter Baldwin (Boston: Beacon Press, 1990), 251–61.

32. Meyerhofer, *Thomas Bernhard,* 74. This view is not shared by all German critics. Bernhard Sorg rejects it outright in *Thomas Bernhard* (Munich: Verlag C. H. Beck, 1992), 152.

33. Pierre Nora, "Between Memory and History: *Les Lieux de Mémoire,*" trans. Marc Roudebush, *Representations* 26 (spring 1989): 20. I discuss this at length in chapter 1.

34. This is my translation. Honegger, in *Eve of Retirement,* in *The President and Eve of Retirement,* translates the numbers here as "thousands and thousands into the gas" (195)—thus choosing the easy idiom over Bernhard's pointed historical marker, and losing some of the irony and history.

35. Quoted in Joachim C. Fest, *The Face of the Third Reich,* trans. Michael Bullock (Harmondsworth, Middlesex: Penguin, 1970), 183–84, 177–78.

36. According to Hellmuth Karasek's review in *Der Spiegel,* reprinted in *Thomas Bernhard Werkgeschichte,* ed. Jens Dittmar (Frankfurt: Suhrkamp Verlag, 1981), 216. References to music and concerts appear throughout the play, always in a parodic context.

37. For a discussion of kitsch elements in Nazism see Saul Friedlander,

Reflections of Nazism: An Essay on Kitsch and Death, trans. Thomas Weyr (New York: Harper and Row, 1982).

38. Vivian M. Patraka, "Fascist Ideology and Theatricalization," in *Critical Theory and Performance,* ed. Janelle G. Reinelt and Joseph R. Roach (Ann Arbor: University of Michigan Press, 1992), 336–49, applies Friedlander's critique of the "new discourse on Nazism"—a discourse that, while "intending to interrogate and subvert fascism . . . actually reproduces fascism's aestheticized dualities uncritically" (337)—to (among other texts) Bernhard's *Eve of Retirement.* Friedlander claims that part of Nazism's appeal was aesthetic: "a matter of the juxtaposition of opposing images of harmony (kitsch) and death, and of such violently contradictory feelings as harmony and terror" (*Reflections of Nazism,* 50), an appeal replicated in the "new discourse." As examples he cites, among many other texts, R. W. Fassbinder's film *Lili Marleen* and Hans-Jürgen Syberberg's postmodern film *Hitler: A Film from Germany,* which "allow us to perceive something of the psychological hold Nazism had in its day" (18) but also uncritically reproduce that fascination. Friedlander makes clear that texts that employ this "new discourse" create a totalized and hypnotic vision through "a massive use of synonyms, an excess of similar epithets, a play of images sent back, in turn, from one to the other in echoes without end" (50). Such emotional and textual unity is certainly inapplicable to Bernhard's highly self-conscious and ironic play. Patraka describes *Eve of Retirement* as though it were realistic and totalized: all of one discourse. She does not see the comedy, the parody of kitsch, the provocative exposure of taboos. Most important, the political context of the play's presentation is absent from her critique. Patraka writes that the play "unintentionally accedes to fascism's own theatricalizing instead of framing it by an informing context" (338); I will claim that the "informing context" is to be found in the audience.

39. Donna L. Hoffmeister, "Post-Modern Theater: A Contradiction in Terms? Handke, Strauss, Bernhard, and the Contemporary Scene," *Monatshefte* 79, no. 4 (1987): 432–33.

40. Hoffmeister, "Post-Modern Theater," 436.

41. Joseph A. Federico, "Millenarianism, Legitimation, and the National Socialist Universe in Thomas Bernhard's *Vor dem Ruhestand,*" *Germanic Review* 59, no. 4 (1984): 147.

42. Steven Connor, *Postmodernist Culture: An Introduction to the Theories of the Contemporary* (Oxford: Basil Blackwell, 1989), 227.

43. Hoffmeister, "Post-Modern Theater," 436.

44. See, for example, Bruce F. Pauley, *From Prejudice to Persecution: A History of Austrian Anti-Semitism* (Chapel Hill: University of North Carolina Press, 1992), 286–89, on "The November Pogrom."

45. See, for example, Egon Schwarz, "*Helden*platz?" *German Politics and Society* 21 (fall 1990): 36.

46. Most critics suspected Peymann and Bernhard of orchestrating the scandal by leaking the passages themselves, and of purposely postponing publication of the text until the premiere in order to increase tension and interest.

47. Quoted in the wide-ranging book published by Peymann and the Burgtheater, documenting the scandal, the play, and subsequent reactions, from August

1 to December 31, 1988, *Heldenplatz: Eine Dokumentation* (Vienna: Burgtheater, 1989), 220.

48. Schwarz, *"Heldenplatz?"* 38.

49. Bernhard Sorg, "Die Zeichen des Zerfalls: Zu Thomas Bernhards *Auslöschung* und *Heldenplatz,"* *Thomas Bernhard,* series editor Heinz Ludwig Arnold, 3d ed., *text + kritik* 43 (1991): 84.

50. This is a bit of dramatic license on Bernhard's part, since no apartments border the real Heldenplatz, although some are within hearing distance.

51. In the text, Bernhard writes that from the garden we can see the Burgtheater "through a fog." In production, Peymann and Bernhard changed the perspective, placing the theater wall right by the bench where the characters were sitting.

52. Gitta Honegger, "Thomas Bernhard," *Partisan Review* 58, no. 3 (1991): 495.

53. In Bernhard's short "dramolette" *Der deutsche Mittagstisch* (*The German Lunch Table: A Tragedy to Be Performed by the Burgtheater when Touring Germany*), which premiered in Bochum in 1981, Bernhard develops the connections between soup and ideology. A couple named Mr. and Mrs. Bernhard try to eat a lunch of hot soup with their great- and great-great-grandchildren, but keep on finding "Nazis in the soup." This dramatized verbal coin—the equivalent of finding a Nazi under every bush—stands, in this short, mock-Expressionist play, for the invasion of a still-open past into the most basic rituals of daily life.

54. Honegger, "Thomas Bernhard," 496.

55. Jean Améry, *At the Mind's Limits: Contemplations by a Survivor on Auschwitz and Its Realities,* trans. Sidney Rosenfeld and Stella P. Rosenfeld (Bloomington: Indiana University Press, 1980), 77. My reading here is influenced by Dowden, *Understanding Thomas Bernhard,* who writes with great insight on the connections between Améry and Bernhard, 80–82.

56. Améry, *At the Mind's Limits,* 80.

57. Améry, *At the Mind's Limits,* 81. For an essay on Améry and the morality of "witnessing" see Alvin Rosenfeld, "Jean Améry as Witness," in *Holocaust Remembrance: The Shapes of Memory,* ed. Geoffrey H. Hartman (Oxford: Blackwell, 1994), 59–69.

58. Friedrich Nietzsche, *On the Genealogy of Morals,* in *Basic Writings of Nietzsche,* trans. Walter Kaufmann (New York: Modern Library, 1966), 472.

59. Nietzsche, *Genealogy of Morals,* 475.

60. Michael André Bernstein, *Bitter Carnival: "Ressentiment" and the Abject Hero* (Princeton: Princeton University Press, 1992), 102.

61. Bernstein, *Bitter Carnival,* 102.

62. Améry, *At the Mind's Limits,* 81.

63. Although Bernhard does not refer to him directly, it is clear that Bernhard was acquainted with this famous intellectual whose temperament was so similar to his own. Améry published an appreciative review of Bernhard's memoir *The Cause* and his novel *Correction* in 1976, "Morbus Austriacus," *Merkur* 30 (1976): 91–96; and another before his death in 1978, "Atemnot," *Merkur* 32 (1978): 947–49. Like Bernhard, Améry was preoccupied with aging and death. A few years before his suicide he published a book on the subject: *Hand an sich legen. Diskurs über den Freitod* (Stuttgart: E. Klett, 1976).

64. Quoted from Heinrich Wille, "Wunsch oder Bedingung? Zum Rechtsstreit über Thomas Bernhards letztwillige Verfügung," *Der Standard,* March 7, 1989, 19.

Conclusion

1. This is one of the opening lines of Richard Terdiman's *Present Past: Modernity and the Memory Crisis* (Ithaca: Cornell University Press, 1993), 3; cited also in my introduction.

2. Patrice Pavis, "The Classical Heritage of Modern Drama: The Case of Postmodern Theatre," in *Theatre at the Crossroads of Culture* (London: Routledge, 1992), 66–68. This chapter appeared previously in *Modern Drama* 29 (1986): 1–22.

3. See, for example, Philip Auslander, *Presence and Resistance: Postmodernism and Cultural Politics in Contemporary American Performance* (Ann Arbor: University of Michigan Press, 1992); Hal Foster, "Postmodernism: A Preface," in *The Anti-Aesthetic: Essays on Postmodern Culture,* ed. Hal Foster (Seattle: Bay Press, 1983); Andreas Huyssen, *Twilight Memories: Marking Time in a Culture of Amnesia* (New York: Routledge, 1995); and Linda Hutcheon, *The Politics of Postmodernism* (London: Routledge, 1989).

4. Walter Benjamin, thesis 14 of the "Theses on the Philosophy of History," in *Illuminations,* ed. Hannah Arendt, trans. Harry Zohn (New York: Schocken, 1968), 262.

5. "America is the most subjective, the most innocent nation in the Western world," Müller said, in conversation. "There isn't a nation in Europe that didn't experience the Holocaust. This makes a difference in the subconscious" (Arthur Holmberg, "A Conversation with Robert Wilson and Heiner Müller," *Modern Drama* 31 (1988): 456).

6. This is one half of Steven Connor's definition of the double nature of postmodernism (*Postmodernist Culture: An Introduction on the Theories of the Contemporary* (Oxford: Basil Blackwell, 1989), 227) and is discussed in my introduction.

7. *Postmodernist Culture,* 227; this is the other half of Connor's definition.

8. *Eve of Retirement* has had repeated productions in France, England, the United States, Israel, and other countries, with varying degrees of success.

9. I think particularly of Robert Wilson and Pina Bausch, briefly discussed below, who have received extensive attention in a variety of languages.

10. Johann-Karl Schmidt, "Robert Wilson: *Still Life Is Real Life,*" in *Robert Wilson: Erinnerung an eine Revolution* (Stuttgart: Galerie der Stadt, 1987), 6.

11. Description taken from Brigitte Reinhardt, "Zum Environment von Robert Wilson," in *Robert Wilson: Erinnerung an eine Revolution,* 17.

12. Heiner Müller, *A Letter to Robert Wilson* (1987), in *Explosion of a Memory: Writings by Heiner Müller,* ed. and trans. Carl Weber (New York: Performing Arts Journal Publications, 1989), 153; discussed in detail in chapter 3.

13. Heiner Müller, "'The Forest,' a Conversation with Christoph Rüter" (1988), reprinted in Heiner Müller, *Gesammelte Irrtümer 2: Interviews und Gespräche,* ed. G. Edelmann and R. Ziemer (Frankfurt am Main: Verlag der Autoren, 1990), 108; my translation.

14. See Jan Kott, "Kantor, Memory, Memoire," *New Theatre Quarterly* 7, no. 28 (1991): 299–302.

15. Tadeusz Kantor, "To Save from Oblivion," in *A Journey through Other Spaces: Essays and Manifestos, 1944–1990,* ed. and trans. Michal Kobialka (Berkeley and Los Angeles: University of California Press, 1993), 167.

16. George Tabori, "Es geht schon wieder los," in *Unterammegau oder Die guten Deutschen* (Frankfurt am Main: Suhrkamp, 1981), 202; my translation.

17. George Tabori, from his introduction to the 1969 European premiere of his highly subversive play, *The Cannibals: "Die Kannibalen:* Zur europäischen Erstaufführung," in *Unterammegau,* 37; my translation.

18. Tabori, "Es geht schon wieder los," 201; my translation.

19. Elaine Scarry, *The Body in Pain: The Making and Unmaking of the World* (New York: Oxford University Press, 1985), 109–13ff.

20. For a reconstruction of the performance and a discussion of the play, see Anat Feinberg, "George Tabori's Mourning Work in *Jubiläum,"* in *Staging the Holocaust: The Shoah in Drama and Performance,* ed. Claude Schumacher (Cambridge: Cambridge University Press, 1998), 267–80. A comprehensive study of Tabori's theater work—his practice, theory, and plays—is now available in English in Anat Feinberg, *Embodied Memory: The Theatre of George Tabori* (Iowa City: University of Iowa Press, 1999).

Index

Abbott, H. Porter, 39, 53–54
Action (Shepard), 4, 63, 69, 115–17,
    119, 130, 143–51
Ad Herennium, 4–5, 80
Aitmatov, Tshingis, 76–77
Á la recherche du temps perdu (Proust),
    6–7
Alcestis (Wilson), 239n. 89
America Play (Parks), 4, 7, 24, 156,
    160–61, 172, 175–82
Améry, Jean, 212–14, 250n. 63
Anderson, Laurie, *The Nerve Bible*, 25
Angel City (Shepard), 129
Angels in America (Kushner), 25
Angelus Novus (Klee), 88
Anniversary (Tabori), 223
apocalypse, 22, 33–34, 104, 108, 111,
    115–20 passim, 132–33, 136, 143–48,
    191–92, 217, 220–21
Apollinaire, Guillaume, 17
Aristotle, 3
Art of Memory, The (Yates), 2, 23
Augustine, Saint, 26, 45–46, 50, 51, 56
Auschwitz, 25, 27–28, 31–32, 100, 109,
    193, 201, 212, 222, 242n. 56. *See also*
    Holocaust
Auslander, Philip, 215

Baader, Andreas, 96
Bakhtin, Mikhail, 23, 210
Barth, John, 129
Battle, The (Müller), 72, 73, 79–83, 112,
    190
Baudrillard, Jean, 33–34, 124; *The Illu-
    sion of the End*, 33–34
Bausch, Pina, 63, 220–21; *Viktor*,
    220–21, 223

Beckerman, Bernard, 58–59
Beckett, Samuel, 1, 7–8, 14, 19,
    37–69, 74; *Eh Joe*, 37, 57; *Endgame*,
    44, 69; *Ends and Odds*, 19; *Footfalls*,
    37, 56, 59–60, 62; *Happy Days*, 44;
    Krapp's Last Tape, 37, 43–47, 53–54,
    66; *Not I*, 8, 19, 37, 38, 41, 43–54,
    56, 61, 68; *Ohio Impromptu*, 37, 38,
    40, 47, 56, 63–68, 145; *A Piece of
    Monologue*, 41; *Play*, 19, 44, 57;
    Proust, 42, 46; *Rockaby*, 37, 56,
    59–63; *That Time*, 8, 19, 37, 41,
    54–59, 68, 110, 115, 144, 174, 184,
    187, 216, 220, 233n. 53; *Waiting for
    Godot*, 145
Bek, Alexander, 74, 98
Benjamin, Walter, 24–28, 71, 78–79,
    99, 171, 173, 216; on Proust, 7; *The-
    ses on the Philosophy of History*, 25–27,
    88–89, 93–95, 158
Ben-Zvi, Linda, 46, 159
Berger, Thomas, 129
Bergson, Henri, 6, 23, 53, 57, 59, 170,
    203; *Matter and Memory*, 51
Bernhard, Thomas, 1, 4, 7–8, 9, 14, 15,
    20, 28–29, 31, 55, 63, 156, 183–214,
    216–19, 222; *Eve of Retirement*, 13,
    69, 183, 185, 187–88, 191–206, 218;
    The Force of Habit, 203; *The German
    Lunch Table*, 250n. 53; *Heldenplatz*,
    13, 59, 183, 187–88, 198, 206–14,
    218; *Histrionics*, 183–84, 187–92; *The
    Hunting Party*, 186; *The Ignoramus and
    the Madman*, 191
Bernstein, Michael André, 213–14
Betrayal (Pinter), 22
Beyer, Hermann, 110

Beyond the Pleasure Principle (Freud),
    30–31, 66–67
Bigsby, C. W. E., 116, 117, 134
Birringer, Johannes, 74
Blau, Herbert, 43
Bloom, Michael, 143
Body in Pain, The (Scarry), 102–3,
    222–23
Bourdieu, Pierre, 80
Brater, Enoch, 39, 40–41, 48, 55, 67
Brecht, Bertold, 31, 71–72, 88; *Fear and
    Trembling in the Third Reich,* 74,
    80–81, 83; *The Measures Taken,*
    84–85, 89, 94, 108
Brustein, Robert, 156, 160, 172
Buried Child (Shepard), 116, 119,
    152–53
Büchner, Georg, *Danton's Death,* 90

Calvino, Italo, 2
Camillo, Giulio, 2–3, 5; *L'Idea del The-
    atro,* 2–3
Cannibals, The (Tabori), 222–23
Carroll, Lewis, 120
Caruth, Cathy, on trauma, 29–31, 66,
    163–64
Celan, Paul, ix, 214
Cement (Müller), 107
Centaurs (Müller), 98
Century's End (Schwartz), 33
Chaikin, Joseph, 144
Chaudhuri, Una, 153, 177
Chekhov, Anton, 7; *Three Sisters,* 21
Chicago (Shepard), 117
Choderlos de Laclos, *Dangerous
    Liaisons,* 74, 108
Chubb, Kenneth, 127
Cicero, 4–5, 23, 40–41
Cleaver, Edith, 69
Cohn-Bendit, Daniel, 95, 97
commodification, 15, 80, 115–36 pas-
    sim, 152, 154, 216
Communism: and Gerz's *Monument
    against Fascism,* 13; in Müller, 8, 9,
    73–74, 98–108, 110, 112
Connor, Steven, 19–20, 29, 53, 57, 62,
    205, 217

Cosmos and History (Eliade), 196–97
Cowboy Mouth (Shepard), 128
Cowboys (Shepard), 115, 116, 126
Cowboys #2 (Shepard), 116, 117,
    126–28, 131
Curse of the Starving Class (Shepard),
    116, 152, 153

Dance of Death (Strindberg), 195
Dangerous Liaisons (Laclos), 74, 108
Danton's Death (Büchner), 90
Darkness at Noon (Koestler), 102
Dead Class, The (Kantor), 221
Deafman Glance (Wilson), 63
Death Destruction & Detroit II (Wilson),
    75–77
Death of a Salesman (Miller), 20, 154
*Death of the Last Black Man in the Whole
    Entire World* (Parks), 68–69, 134,
    157–59, 161, 166–75, 181
Delbo, Charlotte, 32
Deleuze, Gilles, 47–48, 52, 94, 157–58,
    170; and Félix Guattari, 93
Demastes, William, 154
DeRose, David, 117, 124, 126, 128
Derrida, Jacques, 62–63, 186
*Despoiled Shore Medeamaterial Landscape
    with Argonauts* (Müller), 73, 75, 82
Diamond, Liz, 168, 172
Differend, The (Lyotard), 27–28, 242n.
    56
Doctorow, E. L., 129
Douglass, Frederick, 167
Dowden, Steve, 187
Dream Play (Strindberg), 21
Drukman, Steven, 158
Duel, The (Müller), 98
Dutschke, Rudi, 96

Eco, Umberto, 20
Eh Joe (Beckett), 37, 57
Einstein on the Beach (Wilson), 63
Elam, Harry, Jr., 172
Eliade, Mircea, 192; *Cosmos and His-
    tory,* 196–97
Eliot, T. S., *The Waste Land,* 220
Endgame (Beckett), 44, 69

Ends and Odds (Beckett), 19
Erasmus, 2
Erne, Eduard, 95–97
Eve of Retirement (Bernhard), 13, 69,
    183, 185, 187–88, 191–206, 218
Explosion of a Memory/Description of a
    Picture (Müller), 73, 239n. 89

Fassbinder, R. W., *Lili Marleen*, 249n.
    38
"Father, The" (Müller), 101
Fear and Trembling in the Third Reich
    (Brecht), 74, 80–81, 83
Federico, Joseph A., 205
Fehervary, Helen, 82–83
Feinberg, Anat, 252n. 20
Filbinger, Hans Karl, 194–206 passim,
    218
Fischer-Lichte, Erika, 17–19, 231n. 3
Fletcher, Beryl and John, 66
Fool for Love (Shepard), 116, 145, 152,
    153
Footfalls (Beckett), 37, 56, 59–60,
    62
Force of Habit, The (Bernhard), 203
Forensic and the Navigators (Shepard),
    129, 143, 146
Forest Near Moscow (Müller), 98
Foster, Hal, 17, 215
Foucault, Michel, 10, 137, 228n. 15
Foundling, The (Kleist), 74, 97, 98
Foundling, The (Müller), 69, 73, 82,
    97–109, 111–12, 134, 238n. 74
French, Philip, *Westerns*, 129
French Revolution, 25, 96; in Müller,
    8–9, 35, 38, 84–95, 108, 219; in Wil-
    son, 219
Freud, Sigmund, 5–6, 23, 34, 152;
    Beyond the Pleasure Principle, 30–31,
    66–67; "Mourning and Melan-
    choly," 65–66, 68, 172; "A Note
    upon the Mystic Writing-Pad," 186;
    and trauma, 9, 30–32, 83, 112–13,
    163–64
Friedlander, Saul, 28, 31–32; *Reflections*
    of Nazism, 249n. 38
Fuchs, Elinor, 75

Fuentes, Carlos, 136
Funkenstein, Amos, 140

Gates, Henry Louis, Jr., 160, 163
Gehlen, Arnold, 33
Geis, Deborah, 116, 244n. 67
Genealogy of Morals, The (Nietzsche),
    213–14
Genet, Jean, 89, 108
Geography of a Horse Dreamer (Shepard),
    116–17, 126, 128, 130–31
Germania Death in Berlin (Müller), 19,
    24, 79–80, 82–83, 104, 190
German Lunch Table, The (Bernhard),
    250n. 53
Gerz, Jochen and Esther, *Monument*
    against Fascism, War, and Violence—
    and for Peace and Human Rights,
    11–13
Gilroy, Paul, 160
Girl 6 (Lee, Parks), 156
Gladkow, Fedor, 74
Glass Menagerie, The (Williams), 20–21
Goll, Yvan, 17
Gontarski, S. E., 42
Gotscheff, Dimiter, 93
Grotowki, Jerzy, 4, 222
Guattari, Félix, and Gilles Deleuze, 93
Gundling's Life Frederick of Prussia Less-
    ing's Sleep Dream Scream (Müller), 72,
    73, 190
Gussow, Mel 167

Habermas, Jürgen, 10
Halbwachs, Maurice, 23, 57–58
Hamletmachine (Müller), 27, 63, 72, 73,
    104, 110, 138, 238n. 81
Handke, Peter, 19, 144, 183, 185;
    Insulting the Audience, 203; *Kaspar*,
    185–86, 233n. 53; *Wings of Desire*, 25
Happy Days (Beckett), 44
Hartman, Geoffrey, 15
Harvey, David, 18
Hauptmanm, Georg, *The Weavers*, 79
Hauser, Kaspar, 185
Hawk Moon (Shepard), 128–29
Heinrichs, Benjamin, 197

Heldenplatz (Bernhard), 13, 59, 183, 187–88, 198, 206–14, 218
Heracles 2; or, The Hydra (Müller), 107–8, 110
Heracles 13 (Müller), 105, 108, 112
Herm, Klaus, 58–59
Herrmann, Karl-Ernst, 210
Heuvel, Michael Vanden, 42, 125, 141, 154
Histrionics (Bernhard), 183–84, 187–92
Hitler: in Bernhard, 184, 206–11; in Müller, 29, 38, 73, 80–83, 100; in Syberberg, 69; in Tabori, 223
Hitler: A Film from Germany (Syberberg), 69, 229n. 37, 249n. 38
Hoffmeister, Donna L., 204–5
Holocaust, 11, 27–29, 30, 77, 193, 199–203, 206–14, 222–23; and Gerz's *Monument against Fascism,* 11–13. *See also* Auschwitz
Holy Ghostly, The (Shepard), 143, 146
Honegger, Gitta, 210, 212
Horatian, The (Müller), 72
Horváth, Ödön von, 184
"How Bodies Remember" (Kleinman), 103
Hugo, Victor, *Les Misérables,* 219
Hunting Party, The (Bernhard), 186
Hutcheon, Linda, 20, 187
Huyssen, Andreas, 10, 215

Icarus's Mother (Shepard), 116, 118, 143, 146
Ignoramus and the Madman, The (Bernhard), 191
Illusion of the End, The (Baudrillard), 33–34
Imperceptible Mutabilities in the Third Kingdom (Parks), 27, 156, 161–67, 169, 181
Innes, Christopher, 80–81
Insulting the Audience (Handke), 203
involuntary memory, 6–7, 20, 26, 53, 106
"I Want to Be a German" (Müller), 238n. 74

Jameson, Fredric, 118
Jelinek, Elfriede, 183
Joyce, James, 6, 9, 160; *Ulysses,* 167

Kaes, Anton, 28, 33, 229n. 37
Kafka, Franz, 40, 98
Kalb, Jonathan, 74
Kamm, Tom, 239n. 89
Kantor, Tadeusz, 221–23; *The Dead Class,* 221; *Wielopole, Wielopole,* 222
Kaspar (Handke), 185–86, 233n. 53
Keller, Andreas, 106
Kennedy, Adrienne, 156
Kiefer, Anselm, 13–14
Klee, Paul, *Angelus Novus,* 88
Kleinman, Arthur and Joan, "How Bodies Remember," 103
Kleist, Heinrich von, *The Foundling,* 74, 97, 98
Koestler, Arthur, *Darkness at Noon,* 102
Kojève, Alexandre, 33
Kokoschka, Oskar, 17
Kounellis, Jannis, and *Mauser* project, 27, 109, 111
Krapp's Last Tape (Beckett), 37, 43–47, 53–54, 66
Kreisky, Bruno, 209
Kushner, Tony, *Angels in America,* 25

Lahr, John, 9, 132, 134
Landscape and Memory (Schama), 11
La Turista (Shepard), 116, 117, 129, 131, 141, 143
Lawley, Paul, 49
Lee, Spike, *Girl 6,* 156
Les Misérables (Hugo), 219
Letter to Robert Wilson, A (Müller), 75–78, 106, 220
Levi, Primo, 214
L'Idea del Theatro (Camillo), 2–3
Liebknecht, Karl, 100
Lie of the Mind, A (Shepard), 116, 152, 153
lieux de mémoire (memory sites), 11, 24, 34–35, 75, 80, 200, 210
Lieux de Mémoire, Les (Nora), 6, 10–11, 22–24, 34–35, 74–75, 200, 210

Lifton, Robert Jay, *The Protean Self*, 227n. 7

Lili Marleen (Fassbinder), 249n. 38

Lincoln, Abraham, 156; in Parks, 8, 35, 175–82; in Shepard, 117, 147–48

London, Todd, 175, 181

"Luckless Angel, The" (Müller), 88–89, 93–94

Luxemburg, Rosa, 80, 100, 105

Lyons, Charles, 42

Lyotard, Jean François, 27, 117, 148–49; *The Differend*, 27–28, 242n. 56

Mad Dog Blues (Shepard), 117, 129, 143–44

Mahler, Horst, 96

Marat/Sade (Weiss), 89–90

Marx, Karl, 118

Matter and Memory (Bergson), 51

Mauser (Müller), 107–8, 111

Mauser project (Müller), 105, 107–13

Measures Taken, The (Brecht), 84–85, 89, 94, 108

Mémoire involantaire. See involuntary memory

Meyerhofer, N. J., 200

Miller, Arthur, 7; *Death of a Salesman*, 20, 154

mnemotechnic, 4–5

Modernity and the Memory Crisis (Terdiman), 4, 6

Monument against Fascism, War, and Violence—and for Peace and Human Rights (Gerz), 11–13

Morrison, Toni, *Playing in the Dark*, 158

Mosès, Stéphane, 26

"Mourning and Melancholy" (Freud), 65–66, 68, 172

Müller, Heiner, 1, 4, 7–9, 15, 20, 25, 28–29, 31–38 passim, 55, 59, 71–113, 115, 156, 157, 184, 190, 216–20, 235n. 15; *The Battle*, 72, 73, 79–83, 112, 190; *Cement*, 107; *Centaurs*, 98; *Despoiled Shore Medeamaterial Landscape with Argonauts*, 73, 75, 82; *The*

Duel, 98; *Explosion of a Memory/Description of a Picture*, 73, 239n. 89; "The Father," 101; *Forest Near Moscow*, 98; *The Foundling*, 69, 73, 82, 97–109, 111–12, 134, 238n. 74; *Germania Death in Berlin*, 19, 24, 79–80, 82–83, 104, 190; *Gundling's Life Frederick of Prussia Lessing's Sleep Dream Scream*, 72, 73, 190; *Hamletmachine*, 27, 63, 72, 73, 104, 110, 138, 238n. 81; *Heracles 2; or, The Hydra*, 107–8, 110; *Heracles 13*, 105, 108, 112; *The Horatian*, 72; "I Want to Be a German," 238n. 74; *A Letter to Robert Wilson*, 75–78, 106, 220; "The Luckless Angel," 88–89, 93–94; *Mauser*, 107–8, 111; *Mauser* project, 105, 107–13; *Philoctetes*, 72; *Quartet*, 73, 104, 107–11, 238n. 81; "Raising the Dead," 108–9; *Russian Gambit*, 98; *The Task*, 8–9, 63, 72, 82, 83–97, 110, 219; *Volokolamsk Highway*, 73, 97–98

Native Son (Wright), 167

Naveh, Eyal, 179

Nazism: in Bernhard, 8, 183–214 passim; in Gerz's *Monument against Fascism*, 11–13; in Kiefer, 13–14; in Müller, 8, 9, 73–74, 80–83, 98–101, 106–8, 112; in Tabori, 222–23

Nerve Bible, The (Anderson), 25

Niethammer, Lutz, *Posthistoire: Has History Come to an End?* 33

Nietzsche, Friedrich, 174, 213–14; *The Genealogy of Morals*, 213–14

Night, The (Syberberg), 69

Nineteen-Eighty-Four (Orwell), 101, 103

Nora, Pierre, *Les Lieux de Mémoire*, 6, 10–11, 22–24, 34–35, 74–75, 200, 210

"Note upon the Mystic Writing-Pad, A" (Freud), 186

Not I (Beckett), 8, 19, 37, 38, 41, 43–54, 56, 61, 68

Ohio Impromptu (Beckett), 37, 38, 40, 47, 56, 63–68, 145

Olney, James, 46
Operation Sidewinder (Shepard), 117,
    121, 131–34, 143, 155
Orwell, George, Nineteen-Eighty-Four,
    101, 103
Our American Cousin, 156, 176, 179–80

Paris, Texas (Wenders, Shepard), 152
Parks, Suzan-Lori, 1, 8, 9, 14, 20,
    28–29, 31, 35, 55, 59, 155–82,
    216–19; The America Play, 4, 7, 24,
    156, 160–61, 172, 175–82; Death of
    the Last Black Man in the Whole Entire
    World, 69, 134, 157–59, 161, 166–75,
    181; Girl 6, 156; Imperceptible Mutabil-
    ities in the Third Kingdom, 27, 156,
    161–67, 169, 181; "Possession," 155
Patraka, Vivian M., 249n. 38
Pavis, Patrice, 215, 219
Peymann, Claus, 188, 206, 210–12
Philoctetes (Müller), 72
Piece of Monologue, A (Beckett), 41
Pinter, Harold, 144; Betrayal, 22
Pirandello, Luigi, 17
Plato, 5
Play (Beckett), 19, 44, 57
Playing in the Dark (Morrison), 158
"Possession" (Parks), 155
Posthistoire, 25, 33
Posthistoire: Has History Come to an End?
    (Niethammer), 33
Protean Self, The (Lifton), 227n. 7
Proust (Beckett), 42, 46
Proust, Marcel, 6, 26, 53; À la recherche
    du temps perdu, 6–7

Quartet (Müller), 73, 104, 107–11,
    238n. 81
Quintilian, 4, 23

"Raising the Dead" (Müller), 108–9
Rayner, Alice, 172
Red Cross (Shepard), 116
Reflections of Nazism (Friedlander),
    249n. 38
Reich, Wilhelm, 104

Reichert, Thomas, 91–92
Renan, Ernest, 34, 230n. 61
Rich, Frank, 153
Robinson, Marc, 174, 176–77
Rockaby (Beckett), 37, 56, 59–63
Rock Garden (Shepard), 115, 116
Rorty, Richard, 148–50
Rouse, John, 107, 109, 111
Russell, Charles, 195–96
Russian Gambit (Müller), 98

Sad Lament of Pecos Bill on the Eve of
    Killing His Wife, The (Shepard), 126,
    134–35
Santner, Eric, 32, 112
Savran, David, 147
Scarry, Elaine, The Body in Pain, 102–3,
    222–23
Schabowski, Günter, 96
Schama, Simon, Landscape and Memory,
    11
Schmidt, Ingo, 73
Schmidt, Johann-Karl, 219
Schmitt, Natalie Crohn, 42–43
Schwartz, Hillel, Century's End, 33
Schwarz, Egon, 209
Seghers, Anna, 74, 84, 86, 90, 98
Shaved Splits (Shepard), 143
Shepard, Sam, 1, 8, 9, 28–29, 35, 75,
    115–56, 161, 216–17, 219; Action, 4,
    63, 69, 115–17, 119, 130, 143–51;
    Angel City, 129; Buried Child, 116,
    119, 152–53; Chicago, 117; Cowboy
    Mouth, 128; Cowboys, 115, 116, 126;
    Cowboys #2, 116, 117, 126–28, 131;
    Curse of the Starving Class, 116, 152,
    153; Fool for Love, 116, 145, 152, 153;
    Forensic and the Navigators, 129, 143,
    146; Geography of a Horse Dreamer,
    116–17, 126, 128, 130–31; Hawk
    Moon, 128–29; The Holy Ghostly,
    143, 146; Icarus's Mother, 116, 118,
    143, 146; La Turista, 116, 117, 129,
    131, 141, 143; A Lie of the Mind, 116,
    152, 153; Mad Dog Blues, 117, 129,
    143–44; Operation Sidewinder, 117,

121, 131–34, 143, 155; *Paris, Texas,*
152; *Red Cross,* 116; *Rock Garden,*
115, 116; *The Sad Lament of Pecos Bill
on the Eve of Killing His Wife,* 126,
134–35; *Shaved Splits,* 143; *The Tooth
of Crime,* 7, 116, 121, 124, 128, 129,
130, 136–44; *True West,* 129, 130;
The Unseen Hand, 117, 121–25, 129,
130, 134, 137, 143
Simonides of Ceos, 4, 40–41
Slaughterhouse Five (Vonnegut), 56
Slavery: in Müller, 76, 84, 86, 89, 92,
94; in Parks, 8, 27, 156, 161–67,
170–72, 175, 178; in Shepard, 122;
and trauma, 30
Smith, Adam, 118
Solomon, Alisa, 156–57, 161
Sontag, Susan, 104
Sorg, Bernhard, 209
Stalin, in Müller, 29, 73, 80, 99, 101,
104–6, 112
Stambolian, George, 125
Stanislavsky, Konstantin, 3–4
Stein, Gertrude, 75, 160
Streisand, Marianne, 97
Strindberg, August, 7; *Dance of Death,*
195; *Dream Play,* 21
Syberberg, Hans-Jürgen, 75; *Hitler: A
Film from Germany,* 69, 229n. 37,
249n. 38; *(Die Nacht) The Night,* 69
Szondi, Peter, 21

Tabori, George, 221–23, 252n. 20;
Anniversary, 223; *The Cannibals,*
222–23
Tandy, Jessica, 41
Task, The (Müller), 8–9, 63, 72, 82,
83–97, 110, 219
Teraoka, Arlene Akiko, 87
Terdiman, Richard, *Modernity and the
Memory Crisis,* 4, 6
Teufel, Fritz, 96
That Time (Beckett), 8, 19, 37, 41,
54–59, 68, 110, 115, 144, 174, 184,
187, 216, 220, 233n. 53
Theses on the Philosophy of History (Ben-

jamin), 25–27, 88–89, 93–95,
158
Three Sisters (Chekhov), 21
Tooth of Crime, The (Shepard), 7,
116, 121, 124, 128, 129, 130,
136–44
Trauma, 1, 15, 27–32, 33–35, 40, 52,
78, 83, 85, 97, 101, 103, 112–13,
150–51, 162–64, 171–72, 176,
179–80, 190, 216; and mourning,
65–67; and postmodernism, 9–10
True West (Shepard), 129, 130
Tscholakowa, Ginka, 87
Tzara, Tristan, 17

Ubersfeld, Anne, 86
Ulysses (Joyce), 167
Unseen Hand, The (Shepard), 117,
121–25, 129, 130, 134, 137, 143

Vaßen, Florian, 73
Vattimo, Gianni, 33
Viktor (Bausch), 220–21, 223
Vitruvius, 2
Volokolamsk Highway (Müller), 73,
97–98
Vonnegut, Kurt, *Slaughterhouse Five,*
56

Wackernagel, Christof, 96
Waiting for Godot (Beckett), 145
Waldheim, Kurt, 183, 194, 207, 209
Warnock, Mary, 51
Waste Land, The (Eliot), 220
Weavers, The (Hauptmann), 79
Weber, Carl, 78, 79, 97
Weiss, Peter, *Marat/Sade,* 89–90
Wenders, Wim, 75; *Paris, Texas,* 152;
Wings of Desire, 25
Westerns (French), 129
Whitelaw, Billie, 53
Whitman, Walt, in Shepard, 147–48
Wielopole, Wielopole (Kantor), 222
Wilcox, Leonard, 132, 133, 136
Williams, Tennessee, *The Glass
Menagerie,* 20–21

Wilson, Robert, 59, 62, 75–78, 113, 219–21, 235n. 15; *Alcestis*, 239n. 89; *Deafman Glance*, 63; *Death Destruction & Detroit II*, 75–77; *Einstein on the Beach*, 63

Wings of Desire (Wenders, Handke), 25
Wright, Richard, *Native Son*, 167

Yates, Francis, *The Art of Memory*, 2, 23
Young, James, 11